BORN *to* WIN

The Authorized Biography of Althea Gibson

FRANCES CLAYTON GRAY
YANICK RICE LAMB

Foreword by Bill Cosby
Afterword by Venus Williams

WILEY

John Wiley & Sons, Inc.

Copyright © 2004 by Frances Clayton Gray and Yanick Rice Lamb. All rights reserved

Published by John Wiley & Sons, Inc., Hoboken, New Jersey
Published simultaneously in Canada

Photo credits: page 27, the Bing Studio; page 41, Du Valier; page 80, Max Peter Haas; page 86, Photo Lite, New Delhi; pages 88, 102, 105, and 147, AP Photo; page 100, Le-Roye Productions; page 103, Will Weissberg; page 106, D. R. Stuart; page 110, D. D. and E. P. Schroeder; page 121, United Artists; page 129, Seawell; and page 192, Elise Amendola.

For general information about our other products and services, please contact our Customer Care Department within the United States at (800) 762-2974, outside the United States at (317) 572-3993 or fax (317) 572-4002.

Wiley also publishes its books in a variety of electronic formats. Some content that appears in print may not be available in electronic books. For more information about Wiley products, visit our web site at www.wiley.com.

Library of Congress Cataloging-in-Publication Data:

Gray, Frances Clayton (date)
    Born to win : the authorized biography of Althea Gibson / Frances Clayton Gray, Yanick Rice Lamb ; foreword by Bill Cosby ; afterword by Venus Williams.
        p.   cm.
    Includes bibliographical references and index.
    ISBN 0-471-47165-8 (cloth)
    1. Gibson, Althea, 1927–2003. 2. Tennis players—United States—Biography. 3. African American women tennis players—Biography. I. Lamb, Yanick Rice. II. Title.

    GV994.G53G73 2004
    796.342'092—dc22

                                                    2004004690

Printed in the United States of America

10 9 8 7 6 5 4 3 2 1

Contents

Foreword:
On Althea Gibson

ONE OF THE GREATEST procelebrity events ever was the RFK Pro-Celebrity Tennis Tournament, a one-day affair held at Forest Hills. It started at eight o'clock in the morning and went all day. The finals would be somewhere around four or five o'clock. I don't remember the year or who my pro was. All I know is I played in the doubles final and won the tournament.

As I was saying, it was a long day. After going through about a thousand early pairings, they moved us off of the clay courts and onto the grass courts in the stadium. It was sold out. Jam-packed for the quarter-final match. As I walked onto the court, there on the other side of the net was my buddy Althea Gibson. I don't remember who her celebrity partner was either, but I know they lost because we just kept hitting the celebrity in the head.

Althea is a wonderful and considerate person when playing with celebrities. But Althea also talks the talk. Why? Because she graduated from Florida A&M.

Florida A&M has a great reputation for academics. Besides that, it has the meanest mascot of any school I know. You see, Florida A&M does not fool around when it comes to a mascot. Their mascot doesn't just wander around wearing big, floppy shoes. Their mascot also is not a bull that runs out on the field. And their mascot is not a falcon with covered eyes and a handler who has to wear a thick leather strap on his wrist to keep the claws from ripping his arm off. No, sir. The Florida A&M mascot is a rattlesnake. You cannot put anything over its eyes, and you cannot let it out onto the field. It stays where it stays, and it hisses all the time. So you have to be aware of people with a mascot like that. And since I knew that Althea attended Florida A&M and that the Florida A&M mascot is a rattlesnake, I should have known better than to mess with her the way I did that day.

Anyway, back to this match. It's getting boring because Althea cannot be in two places at once. And her celebrity partner, whom we keep pelting with tennis balls to win the point, now has about seventeen knots all over the head and some on the back. So Althea and I started talking out loud, back and forth, having fun.

"Hey, Bill," Althea yelled across the net at one point. "You can't do this!"

"Yes, I can," I teased.

We're having a great time just talking. Then Althea got ready to serve. The stadium got very quiet.

"Wait a minute," I yelled across the net.

I was wearing a funky-looking, sky blue cotton hat with a floppy, 360-degree brim. I took off my hat and put it in the left corner of my serving box. And then, with great bravado, I said to Althea: "I bet you can't hit that hat."

And I was happy when I said it. I was just jumping all around like Rumpelstiltskin did when nobody knew his name. And the people in the stands went crazy.

Something lit up in Althea's eyes. But this was not humor anymore.

"All right, Bill," she said. "Here it goes."

Althea tossed the ball into the air, swung her racket, and the ball hit my hat. The people in the stands stood and cheered.

Althea could have just brushed the hat with the ball, which would have been sportsmanlike. But since this woman is Florida A&M and a rattler, she hit the ball very hard. So hard, in fact, that when the ball struck my hat, it flew up in the air and turned over.

I looked up at my hat, and I could see that the ball had dug into the turf because now my hat was covered with a big glob of mud and grass, which meant I would not be able to put this hat back on until I cleaned it up.

On the crossover, I stopped Althea by getting in her way. Then I looked at her and said: "All I asked you to do was hit the hat."

And she said to me: "Yes. And I gave it to you the way I want you to wear it."

—Bill Cosby

Acknowledgments

For years, I've felt that many people were unaware of accomplishments and struggles of the great champion Althea Gibson. Feeling compelled to separate fact from fiction, I partnered with journalist Yanick Rice Lamb to introduce the African American Queen of Tennis to a new generation and to revisit, study, and acknowledge her history. When I talked to Althea about *Born to Win*, she became excited and started reminiscing about her accomplishments. She was also excited when she talked to Yanick and as we watched her videos, learning from the master what this is all about.

Through Althea's recollections, interviews with her contemporaries, my personal experiences, and exhaustive research, we seek to bring you into the life and works of this God-gifted woman who came to be known as the "People's Champion." There are many to thank. But before I get too far in front of myself, I must single out the greatest person in my life—a woman dedicated to education, family, children, justice and fairness. This precious woman, M. Lucile Gray, is my mother.

Those of you who gave personal interviews allowed us to put the facts in proper perspective and give dignity to a life well lived. A special thanks to Zina Garrison, Rosemary Darben, Billy Davis, Dr. William Hayling, David Dinkins, Billie Jean King, Pam Shriver, John McEnroe, Leslie Allen, the

United Stated Tennis Association, Neil Amdur, Bill Cosby, Jeanne Ashe, Newark Mayor Sharpe James, and Mrs. Sweeny Price.

For all of you who will continue to help us perpetuate the legacy while bridging the gap, my thanks. This includes the American Tennis Association, the International Women's Hall of Fame, the Women's Sports Foundation, the Jackie Robinson Foundation, Florida A & M University, the Ladies Professional Golf Association, East Orange General Hospital, the Althea Gibson Early Childhood Academy, the Althea Gibson Community and Education Tennis Center, and the Althea Gibson Foundation. The legacy will continue, and education will continue, which is the mandate that Althea gave me: "Fran, educate the children." Your commitment is also reflected in this book.

This book would not be possible without Carol Lorraine Gaither, Althea's good friend, caretaker, and heir. Carol stayed with Althea daily through the years so that she was not alone and that her needs would always be met. I dedicate this book to Carol, a cancer survivor of more than ten years, who taught us how to use our faith in God.

Lastly, thank you, Yanick, for understanding that this life story is one that needed to be retold. I look forward to collaborating with you on the feature film *Born to Win*.

—Frances Clayton Gray

Nine black students bravely integrated Central High School in Little Rock, Arkansas, shortly before my birth on September 27, 1957. While violence and hatred swirled around their acts of bravery, the world was still celebrating two more pleasant and unifying events. Althea Gibson had been crowned the Queen of Tennis after becoming the first black athlete to win the coveted championships at Wimbledon and then at Forest Hills. Because of my love of history and a lifelong interest in the events of 1957, I responded with an emphatic yes when approached about writing Althea Gibson's biography. As a journalist, I've always had a passion for giving voice to the voiceless and telling untold stories. Given Althea's accomplishments and longevity, I found it remarkable that a void still existed to be filled. There was no comprehensive biography on her entire life—one of the greatest stories never fully told.

For this and all opportunities, I first give glory to God, whose hand was truly all over this project. To Althea Gibson, who called me "Professor," thanks for making magical moments and for letting me in to recapture them. Dandrea James Harris, it wouldn't have happened without your enthusiasm. Thanks for keeping Harlem on our minds, turning around transcripts in a New York minute, sharing your invaluable perspective, keeping me on track with all the "chop-chops," and, most of all, blessing me with another precious godson, Wyatt.

Our appreciation to all of the people mentioned in the book and to those who led us to you, especially Mr. and Mrs. Daniel Gibson Jr., Mary Ann Drayton, Sandra Givens, Mattie Bryant, Agnes Green, Mary McFadden, Thelmer Bethune, Dr. Judi Moore Latta, Gordon Parks, Hamilton Richardson, Arvelia Myers, Edwina Martin, Billie Jean King, Marlene Hagge-Vossler, Kathy Whitworth, and Marilynn Smith. Thanks also to the staffs of the Schomburg Center for Research in Black Culture, the Moorland-Spingarn Research Center at Howard University, and the Clarendon County Archives in South Carolina.

A special shout-out to the members of my book clubs, LaView and Color Me Read—especially to early champion

Janice Kee and to Angela Johnson and Monica Norton, two of the most well-read sisters on the planet. To my cousin, poet A. Van Jordan (remember that name), for steering me in the right direction and sharing your formidable, creative writing talent. My eternal gratitude to others who placed their fingerprints on this book in some way and moved it forward: Patrik Henry Bass, Laneta Goings, Ingrid Sturgis, Edwin Lake, Flo McAfee, Carolyn Hardnett, Joyce Davis, Jared McCallister, Angela Dodson, George Curry, Clem Richardson, Shawn Kennedy, Freddie Allen, A'Lelia Bundles, Herb Boyd, Anita Samuels, Brenda Alexander, Roosevelt Wilson, Cleve Dowell, Henry M. Joseph III, Renee D. Turner, Michael Cottman, Charlyne McWilliams, Ed Harris, Trisa Long Paschal, Connie Green Freightman, and Jacci Brooks McClendon.

To my esteemed colleagues at "the Mecca," the one and only Howard University, thanks for your support, especially Phillip Dixon, chair of the Department of Journalism; Dr. Jannette L. Dates, dean of the School of Communications; Dr. Barron Harvey, dean of the School of Business; and my M.B.A. family. To my students, thanks for keeping me young at heart, helping me grow along with you, and keeping it really real!

Monique Greenwood: What a gift! What a blessing! Thanks for granting me the honor of christening your writer's retreat at the Akwaaba Inn in Washington, D.C. How could I not be productive in such an inspiring, stylish setting with Zora, Walter, Toni, and the rest urging me on! An extra, big hug to Vaughn DeCarlos: I'll always cherish your special touches and surprises.

A crystal ball to Manie Barron of the William Morris Agency. Thanks for sharing such a historic opportunity and for years of laughs and support. Here's to many more! Frances Clayton Gray, what can I say? Thanks for an incredible journey into an incredible life. Bill Cosby and Venus Williams, thanks for voicing your reflections. Carole Hall, editor emeritus of John Wiley & Sons, thanks for recognizing that Althea's story needed to be told in its entirety and for setting me on the right path with your "homework." To our new editor, Hana Lane, thanks for such a smooth transition and for sharing our passion. Thanks also to Kimberly Monroe-Hill, Faren Bachelis, Nicole Martone, and Nancy Flynn of Wiley.

To my lifelong champions and extremely biased parents, Carmelie Jordan and William Rice, thanks for your unconditional love and for keeping the bar high. To my super-extended family of Rices, Lemons, Willises, Jordans, Coxes, Pouxes, Clarks, Fords, Streets, Jacksons, and Claytons (especially Dennis), thanks for keeping your arms around me. Thanks to my siblings: Terrence, Kim, and Linda Rice; Tanya Madison; Jeffrey Jordan; and Patrick Jordan in particular. An extra thanks to Gail Jordan and Michelle and Gary Trotter for providing places to rest my head on top of everything else. Most of all, thanks to my son and special assistant, Brandon, and my husband, Michael, for incredible love, patience, support, late nights, and early mornings.

—Yanick Rice Lamb

Chapter 1

"A Traveling Girl"

My friends and I used to regard school as just a good place to meet and make our plans for what we would do all day.

THIS TIME, Althea had really worked his last, good nerve. Daniel Gibson came at his eldest daughter as if she were the Brown Bomber—with every ounce of his 190 pounds behind his fists. He punched Althea so hard that he sent her tall, skinny behind sprawling down the hall outside the family's five-room walk-up in the heart of Harlem. She hadn't just skipped school or stayed out all night; she had been gone for a few days. So Gibson didn't even bother looking for a strap or snatching off his belt. What was the use? No matter how hard he whipped Althea, she always refused to cry. Even when he punched her that time, she pulled herself off the floor, socked him in the jaw, and made use of all the boxing lessons he had given her by fighting him as if she really were the son he had wanted as his firstborn.

Whenever he whipped her, Althea merely gave her father the silent treatment and continued to do *what* she felt like doing *when* she felt like doing it. But she wasn't feeling junior high school and it had been the same in elementary school at

1

P.S. 136, both of which often lost out to softball games in Central Park and other diversions. Althea couldn't sit still. She was in her own words "a traveling girl." School was too confining and boring to be worthy of more than cameo appearances. She paid a high price for playing hooky—paddlings in the classroom, whippings from her father so severe that she'd bypass home for the police precinct, and that punch in the face. But it was a price she was willing to pay to see all that Depression-era New York had to offer. "We'd climb over the fence to a playground, and we'd swing way up, two on a swing," Althea reminisced many years later. "And we'd sneak in the movies." She would also travel the subways night and day; catch a show at the Apollo; shoot some hoops; or lift some ice cream, fruit, or sweet potatoes for roasting.

"My parents were doing their best to raise me, but I wouldn't let them," Althea recalled. "I just wanted to play, play, play. My mother would send me out with money for bread, and I'd be out from morning to dark—and not bring home the bread. I had fun, fun, fun!"

All of this wandering around caught the attention of child welfare officials, who placed her in a home for wayward girls as a ward of the state in lieu of sending her to a reformatory. But it also prepared her for a life on the move as an athlete, playing tennis and golf in far-flung corners of the earth that were quite different from her Harlem neighborhood and especially her birthplace on a cotton farm in Silver, South Carolina. These early days shaped her restless personality, competitive spirit, and zest for life.

It all started on August 25, 1927, when Althea came screaming into the practiced hands of her great-aunt Mattie Davis, a "middoctor" who had delivered many babies throughout Clarendon County. She was born to Annie Bell and Daniel Gibson in a four-room cabin, where they lived with her paternal grandparents, Junius and Lou Gibson, and at least six of their children from current and previous marriages. "Us children knew better than to go near the door," which was off limits, Mary "Minnie" McFadden recalls of her niece's birth.

Word spread all over Silver about "Dush" and Annie Bell's firstborn—"a big, fat one" at eight pounds and long, too. Since Silver wasn't but that big, word didn't have too far to go. Both Annie Bell and Dush had grown up in Silver, which folks have always described as less of a town and more of a community. Silver, named for John S. Silver, cofounder of the Charleston, Sumter & Northern Railroad, stretched maybe three miles in any direction. Everybody knew everybody and everything, since most of them could say they were cousin so-and-so's daddy's sister's people whether they were Gibsons or Tindals or Stukes or Durants or Bethunes or Washingtons. Annie Bell was a Washington.

"While we were courting, I used to walk a mile over the bridge to see her once a week; every Sunday night I went," Dush once told Althea. "That's all her people would allow." Once a week wasn't enough for the young sweethearts. They would sneak around behind their parents' backs to see each other. "Mama used to talk about how they used to pick cotton, and I guess Daddy, he was making corn liquor in the woods somewhere, and they would always run across each other some sort of way," remembered Daniel Jr., better known as Bubba. "It must have been romantic, because something developed out of it." By the time they jumped the broom, Dush was nineteen and Annie Bell was eighteen. She kept house, while he farmed cotton and corn on the land passed down to his father, Junius, from his grandfather, January.

January Gibson is the oldest known member on the paternal side of Althea's family. "His mother came over here on the ship," according to his grandson, Thelmer Bethune, the sole surviving child of Mary Gibson Bethune, the fifth of January's eleven children. The story told to Bethune, Dush's

Althea's parents, Annie Bell and Daniel "Dush" Gibson, celebrating her 1957 Wimbledon victories at Gracie Mansion in New York City, after Althea had gained international prominence.

first cousin, and other Gibsons was that January was born to a sixteen-year-old girl and a slave owner who had purchased her on an auction block down on the coast in Charleston. The slave owner told his wife that he had deprived the girl of breakfast and supper for disrespecting him but that he was ready to feed her in exchange for an apology. He gave her not only a meal but also his seed, fathering January and eventually a daughter. The slave and her two children were later sold to another slave owner, Thelmer says. "And then that slave owner, he had two children by her."

Under the chattel for W. J. Gibson, Clarendon County's 1860 slave schedule lists an eight-year-old mulatto boy and a twenty-four-year-old black woman who fit the age span that Thelmer described. A five-year-old girl is also recorded among Gibson's eight slaves. Two decades later and seventeen years after the ink dried on the Emancipation Proclamation that

Abraham Lincoln signed to free slaves like January, his name shows up on the 1880 census as the head of his own household. January is listed as a twenty-nine-year-old farmer with a wife, Adrianna, twenty-seven, and four children, including two-year-old Junius, Althea's grandfather. The 1880 census also lists a forty-five-year-old single black woman named Rachel, living with five children ranging in age from one to fifteen. January's and Rachel's names turn up again on the tax rolls of 1898. These and later public records consistently show that January was probably born around 1852 and most likely in the month that bears his name, a common practice at the time. The last reference for Rachel, who may or may not have been January's mother, indicates that she was probably born in 1835 and lived at least until the age of sixty-three.

It is known, however, that January died on January 12, 1928, four and a half months after the birth of his great-granddaughter Althea, according to the inscription on his tombstone at Mount Zero Missionary Baptist Church in Paxville, just north of Silver. Over his grave, a limestone obelisk, dark and mottled along the edges by decay, lists his birth as occurring in 1842—ten years earlier than decades of census records show. Historians note that people often "aged" more than once a year because of the reverence bestowed upon elders. Exact ages are also iffy due to faulty memories or, more typically, nonexistent birth and death records. Whether January was seventy-six or eighty-six, he lived a long and fruitful life, boasted descendants who took to heart the inscription on his tombstone: "Gone but not forgotten."

January was a farmer, a Freemason, and a deacon who served forty-six years at Mount Zero, which was founded on the land owned by James E. Tindal, for whom his first wife, Adrianna Tindal, was named. Shortly after the Civil War, newly freed slaves had taken to the woods to hold worship services for what became Mount Zero. They gathered at

Bush Arbor near Tindal Mill Pond, where many Gibsons were baptized well into the 1970s, Minnie McFadden remembers. Like January, some of his descendants became leaders in local churches, including the Reverend Purdy Gibson, a grandson who was pastor of Friendship AME Church, founded on the Ridgill plantation in 1901. January also established a legacy of land ownership that survives today and grew acres upon acres of corn, cotton, and tobacco. "He couldn't read or write, but during his time he bought and paid for four hundred and sixty-eight acres of land," Thelmer pointed out with pride. "I tend some of it now." According to county tax records in 1898—thirty years before January's death—he owned 193 acres and four buildings worth $650 plus $200 in other possessions. That November, he paid $13.11 in taxes on his $850 property. Historians say his holdings were significant for a Negro man of that era.

Through the land, January provided sustenance, homesteads, and a way for his heirs to put in an honest day's work. Althea would eventually develop a work ethic as strong as her great-grandfather's and a desire for self-sufficiency that some came to view as an obsession with making money. January's holdings also created a buffer against Jim Crow for some of his descendants, but unfortunately not for Althea, who had to withstand the racism in the sports world alone. All over Clarendon County, for instance, Negroes lost jobs, banking privileges, access to farming equipment, and customers in the 1940s and 1950s for supporting school equality and integration resulting from *Briggs v. Elliott*, the first of five lawsuits that made up the 1954 landmark Supreme Court case *Brown v. the Board of Education*.

But Thelmer says that he was able to withstand the pressure to simply go along to get along. Thanks to January's holdings, he was his own man with his own land—even if he sometimes had little to show financially after meeting his expenses. "I'm the first man that sign the petition to have the schools," noted Thelmer, now in his nineties and one of Althea's oldest living relatives. "They couldn't hurt me because I was on my own place." January also provided land for Oak Grove School, which Thelmer and the other Gibson children attended when they weren't farming. "Sometimes I'd get two lessons in a week," Thelmer recalled wistfully. "I made up my mind that if I ever growed up and get to be a man, I'm going to see to it that my children got a better education."

Dush, Minnie, and Junius's other children learned to read and write. Minnie described attending a school for Negro children called Ram Bay until the fourth grade and then the two-room Hamilton-Brailsford Road School at the old Gum Springs Baptist Church. "School lasted three months," she said. The rest of the time she joined Dush on the farm, help-ing their father, Junius, milk their two cows, plant wheat for flour, chop cotton, and pick corn, tobacco, and soybeans—some of which they sold. Their older sisters would transform the fruits of their labor into hearty meals, keeping the wood-stove burning to cook peas, corn bread, collard greens, and es-pecially sweet potatoes, a family favorite. "You don't have that; you don't have nothing," said Minnie, who was also partial to bread with milk and syrup. "We used to raise our own chick-ens," she added. "The goats would walk up the steps and come right in the house. They would get in the bed, too!"

Junius stretched the meals by hunting. A prankster with a "devilish" streak that made its way down to his granddaugh-ter Althea and her siblings, nieces, and nephews, Junius once passed off a fox to his wife as a sand hill coon. "Mama had it cooked up real good with black pepper and onions and stuff," Minnie chuckled, her eyes watering from laughter as she retold the story. "Then Papa told her, 'Lou, that ain't been no coon; that was a fox.' Boy, did Mama get mad and get on Papa! I don't think I ever seen her mad."

Since Junius wasn't particularly fond of farming, a good deal of it fell to Dush and the rest of his offspring. Sometimes Junius found other ways to occupy his time and bring in extra money. "He used to go into the woods and saw blocks and logs and take them to Sumter to sell them," Minnie remembered. Silver was smack dab in the middle of logging and lumber operations stretching from Sumter to the north and the Santee River farther south. Some of the railroads that serviced them paid local farmers and woodsmen roughly 12 cents for each pine or cypress crosstie.

When Junius wasn't chopping wood or hunting, he made beer and moonshine. "He used to make some nice moonshine liquor," Minnie said. "People would rather buy that than buy label liquor." Mattie Bryant, Althea's cousin and childhood running buddy, was even more emphatic. "He made the *best* corn whiskey in the world," she said of their grandfather. "Everybody came to him." Thelmer pointed out that Junius wasn't alone. "Plenty of people were making whiskey," he said. "All they do is have to duck the law; that's all." At one point, as many as forty thousand people made a living as "bootleggers, moonshiners, and rumrunners" in South Carolina, according to the historian Walter Edgar.

Althea's other grandfather, Charles Canty Washington, also made moonshine on the side. But Charlie, a loud-talking man, was mostly a father, a farmer, and a preacher. "He was a good grandfather and provider," recalled Althea's first cousin Agnes "Aggie" Green, who was raised by Charlie and his second wife, Miss Josephine, after her mother died when she was a baby. "My grandfather ran a big farm," said Aggie, the daughter of Willie Washington, one of Annie Bell's older brothers. Aggie described Charlie as a tenant farmer, working the land owned by Levy Tindall with help at one point from Althea's father, Dush. "We worked so hard until I couldn't think straight," Aggie reflected on her days in the field, picking everything from string beans to watermelon. Charlie didn't have his own church, but he was a popular preacher who stirred souls with his powerful delivery of the Word. He tended to preach close to home at Friendship AME, which was only a mile from his house. Aggie still worships there along with other relatives, traveling seventy-five miles east from Columbia, South Carolina.

Charlie Washington also ran one of Silver's three stores. "He was the first man opened up a store in Silver," Thelmer said. A master butcher, he sold everything from dresses and shoes to beef and fish that arrived each Friday by train from Charleston. As a girl, Aggie cooked fish and sold clothing at her granddaddy's store, which was located in the center of whatever hustle and bustle the small town could muster up. At its peak, Silver had the trio of stores, a sawmill, a corn mill, a cotton gin, a post office, and a train depot with an agent. The town rode along with the fortunes of the railroad and the crops it carried. By the forties, the only thing moving along Silver's railroad tracks were local folks walking north to Paxville and Sumter or south toward Summerton and Manning. Overgrowth and dusty farm roads conceal those tracks today, and Silver's businesses center on a small nightclub, a nursing home, and one store—Sunny's—owned by Harold "Sunny" Billie, another of Althea's cousins.

No one remembers exactly when Charlie's store went bust; his third wife, Rosa, tried to keep it going after he died. Lots of businesses in South Carolina went under in the early years of the twentieth century, from stores and banks to lumber mills and farms, including those owned or managed by relatives on both sides of Althea's family—especially those who grew cotton. For a time, cotton was truly king in the state and spread its riches throughout the local economy, accounting for two-thirds of the cash value of South Carolina's crops. Better seeds and fertilizer spawned record harvests that grew from 747,000 bales in 1890 to 1,280,000 bales in 1910. Although South Carolina was the smallest of the cotton-growing states, its farmers picked enough for it to rank third behind Georgia and Texas.

But no matter how promising things looked time and time again, any hopes that the Gibsons and Washingtons had of getting ahead were repeatedly dashed. The war in Europe was a boon for the cotton market and gave everyone hope, but in the long run it proved to be a mixed blessing. South Carolinians found themselves with too much cotton and not enough places to sell it or even store it. With overproduction, a tight export market, and cotton exchanges shuttered for at least three months, prices plunged as low as $6^1/_2$ cents a pound in mid-1914. After the United States entered World War I in 1917, prices for both cotton and tobacco rose to roughly 40 cents a pound. By Christmas of 1921, however, cotton prices fell again, this time by two-thirds to $13^1/_2$ cents a pound, thanks in part to the one-two punch of a drought and a boll weevil plague that had worked its way up from Mexico. Long before Black Tuesday—when the historic stock market crash of October 29, 1929, signaled the official start of the Great Depression—South Carolina was already suffering from a rural depression that was just as great and devastating.

It is against this backdrop that Althea Gibson was born in August 1927. With a new wife and new baby, Daniel Gibson was having a hard time making unruly ends meet, especially with three years in a row of bad weather. "The depression hit Silver, South Carolina, quicker than it did most back around 1929, and things were tough all over, even if I was working my father-in-law's farm then," Dush recalled. With the drought and the boll weevil, many farmers harvested less than 10 per-

cent of their typical yields. Overall, average cotton production in the state dropped from about 1,365,000 bales a year to
801,000 bales. The common refrain, Edgar said, was, "Ten-cent
cotton and 40-cent meat; how in the hell can a poor man eat?"

Dush could certainly relate.

"I worked three years for nothin'," he remembered.
"That third year, all I got out of it was a bale and a half of
cotton. Cotton was sellin' for fifty dollars a bale then, so I
made seventy-five dollars for the year's work. I had to get out
of there." So when Annie Bell's sister, Sally Washington,
came home for their sister Blanche's funeral, Dush decided
that they would follow her back to New York City. His plan
was to send Althea first with Aunt Sally, and he'd take the
train up to do some job hunting as soon as his cotton money
came in. Once he got on his feet in New York, he would send
for his wife. The Gibsons and Washingtons became part of a
mass exodus in which half of South Carolina's forty-six coun-
ties lost as much as 15 percent of their population. More
than fifty thousand black farmers left early on. "Back then,
everybody was catching the devil," Thelmer said. "How I
came through that, sometimes I don't believe it." Black farmers made even less for their crops than white farmers did,
Thelmer recalled, shaking his head. "You could pick a hundred pounds, but you wouldn't make no money. The big man,
he buy the cotton. He gave you the lowest he could give you
for it. And one time I know it ain't been but five cent a
pound for a bale of cotton. It take fifteen hundred pounds of
seed cotton to make you a bale."

"Those were the draining years on the cotton farms," wrote
Ben Robertson, the author of *Red Hills and Cotton*. "Nearly all
of the strongest tenant families left the cotton fields. Only the
old and the young and the determined stayed on." Although
Dush was certainly young and determined, when his money

came through, he was out of there, joining the nearly thirty-four thousand others who left South Carolina for Harlem in 1930. "I bought me a cheap blue suit for seven-fifty," he said. "I paid twenty-five dollars for the fare, I left some money with the wife, and I took off for New York City."

Charlie's daughter, Daisy Kelly, is believed to have been the first of Althea's kin to head north, according to Mattie. Many relatives and neighbors tested out life in New York by taking on short-term jobs that they'd hear about through the grapevine. Daisy, whose husband held a coveted job as a Pullman porter on the railroad, lived in Philadelphia for a time, before relocating to Bronx, New York. Even Althea's grandfather Junius migrated north when he got up in years, living down in the Bowery in lower Manhattan, where he was the superintendent of an apartment building on Irvington Street. Although Junius spent most of his life in a warm climate, he walked around New York in the winter wearing only rubbers on his feet. Sometimes he wore nothing on his full head of hair that he usually kept parted down the middle in two lengthy braids of a glistening silver that Althea longed for in her later years, but that only blessed Bubba's crown.

"He'd run his hand through his hair and say 'if a fly come on my head and slip up, he'll slip and break his darn ass,'" Minnie recounted. His skin was so light, she added, that he had gotten away with sitting in the front of South Carolina's buses with the white passengers rather than in the back with the other black riders. Junius would come to Harlem to visit Althea and Bubba's family and then moved there permanently with his daughter, Sweetie, when he became ill. Sweetie and her husband were the parents of Claude Brown, who chronicled his family's adjustment from country life in Silver to their hard-knock life in Harlem in his critically acclaimed memoir, *Manchild in the Promised Land*.

Dush, indeed, saw New York as the promised land—even though his introduction to the big city entailed being hustled out of five dollars by a train porter who offered to spare an hour to accompany him on the allegedly tricky trip to Harlem. The porter kept his word, so to speak. But Dush paid a huge markup for the nickel subway ride, which had a fairly direct route north from Pennsylvania Station at West 34th Street in midtown Manhattan to West 125th Street in Harlem. Roughly twenty minutes after they entered the subway car, the porter walked Dush up a few flights of stairs to the sidewalk and said: "Here you are, Mr. Gibson. This is Harlem." Dush was so happy to be in New York that he shrugged off the con job and joined three-year-old Althea at the apartment his sister-in-law Sally shared with a boarder on West 145th Street, while Annie Bell waited in Silver with their new baby, Mildred. "I got me a job right away," Dush said. "Handyman in a garage for big money. Ten dollars a week. I didn't have nothin' to worry about no more. I sent for my wife, and we were in business."

Despite its fledgling "Don't Buy Where You Can't Work" campaign, the Harlem that the Gibsons and other transplants encountered lived up to its reputation for good times and what they considered to be good jobs. It was a Harlem that buzzed with blackness, borne of a "Negro invasion" that fleeing white residents despised and tried unsuccessfully to block with restrictive real-estate covenants and fear tactics. Blacks migrated not only from the Deep South, like the Gibsons and Washingtons had done, but also from the near South, leaving chocolate clusters in Greenwich Village, the Tenderloin and San Juan Hill on the west side of Manhattan, and Five Points, now City Hall, in the lower part of the island. Add to this the immigrants who had sailed into Ellis Island from the Caribbean after boarding boats of their own volition unlike the grandparents of their new American neighbors who had been forced onto slave ships.

It was a Harlem reveling in a renaissance that calls to mind the poet Langston Hughes, the author Dorothy West, and the sculptor Augusta Savage. It was a Harlem swinging to the sound of Duke Ellington and singing the blues of Bessie Smith. It was a Harlem that had witnessed the business acumen and philanthropy of a Madame C. J. Walker. It was a Harlem inundated with "leaders" of every stripe, including W. E. B. Du Bois of the NAACP; the Reverend Adam Clayton Powell Sr. and his son at Abyssinian Baptist Church; A. Philip Randolph, the founder of the Brotherhood of Sleeping Car Porters; as well as more controversial figures such as Bishop Charles Emanuel Grace, better known as Sweet Daddy Grace, at the United House of Prayer; George Baker, dubbed Father Divine for his reputed mystical powers; and Marcus Moziah Garvey, who had spent much of the twenties trying to move the masses back to Africa. Before his deportation to Jamaica, Garvey had captivated many in Harlem with the power of his message, "Up you mighty race! You can accomplish what you will"; the pageantry of his parades; and the sheer size of his empire, for which he used its millions to amass hotels, factories, restaurants, stores, and the Black Star Line intended to transport the masses to the Motherland.

It was a Harlem that captivated the Gibsons, who got off to a comfortable start at Sally's place with Annie Bell and Millie settling in just months after Dush's arrival. "There was always lots of food to eat in her house, the rent was always paid on time, and Aunt Sally wore nice clothes every day in the week," Althea recalled. "She did all right for herself." Sally, who worked as a domestic, also sold bootleg whiskey on the side, just as her father, Charlie, had back home. Once, Althea inadvertently had a taste when she woke up thirsty for water and turned up a jug on the kitchen table, while Sally entertained company in the parlor. "The next thing I can remember is Aunt Sally holding me down in the bed while the doctor pumped my stomach out," Althea said. It wouldn't be her last drink, for her father would have to purge her periodically of the whiskey that her uncles and Sally's visitors would share. But these early experiences convinced Althea that she'd never "disgrace" herself by getting drunk in public.

From Aunt Sally's place, Althea moved to Philadelphia, where she lived on and off with Aunt Daisy. In Philly, Althea began to show the spunk that would mark her childhood. Never one to sit still—even in her Sunday best—Althea once jumped back and forth over a bucket of automotive grease while a friend of Aunt Daisy's worked on his secondhand car. Since Althea was so drawn to Aunt Daisy's friend and to his car, she didn't pay enough attention to her footwork while jumping the bucket. After one false move, she wound up with grease all over her skin and the immaculate white dress that matched her stockings and the silk bow in her hair. It took Aunt Daisy a while to degrease her niece, whom she said was transformed from a picture of beauty to an *Amos 'n' Andy* character. And the outfit—it was ruined. Another time, Althea had a fit when she couldn't go somewhere with Aunt Daisy and her cousin Pearl. Little did they know that she accompanied them the entire trip by ducking below the car window on the running board and holding onto the door handle for dear life. "When the car pulled up at the house they were going to and Aunt Daisy and Pearl got out, I was standing on the sidewalk."

And then there were the fights, where Althea was swinging either fists or branches at boys chasing her around the neighborhood. But all of this was nothing, she admitted, compared to the ruckus her wandering ways caused in Harlem at her family's railroad flat on 143rd Street, between Lenox and Seventh Avenues. "I was a traveling girl, and I hated to go to school," Althea explained. "I played hooky from school all the time. It was a habit I never lost. Later on, when I was older, my friends and I used to regard school as just a good place to meet and make our plans for what we would do all day. What's more," she added, "I didn't like people telling me what to do."

So she did what she wanted.

"I guess about the worst thing we did was snitch little packages of ice cream while we were walking through the big stores like the five-and-ten or pieces of fruit while we were walking past a stand on the street." A cop once caught her with a sweet potato in hand but released her after lots of pleading and begging. But as soon as she was free, she reclaimed it on a dare from her girls, and they roasted the "mickey" on burning milk crates at a nearby empty lot. "Snitcher's heaven," Althea said, was over the 145th Street Bridge at the Bronx Terminal Market. There, they'd fill empty baskets with rejected peaches, bananas, tomatoes, and lettuce. "Once, I carried a whole watermelon in my hands over that bridge."

While she was determined to be in the thick of things, all that was new and exciting and hot, Althea was oblivious to what the times truly represented. It wasn't until adulthood that she realized the true depths of the Depression and how it had affected her family. "I remember you could get fish-and-chips for fifteen cents and soda at five cents a quart," she recalled. "If there was any poverty, I wasn't aware of it. How could you think that when you could get soda for five cents?" She lived a carefree existence—"a very happy child's life," her cousin Mattie said. "She was very playful. She was pleasant, very active. Nobody would bother us. We'd take up for one another." Life wasn't so easy for their parents, however. "It was just hard times," Mattie said. "People were on WPA;

they call it welfare today." Mattie's mother used help from the Works Progress Administration to supplement her income as a hospital laundry worker, while Althea's father worked nights as a mechanic. The median family income in Harlem fell 43.6 percent in the first three years of the Depression, from $1,808 in 1929 to $1,109 in 1932, while the national median was $2,335. And, even as incomes continued to fall, rents rose above 125th Street in Harlem and were up to $30 a month higher than the rest of Manhattan.

The Gibsons made sure that Althea and Bubba and their sisters, Millie, Lillian, and Annie, lived richly even if they weren't. They kept them fed and clothed, making their daughters' wardrobes a priority over their son's. "I said, 'Mama, you know what? You don't have to buy me any more clothes. You don't have to buy me anything.' I said, 'I'm going to get my own,'" Bubba claims he promised as a nine-year-old. "Whatever I was doing," he added, chuckling with raised eyebrows, "I never got caught."

Annie Bell could burn in the kitchen—always cooking two meats on Sundays—and knew how to stretch a meal. She had to, since there were always extra mouths to feed. The Gibson home was the place to be. It was full of life, making outsiders long to be on the inside where they thought all the laughin' and fussin' meant a party was going on. But it was usually just family. Lots of 'em. Dozens for Thanksgiving and other holidays. And nearly a dozen just because. Just because it was the weekend. Just because they were in the neighborhood. Just because they up and decided to leave the South and needed a place to rest their heads until they got on their feet. Some stayed, like Annie Bell's baby sister, Hallie, and her dog, Ruth. Millie also stayed along with her girls, Mary Ann and Sandra, after she got married. Annie Bell wouldn't have it any other way—even when Hallie would argue with

Dush over any little thing, drink, curse, or show her behind—literally pulling down her pants and telling her brother-in-law to "kiss my ass!"

"Mama was a sweet lady," Bubba said. "She was a softy." Many a niece and nephew claim to this day that Annie Bell was their favorite aunt. To a person, they use the words *sweet* or *nice* or *quiet* when describing her. One of her favorite pastimes, Bubba recalled, was playing popular ragtime tunes on the piano.

Dush, on the other hand, was characterized as an easygoing family man but not the "huggy-kissy" type. After working long hours at various garages around town, he'd return home, wash up and brush his teeth with Octagon soap, and fix one of his favorite meals: grits and eggs with fish, sardines, or bacon—polished off with a nip of Four Roses whiskey. He also liked Brown Mule chewing tobacco, the one thing that the Gibson and Washington children wished that their elders would have left down South. They found it embarrassing and disgusting, but they were in good company. With so many transplants in Harlem, nearly everyone had someone in his family who chewed tobacco, like it or not.

Although Althea was fond of her father, she kept him riled up. "He was the quietest man I've ever seen," Mary Ann said. "But when he got mad," Bubba added, "get out of his way! When he talked, you listened—and he didn't repeat himself." Annie Bell would try to smooth things over when Althea, Bubba, or another child stirred up her husband's wrath. She'd stand between Dush and the offending child—sometimes catching errant swings—or she'd "administer" the discipline herself. Typically, her children and grandchildren said, she'd make much ado about nothing—fussing and whipping the bed more than the child so that Dush would hear the commotion through the walls and be satisfied that the rod had not been spared. Now Dush's punishments were the stuff of legends, often coming at full force from an ironing cord or an open hand. "He would slap the hell out of you," Bubba recalls, wincing. As severe as they might have been, his whippings were no different than those delivered in many households. Dush considered himself a good father who wanted what other parents wanted: to keep his offspring in line and out of harm's way. "I feel a lot of those whippings helped," Althea admitted. "Somebody had to knock a little sense into me." And the whippings were avoidable, Bubba said. "You could be around that man for a whole week or a month; as long as you are doing the right thing, he wouldn't bother you." Bubba chuckled at the memory. "Sometimes he wouldn't even say anything to you. He'd look at you."

As long as Althea and the rest could steer clear of drugs, alcohol, fights, and Daddy's quiet fire, they were fine. Thanks to Dush, Althea could hold her own on the streets and was among the few trained boxers in her neighborhood. "Daddy used to take Althea and I on the roof," Bubba said. "He told Althea: 'I'm going to teach you how to fight.' He would hit her like he would hit a man. He would teach her, but he would knock the hell out of her until she couldn't take no more. Althea turned around and beat Daddy's butt. After all that, he said, 'Lesson's over.'"

Dush was pleased with Althea's progress. "The minute I saw this natural left hook that Al had, I started teaching her how to mix it up with a right cross," he said. "It was a beautiful combination from the beginning."

"She could beat the hell out of anybody in the block, including all of us," Bubba acknowledged. "So we never had to worry about anything." That protection extended from children to adults, he added. "There was a guy named Ellis. He was over six feet tall, and he was a little husky, too. One day we were out in the street arguing, and he called Mama a name. I ran to get Althea. I said, 'Althea! He's talking about our mother!'" Althea was about fourteen, and Ellis was about eighteen, but the age difference didn't matter. "She hauled off and hit him and knocked him down," Bubba said, beaming. With a black eye from a younger teenager—a girl at that—Ellis left the Gibsons alone.

Althea also came to their inebriated Uncle Junie's defense when the leader of the Sabres gang on 144th Street tried to jump him in a stairwell leading to their Aunt Sally's apartment. "That's my uncle," Althea yelled at the gang leader. "Go bother somebody else if you got to steal!" As she helped Uncle Junie to his feet, the gang leader threw a sharpened screwdriver at her. "I stuck my hand out to protect myself and got a gash just above my thumb," she said. After escorting Uncle Junie to Aunt Sally's place, Althea ran downstairs to beat up the boy in a bloody fight that became the talk of the neighborhood. "She was going blow for blow with this guy," Bubba remembered. "They were battling!"

"You didn't mess with the Gibson family in those days," Bubba boasted. "Althea had a reputation. I got a kick out of it!" Besides her fighting ability, Althea hung with a tough crowd. Some of her friends lived behind them on 144th Street, and they would go to the back windows to talk across the alley. "They were some rough girls," Bubba explained. "When you saw them coming, you got on the other side of the street."

"If Daddy hadn't shown me how to look out for myself," Althea pointed out, "I would have got into a lot of fights that I would have lost, and I would have been pretty badly beaten up a lot of times.

"Sometimes, in a tough neighborhood, where there is no way for a kid to prove himself except by playing games and fighting, you've got to let them know you can look out for yourself before they will leave you alone. If they think you're helpless, they will all look to build up their own reputations by beating up on you. I learned always to get in the first punch."

"Althea carried herself very well," Bubba said. "She would never back down. She'd say, 'Kiss my ass!' I heard her say that many times."

Besides building street savvy, Dush was also motivated by the possibility of boxing stardom. "You see, back in those days, you could read in the papers about the big money that lady boxers were making," he explained. "And I knew right away that Al would make a world's champion." Women boxed at the Moulin Rouge in Paris and in boxing booths that traveled to fairgrounds in some parts of Europe. In 1904 women's boxing was showcased in an exhibition at the Olympics in St. Louis and began spreading across the United States. One of the popular boxers of the 1930s was Ruby Allen, who made as much as $1,000 fighting other women. Allen boxed each Thursday at the Liberty Theater in St. Louis and wrestled on Mondays. But it remained a controversial pastime, because it wasn't considered ladylike and could lead to severe injury or death.

But things didn't work out quite as Dush had planned. "There was no way for me to know then that the fad for lady boxers was going to run out. But it did," he said. Still, he was right about his eldest daughter one day becoming a world's champion. The signs might have been there all along when she was hitting a ball with a stick as a toddler back in Silver. As she grew older, she played sports with her brother or stickball and basketball with her cousin Mattie. "I mean that girl would play ball in the street," Mattie said. "We loved to play ball. It was basketball all the time." Althea would also shoot hoops for Cokes and hot dogs with her best friend, Alma Irving.

"At night, we used to go to the school gymnasium and challenge anybody, boy or girl, man or woman, to play us in what we used to call 'two-on-two,'" Althea recalled. "We'd use just one basket and see which team could score the most baskets on the other. We played hard, and when we got finished, we'd go to a cheap restaurant and get a plate of turnip greens and rice, or maybe, if we had a little extra money, a hamburger, steak, or fried chicken and french fried potatoes. In those days, of course, you could get a big plate of food like that for only thirty-five cents. Fish-and-chips were only fifteen cents, and soda was a nickel a quart if you brought your own can."

Althea filled her time with games and postgame celebrations, which left little time for school or home. "I played it all—basketball, shuffleboard, badminton, volleyball," Althea said. "Mama could never get me up from the street. I was down there from morning to night."

The teenager became even less interested in school after graduating from junior high in 1941. Being assigned to Yorkville Trade School didn't help matters. She tried to obtain a transfer to the high school downtown where her friends were enrolled, but it didn't work. Althea was pissed. She initially tried to make the best of it, but the novelty of sewing and fixing sewing machines soon wore off. "From then on, school and I had nothing in common at all. I began to stay out for weeks at a time." Her "vacations" from school spilled over into her home life, and soon she was dodging not only the truant officer but also her father.

"I would go to the police station on 135th Street and tell them that I was afraid to go home because my father was going to beat me up," Althea explained. "Once a girlfriend told me there was a place on Fifth Avenue at 105th Street, called the Society for the Prevention of Cruelty to Children, that would take in kids who were in trouble and had no place to go. The next time I stayed out so late that I didn't dare go home, I asked them to take me in. . . . The trouble was, they notified

my mother and father, and Daddy came for me in the morning. I promised him I wasn't ever going to run away again,
but he licked me anyway, and a week later, I took off again.

"I went straight to the SPCC," Althea continued. "I
skinned off my shirt and showed them the welts on my back.
They took me in again. When Daddy came after me, they
asked me if I wanted to go back with him. When I said no,
that I was afraid to, they said I could stay. That place was a
regular country club. I had to do a little work, like making
my bed and helping clean up the dormitory and taking my
turn scrubbing the toilets, but mostly it was a snap."

However, the novelty soon wore off, and Althea asked to
return home, promising to stay out of trouble. Before allowing her to leave with Dush, the woman in charge warned
Althea that if she reneged on her promise, the next stop
could be a reformatory. Althea kept her word—for a little
while—but it wasn't long before she was back out in the
streets. When Althea seemed to forget where she lived, Millie had to lead the search parties. "We used to have to drag
her back in the house," she told *Time* in an interview. "When
the other girls were putting on lipstick, she was out playing
stickball." Sometimes Annie Bell went out herself to find
Althea. "Mom says she used to walk the streets of Harlem
until two or three o'clock in the morning looking for me,"
Althea said. "But she never had much chance of finding me.
When I was *really* trying to hide out, I never went near any
of the playgrounds or gymnasiums or restaurants that I usually hung out at.

"I sneaked around to different friends' houses in the daytime or sat all by myself in the movies, and then, if I didn't
have anyplace lined up to sleep, I would just ride the subway
all night. I would ride from one end of the line to the other,
from Van Cortlandt Park to New Lots Avenue, back and forth
like a zombie. At least it was a place to sit down."

Chapter 2

Holding Court

I knew that I was an unusual, talented girl through the grace of God. I didn't need to prove that to myself. I only wanted to prove it to my opponents.

NO ONE COULD BEAT the princess of paddleball. She even trounced her brother, Bubba, who had gained notoriety by winning tournament after tournament long before she took an interest in the game. Bubba said that he was able to rise to the top because Althea was "running around" so much even during her adolescence. But once she slowed down long enough to learn the game, she ruled her block and other play streets cordoned off by the Police Athletic League. And together, the Gibsons were a formidable team. Paddle tennis and other PAL activities kept Althea closer to home at least, though not in it.

PAL days meant early days for grown-ups who had to move their cars so they wouldn't be towed and for children impatiently gathered outside the apartment of the man who stored the treasured equipment. Althea, Bubba, and their playmates would descend into their neighbor's basement to help retrieve balls, jump ropes, poles, paddles, and pucks.

After helping him set up, they could run up and down West 143rd Street between Lenox and Seventh Avenues playing everything from shuffleboard to Ping-Pong and cooling off periodically in the spray of water from the sprinklers placed on the fire hydrants. Althea held court in front of her building, where a net had been strung tightly across the painted lines of asphalt to the sidewalk on the south side of the street. "When she first picked up the tennis paddle, she fell in love with it," Bubba recalled. "When she learned to play, she beat my ass."

"The fellows in the block were more fun to compete with than the girls; they made it worthwhile," Althea explained. "The young boys who played on another court up the block heard about me and challenged me. And I accepted." Never one to back down from a challenge, Althea relished making her opponents regret that they had taken her on. "She could out-hit everybody," Bubba said. "They could never return her serves." Some players didn't even try. They just stood there on the court—about half the size of a regulation tennis court—and watched the ball zip by them. "She'd be out there all day long playing tennis," Bubba added, "without stopping to eat." When the PAL equipment went back in the basement, she'd switch to stickball, whacking the life out of a 29-cent Spalding ball with a broom handle. Her skills won her awards presented by New York Mayor Fiorello La Guardia, as the citywide champion of paddleball and as the pitcher—and only girl—on the number-one softball team. In fact, she was the PAL paddleball champion from 1938 to 1942.

"Her aggressive strokes and swift movement caught my attention immediately," said Buddy Walker, PAL play leader by day and bandleader by night. The popular yet struggling saxophonist figured that if young Althea could win at paddle tennis, she could take on regular tennis, too. Some of his tennis friends snickered when he invited them to play this tall, skinny kid he'd been bragging about, but the laughter ended once they came to the block where Althea reigned and left as losers. Walker was pumped up even more. He gave five bucks to a racket stringer named Van Houton for a used pair of wooden rackets and took Althea to Mount Morris Park to hit balls against the wall.

They moved on to the Harlem River Tennis Courts at 153rd Street and Seventh Avenue, where he again asked a friend to hit a few balls with her. "After about ten minutes, all the players on the other courts stopped their games to watch her," Walker later told Ted Poston, the dean of black journalists and a reporter for the *New York Post*. "In about an hour, spectators had lined up on both sides of her court."

"It was wonderful to see this twelve-year-old kid hypnotize so many people with her speed and power strokes the very first time she had ever been on a tennis court." Althea had no idea—and probably couldn't have cared less—that she was mesmerizing members of the Sugar Hill elite. Unbeknownst to her, she was at a turning point that would forever change her life. Just as Walker had hoped, one of the spectators literally picked up the ball and ran with it. It was Juan Serreals, a schoolteacher and a member of Harlem's prestigious Cosmopolitan Tennis Club, which had a clubhouse and five courts enclosed in a fence at 149th Street and Convent Avenue through the midfifties. Serreals told Fred Johnson, the club's one-armed pro, about Althea and took her up there to meet him. "They all said she was a natural athlete," Johnson said, "but I was skeptical."

Johnson was one of the best coaches in the city and a champion in veteran's singles of the American Tennis Association (ATA), founded in 1916 to increase the field of black athletes. He had been honing his skills since 1906, when he turned to tennis as his sport of last resort after losing his left arm in an industrial accident during his youth. Competing

Fred Johnson (far right), one of the best tennis coaches in New York City in the 1940s, was an important early influence. Bertram Baker (far left) was the executive secretary of the ATA and a Brooklyn assemblyman.

with one arm was no hindrance for Johnson, who won a singles championship in New Jersey and a doubles title in Nassau, Bahamas, as a member of the Ideal Tennis Club, an early ATA affiliate. Since Johnson was renowned inside ATA circles and beyond, anyone who was even halfway serious about tennis wanted to be his pupil. Johnson's students included the filmmaker Gordon Parks, the journalist Evelyn Cunningham, and many an ATA standout, such as Billy Davis, a boy's and men's champion. Johnson knew talent when he saw it. The question was, would he see enough of it in Althea? His question was answered after hitting a few balls with her. He was impressed and so were the Cosmopolitan members who chipped in to pay for a junior membership for Althea. One member put up $5 for a new racket, and Johnson doubled it with $10. That evening, the coach headed down to Warren

Street to buy a Dreadnought Driver from the Harry Lee Company at the $15 professional rate. On the way, he made a detour to Althea's apartment to ask her parents for permission to coach her. Annie Bell asked Johnson, "How much money is there in it?" He replied, "None now, but probably some later."

Johnson tried to smooth out Althea's rough edges and tone down her cockiness. "I really wasn't the tennis type," Althea said. "I kept wanting to fight the other player every time I started to lose a match." But she learned to suppress these feelings, which were tested throughout her athletic career with Jim Crow circling so strongly all around. One of the first people to take on refining Althea's behavior on and off the court was Rhoda Smith, who met her at the same time as Johnson did. "I was the first woman she ever played tennis with, and she resented it because I was always trying to improve her ways," said Smith, who had been a top-ranked ATA player and purchased Althea's first white tennis outfit. "I had to keep saying, 'Don't do this' and 'Don't do that,' until she would cry out: 'You, Mrs. Smith, you're always [picking] on me!'"

"When balls came onto her court from the other courts," Smith related, "she would simply hit them out of the way in any direction instead of politely knocking them back to the players who wanted them, as is done in tennis. But, after all, she had played in the street all her life, and she didn't know any better."

The Cosmopolitan club was made up of people who knew better. Its members included professionals, intellectuals, and society types like Smith, the kind of people whom W. E. B. Du Bois described as the "Talented Tenth." They counted race-conscious men and women among their ranks. They had money—and it was "old." Few of them knew just how rough Althea was around her edges. They had no clue that one of their newest and youngest members was so drawn to the theater of the streets, spending most of her time there when she wasn't on their courts. The teenager eventually dropped out of high school and found herself living temporarily in a furnished room with a family that provided safe havens for girls like Althea who were a step away from being sent to a reformatory school. Althea's close call stemmed from her chronic absences from school and home. By this point, she had reneged on a deal she had cut with Yorkville Trade School to get her working papers ahead of schedule if she attended night classes.

"I went for a couple of weeks," Althea said of the night classes. "But then I stopped, and nobody ever came after me. So that was that. I was officially a working girl; I liked it, too. I felt better working. I had the feeling of being independent, like I was somebody, making my own money and buying what I wanted to buy, paying in a little at home, and doing what I wanted to do instead of being, what you might call, dictated to. It was very important to me to be on my own.

"I must have worked at a dozen jobs in the next few years, maybe more," she explained. "I was restless, and I never stayed in any one place very long. If it wasn't to my liking, I quit. I was a counter girl at the Chambers Street branch of the Chock Full o' Nuts restaurant chain. I was a messenger for a blueprinting company. I worked at a button factory and a dress factory and a department store. I ran an elevator at the Dixie Hotel, and I even had a job cleaning chickens in a butcher shop. I used to have to take out the guts and everything." Her favorite (and longest) job was working as a mail clerk at the New York School of Social Work, complete with her own tiny office. "I liked the job, because it was the first one I'd had that gave me some pride—that made me feel like I was somebody." But she lost it in six months, after skipping work on a Friday to join some friends at the Paramount Theatre in Times Square to see her favorite singer, Sarah Vaughan.

She didn't spend much time looking for another job. "I was too busy playing tennis in the daytime and having fun at night," Althea said of her schedule, which would grow even more hectic and begin to overshadow not only work but also family time, friendships outside of sports, and romantic relationships. "The hardest work I did, aside from practicing tennis, was to report to the welfare ladies once a week, tell them how I was getting along, and pick up my allowance. Then I would celebrate by spending the whole day in the movies and filling myself up with cheap food."

Gordon Parks was one of the few Cosmopolitan members who had a clue about Althea's other life. In fact, their friendship blossomed because he had gotten in the middle of it one day to come to her defense. Parks was standing in front of the 135th Street YMCA with a few friends. Like a streak of lightning, Althea shot past him wearing a pink and blue gingham dress with loafers. "She looked anything but like an athlete at that particular moment," Parks recalled. Two angry boys were in hot pursuit, and fear was in her eyes—eyes that pleaded for Parks's intervention. Parks got the message and stepped in with his boys. Clearly outsized and outnumbered, Althea's pursuers gave up the chase. "She appreciated it, and I don't think she ever forgot it," Parks said. "I was always her buddy after that. She called me Parksy, and I called her Thea Babe." To this day, he still has no idea why Althea was being chased. Whatever the reason, it probably would have raised eyebrows at the Cosmopolitan.

"Those days, I probably would have been more at home training in Stillman's Gym than at the Cosmopolitan club," said Althea, referring to the legendary boxing ring where Joe Louis, Sugar Ray Robinson, and Jersey Joe Walcott battered bags, ribs, and jaws with their upper cuts, jabs, and hooks. "The Cosmopolitan members were the highest class of Harlem people, and they had set ideas about what was socially acceptable behavior. They were probably stricter than white people of similar position." While Althea was responsive to tennis instruction, she was hardheaded about lessons on life from Johnson and the rest. "I was willing to do what he said about tennis, but I figured what I did away from the courts was none of his business," she maintained. "I wasn't exactly ready to start studying how to be a fine lady." She didn't even want to play against ladies. But after joining the Cosmopolitan club, she began to learn that female competition could be as challenging as male competition. "After a while," she added, "I began to understand that you could walk out on the court like a lady, all dressed up in white, be polite to everybody and still play like a tiger."

"We were sort of all in awe, because of her taking to tennis so rapidly," recalled Billy Davis, who became Althea's warm-up and sparring partner at the Cosmopolitan as well as a lifelong friend. "She was tall for her age and a great athlete, so we had to admire her."

"I got a regular schedule of lessons from Mr. Johnson, and I began to learn something about the game of tennis," Althea said. "I already knew *how* to hit the ball, but I didn't know *why*. He taught me some footwork and how to plan where to hit the ball." She tried to model her game after that of the national white champion, Alice Marble, whom she saw play in one of the few interracial matches at the Cosmopolitan or anywhere for that matter and who was considered one of the first "big" power hitters in women's tennis.

A year after Althea's first lesson with Johnson in the summer of 1941, she entered her first tournament: the 1942 New York State Open Championship. She won the girls' singles, and the victory was "all the sweeter" because she had defeated a white girl, Nina Irwin, in the finals. She was on a roll.

"I knew that I was an unusual, talented girl through the grace of God. I didn't need to prove that to myself. I only wanted to prove it to my opponents."

That summer, Cosmopolitan members took up a collection to send her to Lincoln University in Pennsylvania for the ATA national girls' championship. She lost in the finals to Nana Davis, her only defeat in the ATA girls' division. "Althea was a very crude creature," Davis said. "She had the idea she was better than anybody. I can remember her saying, 'Who's this Nana Davis? Let me at her.' After I beat her, she headed straight for the grandstand without bothering to shake hands. Some kid had been laughing at her, and she was going to throw him out."

Althea was disappointed about losing in her first national tournament, and it would be two years before she had another chance to go for victory. World War II and related travel restrictions meant no national ATA competition in 1943. But in 1944 and 1945 Althea won back-to-back girls' titles. With her eighteenth birthday that August, she moved up to the next level of competition as she was now old enough to take on the women. Being eighteen also meant more freedom for Althea. "I was able to run my own life at last," she said. In Gloria Nightingale she found a running partner and alter ego. "Gloria was like me; all she cared about was playing games and having a good time. . . . No responsibilities, no worries, just having a ball." Althea moved in with Gloria's family and paid rent to her grandmother with money she made as a waitress. She and Gloria joined a basketball team called the Mysterious Five. They practiced at the 134th Street Boys Club and played up to four games a week. Afterward, they'd bowl the night away, sometimes until 4 A.M. One night, Gloria introduced Althea to Sugar Ray Robinson. "So you're Sugar Ray Robinson?" she asked her

With Sugar Ray Robinson, Althea's all-time favorite boxer and good friend and supporter.

all-time favorite boxer and told him, "Well, I can beat you bowling right now!"

From that point on, Robinson, who found Althea's cockiness amusing, and his wife, Edna Mae, became like her big brother and sister. Althea hung out at their home and often spent the night there, especially when the boxer was in the army. She also kept Edna Mae company in a cottage three miles from Sugar Ray's cabin at Joe Louis's training camp at Greenwood Lake, New York. "I was what you might call her Girl Friday," Althea explained. "I did everything I could to make our relationship a lasting one." The Robinsons gave her a glimpse of the "good life"—Edna Mae with her lingerie boutique and furs and Sugar Ray with his restaurant and flashy cars in eye-catching hues like flamingo pink. Althea loved to practice driving in these cars, but she loved the Robinsons most of all. And they loved her back. Like Buddy and Trini Walker, the Robinsons offered Althea support and encouragement. They pushed her to excel in tennis.

"Althea used to come over to our apartment and sit on the floor," Edna Mae said. "She was unhappy; she had a gaunt build and she felt that she was the least good-looking girl she knew. She had insecurity and went into herself. She used to talk wild. I tried to make her feel she could be something."

Now on the women's circuit, Althea was on her way to the 1946 national singles competition at Wilberforce College in Ohio. "My New York supporters thought I was a cinch to win," she said. They covered her travel expenses and made arrangements for her to stay in a dormitory. Althea made it to the finals, but she lost to Roumania Peters, a teacher at Tuskegee Institute who held the 1944 women's titles. "It was my lack of experience that lost the match for me," Althea said. "Roumania was an old hand at tournament play, and she pulled all the tricks in the trade on me. I wasn't ready for it." Peters came out of perhaps the strongest program at any black college. Early in the twentieth century, Tuskegee had been one of the first with a tennis program. The institute had an ATA president as a coach and had built a pair of courts just for women. During the Depression, the school had fourteen courts and a thousand-seat covered grandstand. In addition, Peters and her sister, Margaret, known as Pete and Re-Pete, won the ATA women's doubles championship fourteen times between 1938 and 1953—more than any pair of either gender.

Althea admitted that she had been overconfident against her seasoned opponent. "She really worked on me," Althea recalled. "She won the first set, 6-4, and after I pulled out the second, 9-7, she began drooping around the court as though she was half dead. She looked for all the world as though she was so tired she couldn't stand up. Naturally, I thought I had it made. It was quite a shock to me when Roumania managed to keep running long enough to win the third set, 6-3. It was also a good lesson for me."

Some New Yorkers used the occasion to give Althea a piece of their mind, essentially saying that they had had enough. She hadn't lived up to their expectations as a player nor as a person with her attitude and behavior. The normally feisty Althea was crushed. "The people I had expected sympathy or a kind word from, told me they thought I should have won," she said. "It was life's darkest moment. I was sitting in the grandstand alone when a man came up to me and asked: 'How would you like to play at Forest Hills?' I couldn't believe my ears and naturally thought it was a joke until I looked at the expression on his face. Then I knew he meant what he was saying.

"My answer was, and I'll never forget it, 'Of course, I would like to play at Forest Hills, but you know that is impossible.' He replied, 'It is impossible now, but if you are willing to work hard enough, I believe you are the key to unlock the door.' I told him I would do anything to be able to play at Forest Hills."

The man was Dr. R. Walter Johnson, known in tennis circles as "Whirlwind." He immediately consulted with his tennis buddy, Dr. Hubert A. Eaton, to come up with a plan to turn Althea's game and her life around. "She should have won that title easily," Johnson said. "She had agility, power, everything. Everything, that is, but consistency and accuracy." Johnson, a general practitioner in Lynchburg, Virginia, and Eaton, a surgeon in Wilmington, North Carolina, offered Althea training and the use of their private courts. They would also take her into their homes as a family member with her very own room and the same allowance that their own kids received. They had originally offered to put her through

Dr. Hubert A. Eaton (left) and his wife, Celeste (center), took Althea into their home and helped her turn around her life and her game. Buddy Walker (right), another important early influence, spotted the future tennis player when she was playing paddleball in New York City.

college but discovered that she had dropped out after only a year of high school. So the plan was revised to have Althea complete her education by living with Eaton, his wife, Celeste, and their three children during the school year. She'd spend summers with Johnson, who would later serve as benefactor for a young Arthur Ashe.

Although Althea was certainly open to the idea of improving, she wasn't sure about this business of leaving New York and all that she knew and loved to head south, where she'd heard that "terrible things were done to Negroes just because they were Negroes, and nobody was ever punished for them." Her mother, Annie Bell, also had misgivings about her eldest daughter leaving home, knowing that their contact would be reduced to letters, occasional phone calls, and rare visits if Althea were competing in the New York area. Bubba and others tried to quell Annie Bell's fears by emphasizing that Althea loved her family and that she'd never forget who her real parents were. Althea noted that Edna and Sugar Ray, who was training for the world welterweight title, urged her to go for it. "'You'll never amount to anything just bangin' around from one job to another like you been doin',' Ray told me. 'No matter what you want to do, tennis or music or what, you'll be better at it if you get some education.'" Althea decided to give it a shot and sent a letter to Eaton that August accepting the doctors' invitation. In Eaton's reply he suggested that she arrive by the first week in September. "It didn't even leave me time to change my mind," Althea said.

When her train pulled into Wilmington, Althea emerged wearing "a tired old skirt" and carrying a beat-up suitcase secured by a belt with a few pairs of slacks and two skirts inside. She also had the new tenor saxophone that she bought for $135 from Bill's Curiosity Shop in Manhattan with money from Sugar Ray, who as a drummer on the side understood her musical aspirations. When the Eatons' driver dropped Althea off at her home away from home, Celeste Eaton was in the kitchen making lunch. "She hugged me and kissed me as though I were her favorite niece," said Althea, who was quite taken by the house, the maid, and the starched sheets in her very own bedroom. Before her first day in Wilmington had ended, she went outside with Eaton to play on the family's private court. There, she practiced several times a week with Eaton, other black players, and a few whites who were open to socializing with those of a darker hue.

Since Althea was nineteen, Eaton talked the principal at Williston Industrial High School into placing her in the tenth grade instead of the ninth. "I didn't really have enough credits to get into the seventh grade," she admitted, "much less the second year of high school." Although she once hated school, Althea eventually took a liking to it, focusing intently on her studies, becoming captain of the girls' basketball team, and playing sax in the school band. But as an older student and a tomboy, she had problems fitting in. Her deep voice made it difficult to fit into the choir, too. She quit when the snickering became too intense after being switched from the girls' alto section to tenor with the boys.

"It seemed sometimes as though nobody could understand me," she said.

The New York transplant had problems with her new family, too. "At first, she didn't get along too well," Eaton said. "She didn't want to do things like helping out with the dishes. She'd run up to the pool room at the corner and wear slacks downtown. We told her we didn't do those things in Wilmington like they did in New York." Althea wasn't particularly fond of the South. It wasn't just slower than New York; it was backward as far she was concerned. She hated seeing the "white in front, colored in rear" signs on the bus and sat as far forward as possible. Although she liked sitting in the balcony to watch movies, she couldn't enjoy the films because she was forced to sit there. She also didn't like buying a hot dog at the five-and-ten-cent store but having to eat it outside instead of at the counter. Determined to do some of the things she enjoyed, she once took the Eatons' car for a spin without permission to see her boyfriend, a trumpet player. She almost got away with it, but someone saw her and told the doctor. Clearly, she was getting on Eaton's bad side.

"We told her if she didn't change, we'd have to send her back," he said. "She broke down and cried and asked us to give her another chance. We did, and we were always thankful afterwards."

Althea also had some rough spots in Virginia with Johnson's son, Robert Jr., who was roughly the same age. Virtually every day, she and Bobby argued over using the court or the Tom Stowe Stroke Developer, a volleying machine that spit balls across the net. "There was some jealousy," admitted Bobby, who now lives in Richmond, Virginia. "We fought like brother and sister."

"I used to have to make them get off the court," his father said. "They'd play all day if I let them. But each always wanted to grab the machine. She had no backhand then and he had no forehand and they were always trying to develop one."

But Johnson made sure that Althea got a good workout during the summers, placing her in roughly a dozen tournaments at the end of her sophomore year. They drove as far as Kansas City to play in every major ATA competition. On the way back from the Missouri trip, Johnson's Buick was packed with people. Tennis gear and luggage filled the roomy trunk and overhead rack. This time, Johnson had flown ahead to the Kentucky tournament, which was being organized by a friend. Just outside Louisville, the Buick got a flat tire and then the clouds opened up. The downpour made it difficult to change the tire, so Althea, Bobby, and the rest slept "tangled in a bunch." When the tired players caught up with Johnson, he just laughed and asked, "Did you have a nice trip?" The nice thing about those trips is that Althea racked up singles and mixed doubles titles. She beat Nana Davis at the ATA nationals and held the national women's singles title for ten years straight from 1947 to 1956. Althea and the elder Johnson captured the mixed doubles championship every year between 1948 and 1955, with the exception of 1951. Johnson described Althea as a "hard worker who did everything we told her to," but he also said she was stubborn at times and could "get wheels in her head on the court."

With the nurturing of the Cosmopolitan and ATA, Althea had "flourished like a flower," Billy Davis said. She was known for her powerful serve-and-volley game. At five feet eleven, she had the height, speed, and reach to dazzle a crowd by returning shots that seemed guaranteed to get away. And her face never gave away the brilliant strategies she was cooking up to zero in on an opponent's weakness. "I was fortunate enough *not* to draw her as an opponent," said ATA devotee Arvelia Myers, laughing as she reminisced about the early days. "She made things happen. Serve, come to the net, put the point away, end it and that's it. She did not play around. She did not wait for people to make an error. She made you make the error."

The Fine sisters of Kansas City, Kansas, weren't as fortunate. "I gave her a fit with my backhand, but that forehand and that serve were very powerful," said Mary Etta Fine, who lost to Althea in the ATA finals in 1951. "I played her about three times. I never could get more than three games, maybe 6-3 or 6-2. I never could beat her." Fine's sister, Eva Bracy, recalled similar outcomes. "I played her once in Florida. I think it was 6-1, 6-1. That's all I could do with her."

The sisters had better luck in doubles, taking the championship in 1955, 1957, and 1958. And in the latter year, Mary Etta finally captured the ATA singles title. "Althea was gone," Eva explained jokingly. "That's why she won!" However, Mary Etta and their older brother, Leo, stopped what might have been an eight-game winning streak by handing Althea and Dr. Johnson that 1951 loss in mixed doubles. Leo, who now lives in Florissant, Missouri, called the match a "thriller" and said they tried to keep the ball away from Althea by hitting it to Dr. Johnson.

Like the Fine sisters, Rosemary Darben got a taste of Althea's power. It didn't matter that they were best friends if they found themselves on opposite sides of the net. "When she played me, you would think she was playing in Wimbledon," Rosemary said, her voice a mixture of laughter and incredulity. "Althea and I played very hard against each other, and she would try to kill me, because people were going around saying, 'Oh that's the next Althea. I think Rosemary could beat Althea and this and that.'

*Althea and Rosemary
Darben, her best friend,
sister-in-law, doubles
partner.*

"Althea and I looked alike. We were both tall. I was five feet ten; she five feet eleven. We had similar games. We had serve-and-volley, hard forehands, and we played the game like a chess game. And therefore we became closer. I liked her game. I liked how she played tennis. And I liked how she told it the way it was. She was very straightforward. And I'm more or less straightforward, and we had a lot of fun together."

By this point in her development at the game, many people believed that Althea had the potential to make history and break the color barrier in tennis by competing in its premier event: the national lawn championship at Forest Hills in New York. Eaton and Johnson had made major inroads in preparing her for this step; it was now up to tennis officials in both the ATA and its white counterpart, the United States Lawn Tennis Association, to take it to the next level.

"We had wanted for years to break down the unwritten barriers to Negro participation in the USLTA-sanctioned tournaments, but we wanted to be sure we could offer a Negro player who would be worthy of such competition," said Arthur E. Francis, assistant executive secretary of the ATA and a Realtor in Brooklyn. Francis was part of an ATA triumvirate that included Dr. Sylvester B. Smith, president, and Bertram L. Baker, executive secretary for twenty years and a Brooklyn assemblyman. Working with them on the USLTA side were Dr. Ellsworth Davenport Jr., treasurer; Alrick Mann Jr., national tournament chairman; and Charles Hare, a former member of the British Davis Cup Team.

This was a critical moment in the history of the ATA and a goal for increased opportunities that undergirded its very existence. In a sport born during the Renaissance and preserved exclusively for England's upper classes by a decree of 1388, Althea would make it easier for the sons and daughters of slaves to take part by stepping onto the court at Forest Hills. Tennis had come to America in 1874, and by 1890 some black families had built their own courts. Tuskegee, one of a few black colleges that maintained courts for faculty members, began holding tournaments in the mid-1890s. By the end of the century Reverend W. W. Walker had led a group in organizing tournaments in Philadelphia and inviting tennis players up from Washington to compete. Clubs popped up along the East Coast and in places like Chicago, where "Mrs. C. O. Seames, a legendary figure in tennis circles there, began teaching at the turn of the century," wrote Arthur Ashe in his three-volume sports history, *A Hard Road to Glory*. Youngsters were learning to play, and black colleges formed competitive teams. During a banquet at a 1916 interstate tournament in New York, a group of players discussed the idea for a national organization. The Monumental Tennis Club in Baltimore and the Association Tennis Club in Washington, D.C., joined forces to invite representatives from other groups to a planning meeting in D.C. on November 30, 1916. Officers were elected for the new American Tennis Association, still the longest-running black sports organization in history. "They had that thing running like clockwork, just like the USTA," Bobby Johnson said.

The ATA held its first tournament at Druid Hill Park in Baltimore in August 1917. The first champions in men's and women's singles, respectively, were Tally Holmes and Lucy Diggs Slowe, who later became the dean of women at Howard University, where a dormitory stands in her honor on Third Street, NW. Other early women standouts included Isadore Channels, Lulu Ballard, and Flora Lomax, who each held four singles titles. With Althea's ten-year winning streak that began after she lost to Roumania Peters in her first ATA women's final, she broke Ora Washington's record of eight ATA singles championships. Her record still stands today.

Since much of the lodging on the tennis circuit was segregated, many athletes stayed with host families, at black hotels, or in dorms at the black colleges holding the tournaments. Occasionally, they'd play at places like Shady Rest, a black-owned country club in Scotch Plains, New Jersey, that boasted of being the "best permanent tennis site in the East" with "five perfect clay courts including the nationally famous stadium enclosure," the state's "best" golf course, a "beautiful" ballroom, lounge, card rooms, dining rooms, and lodging for a maximum of $1.25 a day. "It was very much a family affair," former president Virginia Glass said of the ATA gatherings. "Many times we didn't even go into the city. We created our own socialization. There were parties practically every night and a banquet with awards. There was usually a fashion show. We played cards and all kinds of other games."

In 1940 the Cosmopolitan hosted the ATA's first interracial exhibition matches when Don Budge visited to play singles against the reigning ATA champion, Jimmie McDaniel. Budge, who held four world titles in 1938, won 6-1 and 6-2 before a crowd estimated at two thousand. He also joined three-time ATA winner Reginald Weir in doubles against McDaniel and his partner, Richard Cohen. And Robert Ryland played Alice Marble during her visit years later. That's as far as black athletes got in competing against white players since the USLTA maintained a cold shoulder given the widespread segregation in society at the time. "You do not become good playing in your own little circle," said Glass, extolling the need to take on all comers worldwide.

While Althea became the ATA's choice for the big push to Forest Hills, she would not be the first to play in a USLTA event. The initial inroads occurred in 1946 when Weir played in the Eastern Indoor Tournament. He was also accepted into the national indoor event in March 1948. That August, Oscar Johnson won the National Junior Public Parks event at Griffith Park in Los Angeles. He also made it to the quarterfinals of the USLTA National Junior Indoors Tournament in St. Louis four months later, after local officials were forced to honor his approved application.

But lawn tennis was the final frontier and one of the few major sports that was still—for the most part—segregated. Jackie Robinson had integrated baseball in 1947. Woody Strode and Kenny Washington had reintegrated the National Football League in 1946, ending a thirteen-year lockout that began in the Depression to protect jobs for white players. William "Dolly" King and William "Pop" Gates played in the Basketball Association of America for a season in 1946, setting the stage for a breakthrough by six players in 1948. And during the same year, the track star Alice Coachman became the first black woman to win a gold medal at the Olympics. Althea was poised to become the newest pioneer—even the armed forces had already been integrated under President Harry S. Truman. Why not tennis?

Althea with Jackie Robinson, a referee at a women's basketball benefit for the Harlem YMCA. Robinson had integrated baseball in 1947—three years before segregation ended in lawn tennis.

In the winter of 1949 the ATA informed Althea that if she applied to compete in the USLTA's Eastern Indoor Tournament, her application would be accepted. She was thrilled that she would be competing in her first all-white tournament that was to be played down the street from her Harlem apartment in the cavernous armory at 143rd Street and Fifth Avenue. "It was an especially good break for me, because I knew the area and wouldn't feel strange," said Althea, who would also have a chance to catch up with her family. "I'd played at the armory lots of times." She made it to the quarter-finals, where she lost to Betty Rosenquest, 8-6 and 6-0. "I was reasonably satisfied," Althea said of her debut. "At least I hadn't been disgraced. I felt even better when I was asked, right after my last match, if I would like to stay over in New York for another week and play in the National Indoor Championships." She submitted her application, and her principal excused her from school for a few days that winter.

In the first round Althea beat Ann Drye, 6-0 and 6-1. She then eliminiated Sylvia Knowles, 6-4, 3-6, and 6-1, in the second round. But Nancy Chaffee put her out in the quarter-finals. "I'm glad I lasted as long as I did," Althea said. "I had been invited to play with the white girls in one of the important tournaments, and I felt good about it. The world didn't have to reform overnight; I was willing to give it a few days."

"I was made to feel right at home by the other girls," she said in her 1958 memoir, *I Always Wanted to Be Somebody*. "It wasn't just that they were polite; they were really friendly. And believe me, like any Negro, I'm an expert at telling the difference. It was as though they realized how much of a strain I was under, and they wanted to do whatever they could to help." Some of them, like Chaffee, remained as friends throughout her tennis career.

A few months later in June 1949, Althea's three years in the Johnson and Eaton households ended, when the former dropout graduated tenth in her class at Williston Industrial at the age of twenty-one. Since all the girls at school were ordering class rings, Althea wanted one, too, but she didn't want to impose further on the Eatons. Sugar Ray came through with the $15 she needed to buy one. About four black colleges offered her scholarships. Florida Agricultural and Mechanical College in Tallahassee offered the best deal and suggested that she come early for a summer of tennis. Two days after graduation, Althea was on her way. "I'm afraid the Eatons were a little bit hurt about the speed with which I left, but I couldn't help being eager to get started on my own," said Althea, who would visit during breaks. "Nobody could have been more grateful than I was to both the doctors for everything they had done for me in those three years, but it was good to feel a little bit independent again. It's a feeling I've always been partial to."

At FAMU, she signed up for two summer classes to get ahead, eventually dropping American history and getting a B in typewriting. A full basketball scholarship for tuition, room, and board made it possible for Althea to attend college. "We didn't have a tennis scholarship, but we knew about her tennis ability and that was a way to get her there," recalled Edwin M. Thorpe Sr., the retired registrar and director of admissions. "I admitted her to the university." In addition to being a star forward on the women's basketball team, eventually helping to win the conference championship against Tuskegee, she played on the men's golf team and the women's tennis team. "We played on clay courts on campus, so to work on quicker surfaces, I used to go play in the gym every morning before breakfast," Althea said. "My teammates were great. They would put down the tape in the gym every morning for the lines." She also practiced with the men to get more of a workout. "I first played against her in the fall of 1949, following her enrollment here at the university," said Henry Singletary, a fellow tennis player who worked out with Althea. "I found that she had very few weaknesses and that she felt right at home on the court with any male member of the squad."

Jake Gaither, the Rattlers' athletic director, got her a job as an assistant to the head of the women's physical education department. She made $40 a month but had few places to spend it. As a freshman, she had to be in her room by nine

The former high school dropout received a basketball scholarship to attend Florida Agricultural and Mechanical College in Tallahassee.

o'clock; seniors had until 11 P.M. "There weren't many places in Tallahassee where the students were allowed to go," Althea said, "and mostly we got along with a radio in our room, dances every now and then in the college gym, and movies in the auditorium." On campus, students could buy hamburgers and Cokes, play cards, and shoot pool. They were welcome at just one theater, which showed mostly old movies. At the sole eatery in town, students could drink beer or stronger drinks, but they couldn't dance to music on the jukebox. This was a big change for Althea, who had lived it up when she was much younger and made her own rules back home in New York. Now, she had to sign in and out, meet curfew, and dress up for chapel three times a week. She even joined a sorority, Alpha Kappa Alpha. Perhaps the biggest irony was being picked to head a student disciplinary committee that enforced rules, of all things. She had to laugh. As a student already in her early twenties, she truly had become "a sort of aunt to the other kids."

"She set quite a good example for the rest of the students," said Thorpe's wife, Annette, who taught English at Florida A&M. "She was well regarded by her dorm matrons, because they saw her leadership skills, and they were glad that she was willing to share and be sort of a big sister to the younger students."

Some of Althea's physical education professors would also give her extra responsibilities, such as leading classmates in tennis drills. Althea took a no-nonsense approach to her duties and would banish students to the bleachers if they goofed off or failed to follow directions, recalled Edwina Martin, who spent a lot of time around Althea as a fellow physical education major, basketball teammate, and chapel usher. "When she spoke, everybody listened," Martin said. "She was serious, just like she was on the tennis court." On one occasion some students asked Althea if they could play "triples" instead of doubles so that they'd have an easier time out on the tennis court. "She said, 'You go sit down! You play triples when you go home, not out here!'"

Popular yet private, Althea would often shed her serious persona. She'd joke around, socialize, and date, but she took her time opening up to others. "I thought she was kind of withdrawn; she didn't jump right in the group with us," recalled Elizabeth McElveen, known as Maggie Swilley when she and Althea were two of the three forwards on the basketball team.

"She was unusual," Martin added. "She was a loner. She wasn't a loner because she was the lonely type. It was just that her mind was so preoccupied with sports. That was her joy." Her independent streak and being a lot older made it even harder for students to get too close.

"She was such a strong person, until I was a little afraid of her," Martin admitted with a chuckle. "I think she liked me because everything she said or did, I accepted." Take their weekly duties as ushers, for instance. Since they were in charge of seating students in the balcony of Lee Hall for the mandatory convocation programs, a few football players offered to pay them a quarter each time they covered their absences. Althea agreed, and soon other students negotiated similar deals.

A quarter was a lot of money in those days, Martin said, but the risks were great, too. Everyone involved faced expulsion if caught, and it was widely known that the dean of students, the Reverend M. G. Miles, would even contribute to the cost of sending a student home. On good days, Althea and Martin made as much as five dollars. But then some students threatened to tell the good reverend if the fee wasn't dropped to fifteen cents. Martin was ready to cave in, but Althea wouldn't budge. Althea wasn't falling for any extortion threats, especially from people who had as much to lose as she did. "If she said no," Martin explained, "you didn't need to ask anymore."

Althea could be controlling and demanding on committees, too. Her decisions tended to prevail by default. "You'd have to go along with her, because she wasn't going to change her mind," Martin said. "She felt strongly about what she said and what she had to do."

Despite the restrictions at college, Althea lived by many of her own rules just as she had during childhood, and she often had special privileges. Since she loved to shoot pool, she hung out around the billiards table in Sampson Hall, a dormitory for male students that was off-limits to women. "None of us could go into the boys' dormitory," McElveen said.

"None of us could ride with boys in cars, and she could do all of that. But it didn't bother us. We went right along with it because Althea was who she was."

"Not a girl got a scholarship, other than Althea," McElveen added. "The coach would say be in at ten, and she'd come in around ten-thirty and the coach wouldn't fire her." Althea would also slip out of her room to smoke cigarettes. She was caught smoking while in Tuskegee for a basketball game, but no one remembers whether she suffered any consequences. But for the most part, she fell in line with everyone else whether she liked it or not. "Our coach would make us duck walk around the gym, and Althea would curse under her breath," Martin recalled, laughing. "She'd curse like a soldier."

Despite her talent and the national attention she was receiving, Althea wasn't boastful or arrogant, Martin and McElveen said. It wasn't that she didn't have a sizable ego, but it was more a sense of entitlement. McElveen describes it as an air that she deserved what came her way, that she appreciated it but that she also felt those who could do something for her should be honored to do so. "She became quite an interesting person to know," McElveen said. "A lot of people can do stuff, but they aren't sure of themselves. She felt very sure of herself."

"Her strengths really inspired me," Martin added. "I learned a lot from her. She gave me more courage to stand up for what I believe and say what I think is right."

"Everybody just loved that girl," Edwin Thorpe said of Althea, who had the solid support of her FAMU family as she ventured deeper into uncharted tennis territory in her attempts to integrate the sport.

In early 1950 she was invited back to the Eastern Indoor Tournament, which she won. At the nationals she made it all the way to the finals but lost again to Chaffee, 6-2 and 6-0. To the college freshman's surprise, she was greeted to a hero's

*In 1950 Althea made it to the finals of the National Indoor Championships
but lost. Nevertheless, she got a hero's welcome when she returned to FAMU.*

welcome upon returning to FAMU. "You would have thought
for sure I had won the tournament instead of losing it." She
stepped off the train in Tallahassee to a "Welcome Home,
Althea!" banner, the marching band playing the school's alma
mater, and a hearty handshake from the acting president.

Despite her good showing, she still needed to sway the
forty-eight-member USLTA committee—especially the southern contingent—in order to make it to Forest Hills. "We
would have waited another year or two if it had been necessary," the ATA's Arthur Francis said, "but we were sure by
1950 that we had a proper candidate in Miss Gibson." Many
in the tennis world and the press felt the same way and wondered what was taking so long for the USLTA to give Althea
its blessing. The public began paying attention, too, as the
four-time national tennis champion Alice Marble found out

as she crisscrossed the country making appearances and giv-ing lectures. She decided to look into it and didn't like what she discovered, prompting her to write a lengthy letter criti-cizing the tennis community in the July 1950 issue of *Ameri-can Lawn Tennis* magazine. Marble revealed that a longtime USLTA committee member had told her that Althea would have to make a strong showing in major eastern lawn tourna-ments—most of which were invitational—before making it to Forest Hills. "If she is not invited to participate in them, as my committee member freely predicted," Marble noted, "then she obviously will not be able to prove anything at all, and it will be the reluctant duty of the committee to reject her entry at Forest Hills.

"Miss Gibson is over a very cunningly wrought barrel, and I can only hope to loosen a few of its staves with one lone opinion," she wrote. "I think it's time we faced a few facts. If tennis is a game for ladies and gentlemen, it's also time we acted a little more like gentlepeople and less like sanctimo-nious hypocrites.

"She is not being judged by the yardstick of ability, but by the fact that her pigmentation is somewhat different," Marble continued. "She is a fellow tennis player and, as such, deserv-ing of the chance I had to prove myself. I've never met Miss Gibson, but, to me, she is a fellow human being to whom equal privileges ought to be extended."

Marble's letter rocked the tennis world.

Invitations were extended, requests for entry blanks were honored, and applications were approved—to a certain degree. Not surprisingly, some diehards refused to budge. Meanwhile, Althea was busy in New York practicing with Sarah Palfrey Cooke, the 1941 and 1945 USLTA champion. Cooke had called her friend Ralph Gatcomb, the president of the West Side Tennis Club, to arrange for Althea to practice on grass. "Two days later, Althea and I, carrying our bags and rackets,

With Sarah Palfrey Cooke, the 1941 and 1945 USLTA champion, with whom Althea practiced for Forest Hills.

took the subway from Lexington Avenue and Fifty-third Street, and arrived at Forest Hills in twenty minutes," Cooke recalled. "On that hot July afternoon, we practiced for almost two hours, and Althea had her first taste of playing on a real lawn tennis court.

"Actually, her style of tennis was ideally suited to grass. With a big serve, good volley and smash, her unsteady ground strokes were not so vulnerable as on clay. Her natural timing and big catlike strides were useful for the faster pace of a grass court. Being tall, she did have trouble bending down for the low bounces. But it was an impressive workout."

Chicago-based Charles Hare, one of the three USLTA allies, wrote a letter to his ATA cohorts saying that he had spoken to officials of the National Clay Court Champion-

ships and that they were open to the idea of Althea participating. Althea made it to the quarterfinals of the clay event at
the River Forest Club in Chicago, winning her first round
and the second against the top-rated Mela Ramirez of Mexico. Her supporters closely followed her progress. "Whirlwind" Johnson obtained the scores and news accounts about
his protégé and ATA doubles partner directly from a local
sportswriter in Lynchburg, Virginia. He sent Althea a West-
ern Union telegram with on- and off-the-court pointers.
"Keep it up, but don't look at any matches until after you
have played," he advised. "Then look at all of them." His
prediction four years earlier that Althea was "the key to unlock the door" to Forest Hills was coming true. Or was it?
He didn't want anything to prevent the door from opening.
"I would not attend any of their social functions," he added
cryptically in the telegram. "Go home and rest. One of the
reasons they don't want you to play at Forest Hills is because
of the social functions. Pass these up to get to Forest Hills.
Concentrate. Your partner, Dr. Johnson."

Althea didn't win the clay tournament in Chicago; she
lost to the No. 1 U.S. player, Doris Hart, 2-6 and 3-6. But
she was accepted into the Eastern Grass Court Tournament
in South Orange, New Jersey, considered next in importance
after the national lawn event. Francis responded to news
of Althea's acceptance into the tournament with a glowing,
almost gushing, letter. He wrote in part: "Your unafraid declaration that merit be recognized as one of the most important
qualifications for an opportunity to play in your tournament,
inspires us with the belief in the doctrine of the fatherhood
of God and the brotherhood of man.

"Believe me when I say that members of my racial group,
and of all groups who believe in fair play, will be everlast-
ingly grateful to you and your colleagues who thought as you
did and who by their actions have attested to the fact that

tennis is a game for ladies and gentlemen, and of ladies and gentlemen."

However, the ATA's request for an application to the New Jersey State Championship at the Maplewood Country Club was ignored. Francis's letter to the New Jersey branch of the USLTA took on a different tone: "We are somewhat surprised at the lack of common decency you have shown by not answering us. Whatever decision is reached, or action taken by your body, can never be justified by your procrastination, evasion, and absolute discourtesy to us in not answering.

"You have exhibited the very thing that you apparently seemed to be afraid of in other people, snobbishness, prejudice and bad judgment, an un-American spirit that should not find its way in any respectable sport, particularly tennis, a game of ladies and gentlemen."

While Althea's eagerly anticipated debut on grass drew lots of spectators to the Orange Lawn Tennis Club, some ATA members claimed that she didn't act like the lady they thought she had become. After beating Virginia Rice Johnson, 6-1 and 6-3 in the first round of the Eastern Grass Court Tournament, Althea lost to Helen Pastall Perez in the second round, 1-6 and 1-6. "She stepped off the court and wouldn't shake hands with the winner," an anonymous accuser told the *New York Post* reporter Ted Poston. "Children had been waiting for autographs, and she refused to give any.

"I told her one child had been waiting all day and begged her to give just one autograph. But she refused, saying, 'I'm thirsty!' Then she glared across the court at her victorious opponent and said: 'I could have beaten her. I could have won that match.'"

One of Althea's defenders said that if the accusation were true, her actions could be attributed to her obsession with winning. Another claimed she knew firsthand that Althea was not only a good sport but also a charitable one. "Althea wouldn't try to show you up on the court," she said. "If she was winning, she would even throw a game your way. I know, because she gave me one once."

All of this was just another act in the ongoing drama to add some color on the national stage. Althea's showing and the whole process of trying to penetrate the net around tennis was such a big deal that the mere receipt of her application to the nationals made news. On August 16, 1950, the *New York Times* reported that "the entry of Miss Althea Gibson has been received, the United States Lawn Tennis Association said yesterday, but it will not be known until next week whether the New York Negro girl will be permitted to play in the national championship starting on August 28 at Forest Hills."

While in Wilberforce, Ohio, for the ATA nationals at Central State College, Althea got the word she had been waiting for on August 21 when the USLTA announced that "Miss Gibson was accepted on her ability" as one of fifty-two women selected for the nationals. "Although the USLTA announced it in a matter-of-fact fashion," Althea said, "there was nothing matter-of-fact about it to me." Like everyone at ATA nationals, she was ecstatic. Signaling "the beginning of a new era," Bertram Baker proudly made the announcement in Wilberforce: "Many of us have worked untiringly for years to witness the day when our players would be accepted for competition in the national championships of the USLTA. That day has come. It was not brought about by senseless agitation or unwarranted demands, but by cultivation of good will thereby acquiring the genuine friendship of individuals without whose aid the door would not yet be open to us. . . . Althea Gibson will play at Forest Hills . . . on Monday, August 28."

ATA officials had been given a heads-up about the decision and talked Rhoda Smith into postponing a nine-week summer vacation in Europe so that she could be Althea's chaperone to Forest Hills. Althea didn't have much time, since the ATA nationals ran from August 21 to 26, and the USLTA championship was just two days later. Some ATA officials wanted Althea to pass on defending her title and head straight to New York to prepare for the opening USLTA match on Monday; others felt it was important for her to remain in Ohio. After all, a good part of the record-breaking crowd ventured to tiny Wilberforce in the middle of the nowhere between Dayton and Cincinnati to see what one newspaper called "the most talked about women's singles tennis player in America." Althea stayed and won her fourth of ten straight ATA singles' titles on Friday afternoon. Hours later, she and Smith caught an overnight train to New York, arriving on Saturday.

While ATA members were thrilled for Althea, many said the organization needed to strengthen its opposition to exclusions based on race or religion at USLTA events. They also felt that the USLTA had an "implied quota" and too many barriers, including the provision that required an ATA recommendation in order for black players to be considered. Fred Johnson was pushing for Althea and Rosemary to play doubles in the USLTA, believing that they would be unstoppable were it not for the unwritten, one-Negro-at-a-time rule. Nevertheless, history was being made despite the deficiencies.

"No Negro player, man or woman, has ever set foot on one of these courts," the journalist Lester Rodney wrote of the West Side Tennis Club at Forest Hills. "In many ways, it's even a tougher personal Jim Crow–busting assignment than was Jackie Robinson's when he first stepped out of the Brooklyn Dodgers dugout."

Chapter 3

"Champion of Nothing"

I made a vow to myself: "Althea, you're not going to look around. You're not going to listen to any calls or remarks. All you are going to do is watch the tennis ball."

ALTHEA WAS TRULY HAVING a Jackie Robinson moment. She knew she was about to make history, but she hadn't fully grasped the magnitude of this next step. The world as she knew it would be forever changed as soon as she swung her racket publicly at Forest Hills on that Monday, August 28, 1950, just as it had changed for Robinson when he stepped onto the diamond at Ebbets Field as a darker Brooklyn Dodger three years earlier in 1947. Althea was thrilled that she had a chance to visit the West Side Tennis Club before the nationals to test out the grass courts by practicing with Sarah Palfrey Cooke. "Just playing with Sarah was a big help," Althea said. "She's one of the finest tennis players I've ever had the pleasure of hitting against. She knows everything about tennis strokes and strategy that's worth knowing." Cooke felt that time was too tight to calm down Althea's "erratic" ground

Practicing at Forest Hills during the first years she played at the tournament.

strokes but that her serve, volley, and smash would work well on grass. And being nearly six feet tall with long limbs was a clear plus for Althea, the former national champion added.

Cooke and Smith did wonders for Althea's nerves, but they couldn't make the jitters disappear entirely. A childless mother who had rebounded from depression after the death of her three-year-old girl, Rhoda Smith took good care of her surrogate daughter on the overnight train ride from the ATA tournament in Ohio and then at her well-appointed brownstone at 415 West 154th Street in Harlem after their arrival on Saturday. The next day, Althea hit a few balls with Nancy Chaffee, who had beaten her in the USLTA's National Indoor Finals earlier that year and in the quarterfinals in 1949. "Mom," as Althea called Smith, rose early on Monday to prepare a breakfast of eggs, bacon, toast, and milk. After the food settled, Althea gathered a small kit bag and two tennis rackets. She and Smith strolled over to the Sixth Avenue subway line and hopped on the D train, changing in midtown Manhattan at Fiftieth Street for the F train to Seventy-first Street and Continental Avenue in the Forest Hills section of Queens. "It was only a short walk, about three long blocks to the entrance of the West Side Tennis Club," Althea recalled. "I couldn't help but think that it had taken me a long time to make the trip."

Not having to search for the clubhouse and ladies' dressing room or ask for directions gave Althea one less thing to worry about in the hours before her first match at one o'clock. It was reassuring to have Smith by her side as she changed into her snow white tennis ensemble and as she became overwhelmed by the buzz of swarming photographers and reporters. "I wouldn't have been able to handle them all alone," Althea said. "The whole thing awed me. All this attention, all these people wanting to talk to me and get me to say things, patting me on the back and telling me that they knew I could do it. It was hard for a girl who had never been through the mill before." Alice Marble also tried to put her new protégé at ease. "Have courage," she said. "Remember, you're just like the rest of us."

From start to finish, everything at Forest Hills was not only new, but it was also a bit unusual. *Sports Illustrated* noted that the USLTA seemed oblivious to the significance of the moment in its selection of an outside court for Althea's big debut. Court 14 could accommodate only a handful of her supporters and others who had wanted to see what all the fuss was about. Those who couldn't get in caught glimpses through the green latticework surrounding the court. On the other hand, Ginger Rogers, better known for matching Fred Astaire step for step in stilettos in reverse than for her tennis, played on a court in front of the clubhouse, wrote Ted Poston in the *New York Post*.

Some observers—conspiracy theorists among them— smelled rats in the USLTA. A few detected hints of racism in the tournament pairings, court selection, and even the free reign of the press covering Althea. "Contrary to all custom," Poston explained, "a small army of photographers was allowed to flank the court and repeatedly pop flashlights in her face as she opened against her first-round opponent, Barbara N. Knapp of England." Wilfred Bugland, a USLTA official, said that it wasn't unusual for still and moving photographers to shoot from the sidelines, but when pressed to cite a previous incident, he said, "I can't think of a specific time, but I'm certain that it has happened sometime before." Buddy Walker, Althea's mentor from her PAL days, said: "The truth is, she didn't know when she was being treated badly. She didn't know, for example, that photographers were not supposed to stand by taking pictures while a player's nerves were tense in the middle of a match."

Nervous or not, it all made little difference as Althea beat Knapp 6-2, 6-2 in a contest she described as being "easy." All in all, day one ended triumphantly for Althea. She was beaming as she left the court, holding a towel and two tennis rackets. She walked side by side with Marble, her most famous supporter, who wore a belted print dress with a scalloped collar and carried a striped clutch, a far cry from today's typical tennis crowd. Women dressed similarly, and men in straw boaters paraded behind them or flanked the sides along the fence. A young boy with a blond crew cut clapped with outstretched arms as the new and old tennis legends approached. After Althea showered and changed clothes, she joined Smith for their return subway trip to Harlem and an early dinner. "I would have liked to have gone to a movie, but I was afraid it might make my eyes tired, and I didn't want to take the chance."

Going to bed early after such a whirlwind week gave Althea the energy she needed to face the formidable Louise Brough, reigning Wimbledon champ and former national winner. This time, the match was scheduled in the grandstand courts just outside the stadium. "Nearly 2,000 spectators jammed the stands, and the Pinkertons had to close the gates," *Sports Illustrated* reported. The overflow crowd was four deep outside the court. Among the spectators were hecklers shouting, "Knock her out of there" or "Beat the nigger!" While such taunts would unnerve many players, Althea blocked them out and maintained her focus. "It did not bother me," she said. "I was too arrogant and anti-social. I was not conscious of the racial difference."

"Althea was like a horse with blinders," Rosemary Darben explained. "She kept her eye on the ball." Althea knew that her performance could have a major impact on the future. She wasn't about to let someone's ignorant behavior or prejudice stand in her way, especially at this key moment.

With her mentor Alice Marble, the woman who was instrumental in breaking down the color barrier at Forest Hills, at her first tournament there in 1950.

Many years later Althea turned out to support Alice Marble at a ceremony marking the naming of a tennis center after Marble.

"Louise was one of the big guns of women's tennis," she said, "and I could hardly ask for a better opportunity to show what I could do."

The big gun came out blazing. "Miss Gibson was terribly nervous when the match began, so that Miss Brough easily won the first set 6-1," said David Eisenberg, then a sportswriter for the *New York Journal American.* "But Althea settled down in the second set. Rarely since Alice Marble's championship reign has a woman shown so much stroking power as she did, especially with her forehand. She won the second set 6-3, and the match was squared."

In the final set Brough won the first three games. "Again Althea rallied, cracking Louise's service three times as she pulled ahead to a 7-6 lead," Eisenberg said. The crowd was in a tizzy. Althea was on fire and felt comfortable enough to end it with this game. All she had to do was break Brough's service again, and the veteran player looked too tired to hold onto it. "The courage and the power of this unknown colored girl had robbed Louise of her poise," Eisenberg explained. "Everyone in the stands sensed that a fabulous upset was in the making."

But then day turned into night, as lightning crackled overhead. The sky opened up and roared with a thunderstorm so violent that it toppled a stone eagle on the corner of the stadium. Drenched spectators scattered, many taking cover beneath the stands. The storm ended almost as soon as it had begun, but it left pools of water all over the courts that brought the day to an early end. "I remember being distraught, because it was an awful experience," said Brough, who never liked Forest Hills as a location because of the distractions from trains and planes.

"I have sat in on many dramatic moments in sports, but few were more thrilling than Miss Gibson's performance against Miss Brough," Eisenberg recalled. "Not because great tennis was played. It wasn't. But because of the great try by this lonely and nervous colored girl, and because of the manner in which the elements robbed her of her great triumph."

After the near upset, the press swarmed around Althea with even more intensity. A black man and woman, both of whom she didn't know, took it upon themselves to intervene and serve as a buffer between Althea and the press. Things got ugly and erupted into a war of words. "The post-match incident left Althea in a state of near shock," Eisenberg noted. Combined with the delay and everything else, Althea said she remained "a nervous wreck" throughout a sleepless night and the next day's face off. "The delay was the worst thing that could have happened to me." But it gave Brough time to regroup somewhat. "I was nervous, and I guess she was even more nervous," recalled Brough, who added that her composure began dissolving with the half-hour delay because of the media crunch surrounding Althea. She had been warned beforehand that Althea's debut would be a big deal; she just hadn't realized how big.

The competitors picked up where they left off in game fourteen. "I remember missing that first volley," Brough said. The score was deuced, or tied, six times before she took over for good, living up to her "big-gun" moniker. "She won three straight games to run out the set, and the match, 6-1, 3-6, 9-7," Eisenberg said.

"Whether or not Althea Gibson would have beaten Louise Brough that dark afternoon had the rain not come will never be known," he added. "But observers of the match could see that she was destined for a great future." She also garnered praise in a *New York Herald Tribune* editorial: "Althea Gibson did not come through the tournament with a crown of victory, but she won something she can cherish throughout her life which never can be taken from her—the respect and admiration of all who saw her play at Forest Hills. She is a credit not only to the Negro race but to all good sportsmen and women who play and love the game of tennis."

Immediately after the nationals and before Althea headed back to school, Bertram Baker of the ATA made moves to build on her future. He set up a meeting over lunch with Althea and Hollis Dann of the USLTA at the Crossroads Restaurant on Forty-second Street and Broadway in Times Square. The topic of discussion was Wimbledon, the place where kings and queens of international tennis were crowned. Everyone agreed that it was a great idea for Althea to compete at Wimbledon the next year in 1951 but that she needed to tighten her game. The USLTA made arrangements for Althea to work with Jean Hoxie, a highly regarded tennis instructor based outside Detroit in Hamtramck, Michigan, to be sure that she was ready for her next history-making moment.

When Althea returned to Florida A&M, she sent a six-page thank-you letter to Marble on the physical education department's letterhead. In the letter Althea also highlighted her background, apologized for the rowdiness of some spectators at Forest Hills, and expressed regret for the backlash against Marble for her article in *American Lawn Tennis* magazine. "I am elated over the opportunity I had to play at Forest Hills," Althea wrote, "but I am sorry for the slurs you received and the friends you lost. I do believe that you gained more true respectful friends than you lost by writing the very fine article you wrote in my behalf in the tennis magazine." On her loss to Brough, she said: "I didn't feel bad when Miss Brough defeated me. She used her experience and confidence to out think and out play me.

"Miss Marble, next year I hope that I am invited to play in more USLTA tournaments," she added. "I don't mind getting beat. The more I am beaten, the more I will learn. . . . I wait with hopeful anticipation for what 1951 might bring."

The new year brought her first opportunity to take home an international title at the second annual Caribbean Tennis Championships in Montego Bay. Jamaicans welcomed Althea with a reception at their Embassy Club, where they showered her with gifts, including chocolates, Chinese slippers, an evening bag, and a powder box. On opening day, Althea's match was the main attraction and she delivered on the hype by beating the U.S. junior indoor champion, Edith Ann Sullivan, in straight sets. Everyone wanted to see all the power she was becoming famous for, but Althea took a soft approach except on her serves. She wore out Betty Rosenquest of South Orange, New Jersey, with drops and lobs that kept the twelfth-ranked player running all over the court. Her errors almost cost her the match, but she nailed it with a "blistering" serve to Rosenquest's backhand. Althea won her first major world title, 7-5, 3-6, 8-6—the same title that California's "Ventura Venus," Nancy Chaffee, had captured the previous year.

In March she had a breakthrough in the South, becoming the first black player not only to compete in a major tournament below the Mason-Dixon line—the Good Neighbor Championships in Miami—but also to win, beating Betty Pratt of Montego Bay. But that same month, observers said, Althea "beat herself" in the USLTA Women's Indoor Singles Championships at the Seventh Regiment Armory off Park Avenue in Harlem. She got off to a good start, easily winning the first two rounds against Nancy Loretta Derenna of the Bronx, 6-0, 6-0, and even the captain of the Wightman Cup team, Marjorie Buck of Boston, 7-5, 3-6, 8-6.

When the moment of truth arrived against the reigning champion Chaffee in the quarterfinals, Althea hit some "dazzling volleys" and drew gasps from the crowd by returning shots determined to get away. "Miss Gibson tried to smash her way to victory with the fastest service of the tournament combined with an overhand that left Miss Chaffee rooted to the court as some shots flashed by her," *The Courier* reported. However, she was pressing too hard. She missed a number of easy shots and sent too many wild ones Chaffee's way. Her opponent stuck to her baseline game while Althea played to excess. In the first set Althea won the third game, in the second she captured the second and fourth games, but in the end Chaffee took it all, 6-1, 6-2. Many fans "who thronged the courts" saw the loss as just a momentary setback. With her performance at Forest Hills, Althea had charmed them—and some USLTA officials, *The Courier* said. "Both with the officials and her fans, it is unanimous that experience is going to be her best friend, as they look forward to her arrival at the top of the tennis ladder."

The next big step came in May. After completing her final exams Althea flew to Detroit to train for Wimbledon. Bill Matney, the managing editor of the *Michigan Chronicle*, a black weekly newspaper, picked her up at the airport. He was cochair of a committee of Detroiters, including boxer Joe Louis, who were raising money to cover her training expenses and trip to Europe to play at Wimbledon as well as other tournaments in England, France, and Belgium. "Every sports-minded person who has read of Althea's tennis playing and feels pride in what she has done should be more than willing to contribute to this campaign," Louis said. The heavyweight champion gave her use of his personal suite at the Gotham Hotel during her two weeks in town and a round-trip airline ticket to London. "What a guy," Althea exclaimed. "I was glad I had a chance to tell Joe how much I appreciated it before I left for England. He bought me some breakfast one morning and talked to me about how I was doing." The Detroit Duffers' Golf Association voted to donate $500, and a benefit at the Flame Show Bar brought in $770. With additional funds raised by supporters at Florida A&M and in the surrounding Tallahassee community, Althea had three new outfits picked out by her basketball teammate Maggie Swilley, along with new luggage—no beat-up, pasteboard suitcase for this special trip. In his sports column, "Jumpin' the Gun," Matney wrote that "the city of Detroit takes great pride in her visit to our town and of the opportunity to help send this amazing young lady further ahead on the road toward a brilliant career in tennis."

Jean Hoxie, a tennis coach at Hamtramck High School and considered a taskmaster, put Althea through three-hour workouts twice a day. "I never worked so hard in my life," Althea said after the first three days. "Probably her greatest fault," Hoxie explained, "and the thing which could ruin her future in tennis, is that she never learned how to practice.

"On the other hand, there's a brilliant future for her if she can conquer her impatience," Hoxie added. "Her serve is harder than that of any woman playing today. This could be her big year with the top-ranked players like [Pat] Todd, [Margaret Osbourne] DuPont, and Brough about ready to step down." The local sportswriter George Puscas went even further saying that "a revolution is developing in women's tennis" and that the "trim, easy-going Harlem girl" along with Nancy Chaffee and Beverly Baker were poised to replace veterans like Brough. Noting that she was the first black person to play in the U.S. lawn championships, he added that "her appearance at Wimbledon will mark a similar precedent."

When Althea's two weeks in Detroit were up, Matney took her to a downtown bank where he withdrew the donated money, purchased a round-trip ticket to London, and gave her the difference. Another ticket from Joe Louis was waiting for Althea in New York at the Idlewild Airport, now JFK. "I felt rich," said Althea, who cashed in the first ticket and gave the refund to Bertram Baker for safekeeping. London newspapers hailed her arrival with such headlines as "Harlem Girl Is a Big Tennis Hit," "First Negress at Wimbledon," and

"The New Gibson Girl"—one of the media's favorite play on words throughout Althea's career and a reference to Charles Gibson's popular illustrations of an early 1900s woman who was serene and self-confident. Noting that Althea had also been dubbed "Harlem's Tomboy Cinderella" and describing her as being tall, slim, "serious-faced and shy," John Walters caught up his British readers on her past and took a few digs at the less-enlightened American tennis officials in the process. "Last summer, the stuffy U.S. Amateur Lawn Tennis Association broke 'sacred' tradition for this girl. She became the first Negro girl to compete in their championships at Forest Hills. . . . Those who watched her said: 'Give that girl a year or two and she will become one of the world's foremost amateurs.'" Continuing the Cinderella analogy, Walters added that another critic predicted "one day she will wear championship slippers."

"She has a mighty service, brilliant sense of timing, and rapid movement about the courts," Walters explained. "Her weaknesses are poor ground strokes and some erratic play." The Brits had a chance to see for themselves during the first week of June when Althea played against the English star Susan Partridge and then began her European tour by competing at the Northern Lawn Tennis tournament at West Didsbury in Manchester, England. Althea was the talk of Europe and much of that talk centered on not only her talent but also her race. "There is one splendid thing about Wimbledon," Bernard McElwaine wrote. "If a man or woman is good enough, he or she can play—no matter what their creed or color. With the entry of Althea Gibson, a coloured girl from Harlem, another dent has been made in the thick hide of international prejudice. Good luck to her. Her path has not been easy." Althea welcomed the greater openness in Europe. "Let me make it quite clear; I have NO colour-bar worries," she told reporters. "In the States it isn't always easy for a

Negress to play tennis, but I had no difficulty about Wimbledon." She described England's courts as being "cute" and said she liked them "just fine and dandy." She was also delighted that the weather wasn't living up to its dreary reputation. "Guess I'll tell the folks back home it's hotter here than they think."

At the Northern tournament, Althea easily won the first two rounds 6-1, 6-1, with serves that frequently left her opponent, Peggy Hodson, just standing there as the ball whizzed by. But she lost to Barbara Scofield of San Francisco, ranked No. 7 in the United States, in the quarterfinals and then to Doris Hart of Jacksonville, Florida, in the finals. Soon afterward, Betty Rosenquest was able to exact some revenge for her loss to Althea in Jamaica, by knocking the rising star out of the semifinals at the Kent County championships in Beckenham. "Yes, sir. It's tough over here," Althea admitted to the sportswriter Ben Phlegar, as she sat with her legs entwined around a folding chair. "You've got to be good to win." Althea continued what was becoming a pattern of starting strong and then fizzling out. Exerting only as much effort as necessary, she made it to the third round of London's lawn tennis championships at the Queens Club, defeating Shirley Partridge 7-5, 1-6, 6-0. Veteran winner Shirley Fry of Akron, Ohio, however, took her out, 6-1, 6-4.

In the days leading up to Wimbledon the British press made a big to-do about the wardrobes of the American women athletes and what *The Star's* Roy McKelvie called the "passing craze for flares and flutes, pants and points." The "London Laughs" comic strip in *The Evening News* showed gawkers gathered in front of Wimbledon with a photographer carrying a page that read "Latest Wimbledon Fashions." The guard standing post tells the photographer: "No, sir! Miss Gypsy Rose Lee may be appearing in London this summer, but definitely not at Wimbledon, I assure you!" Another strip, "Breakfast Cartoon," depicted two scantily clad tennis players, baring their midriffs and cleavage, looking back at another player covered from top to bottom with a hat, long-sleeved jacket, and ankle-length skirt. With her right hand akimbo and a racket dangling in the other, one remarked, "I suppose she is self-conscious about her legs."

"Let us hope for a peaceful Wimbledon," Bernard McElwaine said. "The girls have been earnestly entreated to dress for battle and not burlesque." Chaffee, pegged a "glamour girl" along with Beverly Baker and Gertrude "Gorgeous Gussie" Moran, told *The Evening Standard* that "When I play, I shall wear nothing sensational—nothing to offend." Reporters made a point of noting Baker's custom-made outfits, which included a low-cut cotton dress with a "trellis-worked pattern of three hundred yards of organdie striping," as well as Althea's red jacket and her sea green cardigan. That's about as flashy as Althea got, limiting any splash of color to her outerwear and dressing conservatively in white shorts or skirts. "No Gorgeous Gussie frills and fancies for me," she said, referring to Moran's penchant for wearing lacy panties under her tennis skirt.

"No woman player has yet come along who can concentrate on two things and win both: that is being a public fashion and glamour 'queen' and a great tennis player at the same time," McKelvie said. Althea agreed. She wasn't about to get caught up in clothing, of all things. With the world watching her every move, she had a hard enough time focusing on what to say, how to act, and where to place the ball on the court so that she could win.

On a rainy Monday, Althea made her debut at Wimbledon on Centre Court—not out on the fringes as she did on opening day at Forest Hills in 1950. The enthusiastic crowd included her buddies, the photojournalist Gordon Parks, who was living in Paris at the time, and Sugar Ray Robinson, who was also in Paris training for his upcoming fight against Randy Turpin in England and performing at nightclubs there. Sugar Ray boasted to reporters covering Althea's Wimbledon debut that he'd be rooting for the "swell kid from my neighbourhood." Althea didn't begin playing until 5:30 P.M., since the rain left the courts idle for three and a half hours. Some of the thousands who came to Wimbledon left, but many passed the time by playing canasta, knitting, or eating cucumber sandwiches. Another difference for Althea was that this year's downpour was uneventful, unlike the one that drowned her chances of victory at Forest Hills.

"I made a vow to myself: 'Althea, you're not going to look around. You're not going to listen to any calls or remarks. All you are going to do is watch the tennis ball.' I did that. I didn't acknowledge the referees' calls; whatever they said, okay fine. I won the first set, 6-love. Then I looked around at the nineteen to twenty thousand spectators as if to say, 'How do you like that?' But then after that I lost the second set . . . because I lost my concentration."

The widely anticipated match bounced back and forth between a poker-faced Althea and an occasionally jittery Pat Ward, the local favorite who played for the Surrey County team. They took turns forcing each other into errors. One minute, Ward would outdrive Althea; the next, Althea would storm the net. But all in all, Ward's tepid, British serve was no match for Althea's powerful one—described as both masculine yet magnificent. When play ended on the slippery court, which caused Ward to fall at one point, Althea went home as queen for the day, 6-0, 2-6, 6-4.

It was a different story later that week in the third round, despite Althea's early 40-love lead against Beverly Baker of Santa Monica, California. Known for having "two forehands," Baker had Althea running all over the court. "Even Althea's service, which is the basis of her net-rushing game, was wild and woolly, and her volleying lacked timing and direction," Laurie Pignon said. The three-time Wimbledon champion Fred Perry said Althea's drop-shot lob approach didn't work. "Drobs" is how he described her drop shots—more lob than drop shot. The ambidextrous Baker won in straight sets 6-1, 6-3.

Althea lost the big one at Wimbledon, but her performance at the Frinton open lawn tournament and the Dortmund International Championships in Germany lifted her spirits. She easily won in singles—not even bothering to take off her blue sweater—and did well in doubles. At Dortmund she beat Hannah Kozeluh, a former Czechoslovakian champion who had become a voluntary exile in Berlin, 6-3, 6-2.

Although Althea later summed up her European tour by simply saying, "All I got was more experience," she was a heroine on American soil. She was billed in a "starring role" at the ATA's thirty-fourth national championships in August, winning her fifth of the ten singles titles, and the ATA Guild teamed with *Our World* magazine to honor her during a reception at the Waldorf-Astoria Hotel in midtown Manhattan. In September, however, she had a lackluster return to Forest Hills. She played mixed doubles with the Australian star Don Candy and made it to the second round of women's singles by beating Gladys Heldman of Houston, 6-1, 6-0. But sixteen-year-old Maureen Connolly of San Diego put her out of the game 6-2, 6-4. *The Afro-American* called Althea's backhand "impotent" and said "rarely did Miss Gibson score by virtue of her own strategy." It happened primarily when Connolly "had maneuvered herself out of position."

Two months later Bethune-Cookman College proclaimed November 10, 1951, as Althea Gibson Day. When Althea arrived in Daytona Beach, she was the star of a parade from the Florida East Coast Railroad Station to the campus where she had lunch at Faith Hall. She spoke that afternoon in an assembly in the auditorium, and the choir sang "Every Time I Feel the Spirit" among other selections. After dinner back at Faith Hall she was whisked to a motorcade for a second parade to Memorial Stadium for the Wildcats football game against Xavier University's undefeated Gold Rush, visiting from New Orleans. At halftime she received a slew of gifts and accolades. The day ended with a dance in her honor in the auditorium.

The next year Althea was ranked ninth in the United States, based on her 1951 performance. She came close to pulling off an upset at Forest Hills, as she had almost done two years earlier, telling a reporter, "My game is much stronger in every department." This time the potential victim was Doris Hart, a former Wimbledon winner and the second-seeded player at the nationals. The fourteen thousand fans applauded each of Althea's points as she took the lead 5-3 in game eight of the first set. "Her opponent was running from one side of the court to the other trying to return Althea's brilliant placements," James Edmund Boyack said. Then Hart traded places—not putting Althea on the run but leaving her standing in amazement, which was just as bad. Althea pulled off a short rally before Hart took over and won the match, 7-5, 6-1.

"I have no excuse," Althea said as she left the court. "I should have beaten her. I know I had her in the first set, but I don't know what happened to me. If I'd taken the first, I'm sure I would have gone onto win the match, but I guess I got too careful. She really murdered my lob shots, but I didn't feel sure of my volley and drive."

Hart felt that Althea had a "chip on her shoulder" and said that she made inappropriate remarks to her opponents after she lost a match such as, " 'I don't know why I didn't beat you; you're not that good.' You didn't say anything like that. You'd say 'nice match' or 'congratulations,' " Hart pointed out. "Her remarks annoyed us as players. She was the only one I came in contact with who said those things." The remarks infuriated Hart, but she didn't react. "I'd just bite my tongue and leave it at that."

In Althea's third time at Forest Hills she had struck out as Boyack put it. "Here is a young star who has all the stroke equipment to cope with these seeded stars and beat them," he noted. "She knows every trick in the tennis championship book. Unfortunately, she does not have enough tournament experience on grass courts." Bertram Baker pointed out that Althea only competed on grass in Orange, New Jersey, that year while other players have played lawn tennis all summer. Plus, he said, Althea had academic and work responsibilities at college.

Before one of her visits to Orange, ATA officials asked Rosemary Darben if her parents would allow Althea to spend a week at their home in nearby Montclair, New Jersey, so that she wouldn't have to travel back and forth from New York City. "So she came and she stayed and she stayed and she stayed," Rosemary said. "That became her home more or less." And the time she spent there at 69 Pleasant Way was among the best periods of her life, Althea said, so much so that the family who bought the house years later would occasionally notice her sitting outside reminiscing about all the fun she had in that house and all the fun she had making friends in Montclair—fun that took her mind off her slump in tennis. The Darbens picked up where the Eatons and Johnsons left off. They, too, absorbed Althea into their household with all the highs and lows that come with being a daughter or a sibling. "We didn't treat her like she was anybody but another person," Rosemary said. "We'd tell her to sit down and shut up.

"Everybody thought when Althea came to live with the Darben family in Montclair, she'd learn her social graces, which were enough to get by, but a little ragged," Rosemary recalled. "We had our own napkin holders and this and that. Her coming there really brought Althea out. She became friendlier. She became more graceful." Althea had come a long way from her days in Harlem, where she spent so much time running around in the streets with her friends that she missed out on some of her home training along with whatever else her teachers at school could offer to smooth out her rough edges. By the time she moved to Montclair she needed only a few pointers here and there. "She wasn't the same person who came out of Harlem who went to live with the Eatons or Johnsons," Rosemary said. "They got the ragged end."

Whatever her buddy Ro said was for her own good, Althea believed, so she heeded reminders to say yes instead of yeah or to take a second before speaking her mind. "I think I had a big influence on her," Rosemary said. "Like for instance, she's playing in a tournament in South Orange, and she got put out in the second round. A reporter came up and said to her, 'Miss Gibson, how do you think you lost the match?' She said: 'You saw it! You tell me! What are you doin'? You're sitting there writing!' I said: 'Al, Al, Al! No, No! Don't holler like that to the reporter. The next day, they're going to put it in the paper.' And they sure did— 'Well, she may have talent, but she doesn't show it.' It was all negative. You know? That's the kind of thing I told her: 'Just grin and bear it.'"

Althea learned other lessons at the Darbens', on everything from pinochle to love. She was a quick study on pinochle; a little slow on making a commitment to Ro's brother Will, who would eventually become her husband and the love of her life; and a no-starter in the kitchen, where all she could make was cocoa despite being surrounded by great cooks growing up in Harlem and now in Montclair. "My mother would always make rolls," Rosemary said. "Every Saturday. From the ground up. Parker House rolls. And she'd put them down and by six o'clock, they were ready to go in the oven. By six o'clock, our house was crowded with people. They'd say, 'Oh hi, how are you?' They knew the rolls were coming out the oven."

"After dinner, we'd play pinochle, and Althea was very competitive," Rosemary said. "My father was a great pinochle player so she chose him as a partner, and we all tried to beat them." Rosemary teamed up with her brother, but the pairing ended as Will grew more attracted to her friend. "After that he dropped me for Althea, and they became partners."

"Will had taken a shine to me," Althea said, "and though nothing romantic developed during that time, we saw a lot of each other. He would accompany me to many social functions and the like, and it was therefore rumored that he and I were engaged. But that simply wasn't true."

"They had a lot in common," Rosemary believed. "They liked to play cards, and they had a lot of fun together. I think he made Althea feel good about herself, and he filled her in on a lot of facts, because he read a lot." Will and Althea stayed on each other's minds when she was at school or on the road playing tennis. "When she wrote, she always spoke of him and how she liked him." And when she was in the Northeast, she came home to the Darbens. She also visited her family in Harlem regularly and called every week, said her niece Sandra Givens of Petersburg, Virginia.

In the spring of 1953 Althea graduated from Florida A&M. Jake Gaither, whose reputation for gridiron victories exceeded that of Grambling's Eddie Robinson at the time, used his juice to help Althea land a job teaching physical education at Lincoln University in Jefferson City, Missouri.

It was a good break for Althea, but it put her even farther away from her family and friends. Will sought to close the

Althea and Will Darben at a nightclub in Harlem.

gap a bit by proposing to Althea, but she turned him down. "Out of consideration of my career, I decided then that marriage wasn't for me," said Althea, who *liked* Will but didn't *love* him. Although she also wanted the option of seeing other people, she knew that the weeks and months she spent on the road interfered with any relationship. Will would always hold a special place in Althea's heart, and he carved out more space by being so dependable and reliable whether it was meeting her from a return trip or tending to her affairs when she was away. "During good times and bad, we were never out of touch," Althea explained, "and the little things he did for me along the way are too numerous to recount." In Missouri, however, twenty-six-year-old Althea found a rival for Will's affections in a forty-one-year-old army captain who ran Lincoln's ROTC program. When she wasn't teaching or playing tennis, she was with him. The rest of the time she kept herself busy with everything from Ping-Pong to badminton. She was the only woman on the faculty softball team, where she was the pitcher and an outfielder. She tried to join the basketball team, but the men balked and said she risked injury. However, they agreed to let her practice with them. She also joined the Just Us and Playmore Duplicate bridge clubs, going off on her partners if they were losing. She tried bowling, but only one place would permit blacks and only during off-hours. That, too, ended when one of the co-owners and some of the white patrons complained.

But love is what really held Althea's attention at Lincoln. Althea said she had a "wingding of a time" with the captain, whom she wouldn't name. "On account of him, I almost gave up tennis for good," she admitted later. Her USLTA ranking, which had inched up to seventh place in 1953, had fallen to thirteenth in 1954. It didn't help matters that amid its articles on the death of the activist Mary Church Terrell, the elevation of Ralph J. Bunche to the undersecretary of the United Nations, the appointment of Benjamin O. Davis Jr. as the first black air force general, or the pending Supreme Court decision on *Brown v. the Board of Education*, *Jet* magazine had dubbed Althea "The Biggest Disappointment in Tennis." After the article appeared Sydney Llewellyn offered to coach her. She knew him from the ATA, and they had played mixed doubles in 1950, making it to the finals of the New Jersey Open. "He insisted that I could go all the way to the top," Althea recalled. "I liked his approach. He was so intense and so serious, and I felt I could do well with him."

"She was obviously a potential tennis champion," Llewellyn said. "You could see it from the get-go. She was very competitive. If she come in here, she believed she could spit further than you. Anything you come up with, she could beat you doing it."

Llewellyn, who drove a taxi on the side, kept Althea on the court for hours, practicing his "theory of correct returns." He helped her maximize her wrist action and switch from the multipurpose continental grip to an eastern grip to strengthen her forehand.

Despite Llewellyn's enthusiasm and progress with Althea, a huge question mark hung over her future. She was intrigued by the captain's suggestion that she join the Women's Army Corps—and his comment that she'd look "snazzy" in a uniform. As a WAC she felt that she could become an officer and a provider, making enough money to support herself, build a nest egg, and send some to her family. "I was tired of never having any money," Althea said. She made $3,000 a year—the going rate for teachers—but she had to stretch it to cover her $48.50 in rent and her car note on a secondhand Oldsmobile. All she had to show for her time playing tennis were trophies. "I didn't see any way that things were likely to get better," said Althea, who considered herself "champion of nothing but the ATA."

"The more I thought about it, the more I thought it was a good idea," Althea said of the WAC possibility. "Anyway, it might mean I could stay with the captain for a long time, and that interested me a lot. Being in love and being loved by somebody was something brand new to me." Her desire for dates began to overshadow her desire for tennis. "It's funny," she acknowledged, "but the things that have seemed most important to you can suddenly become very unimportant compared with being with, and pleasing, somebody you love." The fifteen-year age difference along with "the nagging doubt in me about giving up something I'd put so many years and so much sweat into—not to mention what others had put into it"—kept her from crash-landing into the captain's arms. "In the end we both decided we had to be satisfied with being friends," she said. "I won't go so far as to say I was satisfied, but I admit I went along with the decision. Tennis still had that big a hold on me." Nevertheless, she loaded up her blue Oldsmobile with its Missouri plates, leaving the state and its brand of segregation for good.

Back east, she continued to work on her WAC application. Both Rosemary and Sydney pleaded with her to reconsider. She talked Syd into writing a recommendation letter, and he talked her into sending in her entry form for the nationals. One day she stopped by to tell him that she had passed her military physical. "He looked like I'd hit him over the head with a hammer," said Althea, dismissing his talk about her future. "If I was any good, I'd be the champ now. But I'm just not good enough. I'm probably never going to be. And I'm sick of having people support me, taking up collections for me, and buying me clothes and airplane tickets and every damn thing I eat or wear. I want to take care of myself for a change. In the army I can do it."

Rosemary kept the pressure on. "We drove up to Montclair Center, and she was going to put the letter in the mailbox. And I said: 'Don't do it; your chance is going to come.' So she said: 'Well, I have no home, I've finished college, and I don't want to teach, so what do I do?' So we came back home, and my mother and father told her: 'You have a home with three meals a day, so don't worry about a thing.'"

Since Althea didn't view herself as the champ, she didn't become one at Forest Hills that summer. "As we were leaving," Rosemary recalled, "someone called and said Miss Gibson, may I see you a minute? When she came out the room, she said: 'Buddy, guess what? You're right; my break has come.' The State Department was sending her on an Asian tour to play with all the top players." She would help to integrate a foursome of tennis players as a goodwill ambassador during the height of controversy in the United States over McCarthyism; the Emmett Till lynching in Money, Mississippi; Rosa Parks's arrest for refusing to give her bus seat to a white man in Montgomery, Alabama, and the resulting bus boycott there. A win-win situation for America and Althea, this tour would alter her career and her outlook.

Chapter 4

"At Last! At Last!"

I had the best serve in women's tennis. I had the best overhead in women's tennis. And I had the most killing volley in women's tennis.

A NEW ALTHEA emerged in Asia—one with a sharper game, greater confidence, smoother social graces, and even a stronger vocabulary. "Althea was marvelous; I mean she really made quite an impression," said Hamilton Richardson, a champion tennis player and a former Rhodes scholar. "Frankly, she was an inspiration to all of us because she handled herself very well and spoke very well." Although Richardson, Bob Perry, and Karol Fageros were accomplished and talented athletes, Althea was the star of the group. Many Asians in the countries they visited—Burma, Ceylon, India, Pakistan, and Thailand—felt an affinity to Althea as a woman of color and were delighted to see her as part of an official U.S. delegation. With the United States grappling over the question of race, they turned to Althea for answers or at least to get a firsthand perspective. "We Indians have a natural sympathy for all coloured races," a priest at Rosario High School in South Kanara shared in a handwritten note. "May God keep

Touring Asia for the State Department gave Althea a lot of confidence, both in her game and in herself.

you good and sweet as you have been so far, and may greater and greater triumphs crown your career."

She also aroused curiosity in some places because of her skill as a woman athlete and that powerful serve. When Fageros took ill in Dacca, the capital of East Pakistan, Althea had to play the men and beat the local champion, who later surprised her with a gift: the skin of a twelve-foot Bengal tiger from a hunting tale he had shared with the group. "She loved to just smack 'em over the fence, particularly when she had a crowd of all men," recalled Richardson, Althea's mixed-doubles partner on the tour. She also relished the opportunity to hit an overhead smash in mixed doubles, telling Richardson, "Out of the way Hamball; this one's mine!" Playing with top athletes from America and Asia for a solid six weeks on the State Department tour did Althea a world of good. "A lot of the game of tennis is strictly confidence," Richardson said. "She just really didn't know how to win." Richardson, also a member of the U.S. Davis Cup team, worked with Althea on strategy, strokes, and how to make the most of each point. He also encouraged her to do more speaking and singing in public. She had ample opportunity to shine with the flurry of social events: cocktails in Mandalay, lunch with the leader of New Delhi, a reception to meet Martha Graham and her dance company in Calcutta, to cite just a few examples from their stack of invitations.

Once the whirlwind trip to Asia had ended, Althea continued to crisscross the globe on an extended goodwill tour on the road to Wimbledon. Now traveling alone, the pressure of the spotlight grew. "It was a strain, always trying to say and do the right thing, so that I wouldn't give people the wrong idea of what Negroes are like," Althea said. "No matter how hard I tried to think of myself as just another person, I was constantly being confronted with proof that I wasn't, that I was a special sort of person—a Negro with a certain amount of international importance. It was pleasant to think about but very hard to live with." Nevertheless, she maintained her focus on trying to be a winning tennis player with a winning personality. During her eight months abroad she won sixteen of eighteen tournaments from Rangoon to London. In Europe, Althea targeted key tournaments that would pit her against competitors she was likely to face at Wimbledon, especially contests on grass. She won her first grand slam against the British player Angela Mortimer in France, prompting the boxer Archie Moore to send her flowers—from one champion to another he said—and to invite her to his fight against Yolande Pompey. It was the first time a black tennis player had won one of the world's top four singles titles, consisting of the grand slams held in Australia, England, France, and the United States. "I was very, very proud of her and pleased for her," Richardson said.

Winning the French title had been a challenge. The eight thousand Parisians at Roland Garros Stadium had unnerved

Making history as the first black woman to win a Grand Slam at the French Open in 1957.

Althea with all the booing, clapping, and whistling. Her British friend Angela Buxton won the first set of their face-off in the semifinals, but Althea regained her composure enough to win the second. Then her bra strap snapped. The crowd roared as Buxton accompanied her to the dressing room for a quick repair job. After Althea lost the next game she suddenly left again with Buxton in tow. When she returned, she kept double-faulting and hitting easy shots into the net. At one point she lost it and threw her racket on the ground, but she pulled off the match, 2-6, 6-0, and 6-4. However, the tournament referee-in-chief later chastised Althea about walking off the court without permission and said Buxton could have claimed the match. "Though it was funny, it didn't help concentration," said a smiling Buxton, who endured a repeat of the sudden exits as Althea's doubles partner because of the strap problems. "Naturally, I couldn't dream of her disqualification." Mortimer, who witnessed the goings-on, was also amused. "I'm going to insist on Althea bringing a spare brassiere to the court for the final on Saturday." Althea won the crowd over at the final, with a strong ovation when she beat Mortimer 6-0, 12-10 in an hour and thirty-five minutes. She got the same reaction when she and Buxton won in doubles against Darlene Hard and Dorothy Knode, 6-8, 8-6, 6-1. "I think this is my best yet," Althea said. "All along, I have figured I could not only win Rome and Paris, which I have done, but make the grade at Wimbledon."

In the semifinals of the northern England lawn championships in Manchester, a warm-up for Wimbledon, Althea beat the top-ranked Shirley Fry, with whom she had a friendly rivalry. Then at the finals, she defeated Louise Brough—the world champion whom she had almost upset in her debut at Forest Hills. She also won the Surrey County lawn tournament, her eighth straight European title, against Anne Shilcock of England. In just two years she had gone from being labeled by *Jet* as "the biggest disappointment in tennis" in her darkest days, to being described as "hot as an exploded A-bomb," as *The Pittsburgh Courier* proclaimed to its readers. The key difference was that Althea now had better control of her power and the game. She wasn't as erratic. She wasn't as nervous. She wasn't to be taken for granted. "The crowds came out to see this girl who played tennis like Joe Louis slugged in the ring," said the *New York Times* sportswriter Arthur Massalo. "They were intrigued by her cool killer instinct."

As a player, she was ruthless. But as an ambassador for her country, she was a kinder, gentler Althea. Following a sweep of five tournaments in the Mediterranean area, including the Rome International Tennis championship, the *New York Times* published an editorial titled "A Good Envoy." "We are fortunate to have in Althea Gibson the sort of representation that we need and want," the editorial said in part. "She is part and parcel of the real America that works for what it gets and plays hard and well to win. We are happy in her success and proud of her." Harold E. Howland, an official in the U.S. State Department's International Educational Exchange Service, expressed similar sentiments in a letter to Althea dated June 28, 1956. "It is universally agreed that your sterling efforts, on and off the courts, have gained immeasurable goodwill and understanding, and enhanced respect for our country," Howland wrote. "The success of your tour abroad must not be attributed only to your prowess on the tennis courts but also to your genuine wholesomeness, your personal charm, and your many friend-winning attributes. Never did an athlete on a tour abroad win more respect and understanding for his country."

The string of titles and the latest victory in Manchester had created such a stir that there was talk Althea might again upset Brough, the reigning Wimbledon champion. Despite a five-year absence from the All-England Club, Althea was now ranked fourth to win Wimbledon while Fry was seeded fifth. "On current form, Miss Gibson stands as the best American player, which is the same as the best in the world," said Lance Tingay of *The London Daily Telegraph*. When she hit a ball, it traveled "like a bolt out of a crossbow," another observer said. But Althea, the two-to-one favorite to win the singles title, said she was "stale" by the time she reached Wimbledon and worn out from all the traveling. Her weight had dropped from 150 to 139 pounds, and she lost the quarterfinals to Fry, whom she had just beaten three weeks earlier in Manchester. "Maybe my game was off; maybe I was just tired," she said. "But I certainly am not making excuses." Althea played "scared tennis," wrote Milton Gross of the *New York Post*. "She was cautious when she should have been daring. She was concerned when she should have been comforted." Although Althea didn't go home with the singles crown, she won doubles with Buxton, earning her the first of three Wimbledon doubles titles.

All in all, Althea's world tour was such a success that New York Mayor Robert Wagner gave her an official welcome home at City Hall. As far as tennis and governmental officials were concerned, Althea said and did all of the right things abroad, and she didn't worsen the country's race problem. "I am just another tennis player, not a Negro tennis player," she told reporters. "Of course, I am a Negro—everybody knows that—but you don't say somebody is a white tennis player. Do you?

"It is my personal feeling that my success may help produce finer and better Negro players," she added. "You need top-flight competition to reach the top. My own development this year was greatly enhanced by the players I was pitted against."

She also got a few pointers on her development from a fan, who noted that she was "overtennised" and urged her to take a break so that she could win the U.S. nationals. "You are at a great disadvantage in overdoing the amount of tournament tennis you play," wrote Manfred Goldman, a New Yorker who had followed her career from the beginning. "When you got to England, you should have played in one grass tournament only to familiarize yourself with this court, after the long layoff on such surface, which would have been sufficient to put you in good shape for Wimbledon." Fry, Goldman pointed out, limited her tournament play and came to Wimbledon "practically fresh." Don't play singles and doubles and mixed doubles in the same tournament, he advised. Pick just one. That was actually the same philosophy of her buddy Ham Richardson. Competing in all three events—and sometimes two—"was too much work," he believed.

While Althea acknowledged that she was overtennised, a break was out of the question. She had a few tournaments to enter in the month leading up to Forest Hills. Repeating the scenario at Wimbledon, she lost to Fry at the clay championships in Chicago. With just two hours to spare after her late arrival from the Windy City to the Pennsylvania and Eastern States Tournament in Haverford, she hit the court prepared to do business. She lost no sets over the four days and won her first major grass title at home by defeating Margaret Osborne DuPont, the former national and world champion and the Davis Cup captain. In a move that characterized Althea's play in Haverford, she slammed the ball deep into the baseline and then plopped her next shot just over the net, beating DuPont 6-1, 6-4. She beat Brough again at the eastern grass singles, 6-1, 6-3, and won doubles with Darlene Hard. At the ATA tournament, she won her ninth championship, 6-1, 6-1, vanquishing Nana Vaughn who had called her a "crude creature" and beaten her at the girls' championship back in 1942.

In terms of Forest Hills, Althea's fan mail turned out to be prophetic. Unlike Althea, Fry had skipped most of the tournaments preceding the nationals. She beat Althea in the finals, 6-3, 6-4. "They were the only two sets I lost in the whole tournament, but they were the ones that counted," Althea said. "I kept rushing the net, as I always do, and Shirley calmly let me play my way into error after error." After the nationals Althea accepted an invitation to play in the thirteenth annual Pacific Southwest Championships in Los Angeles. In the finals she played Nancy Chaffee, who had beaten her routinely when she first started playing in USLTA tournaments in the early fifties. But it was a new day, and this time Althea defeated Chafee, 4-6, 6-2, 6-1. Althea celebrated as the guest of honor at a Hollywood party at the Town Club. Nat "King" Cole presented a 35 mm camera to Althea as a memento of the tournament. She had another victory at the Pan-American Games in Mexico City, where she defeated Darlene Hard.

While she was on the road, Will sent a letter saying that he missed her "terribly," inquiring about her tennis activities, and updating her on his father, Poppa, who was in the hospital recovering from a minor hernia operation. It began: "Darling, I received your awaited note yesterday and was really glad and happy to hear from you. As you mentioned in your note, I did kiss the picture in the clipping good night— and really wished for you more than once. However, I will be seeing you Monday, so I really have something to look forward to."

Althea's return to New York was brief, for she soon left for a four-month tour of Australia with Shirley Fry. "We are each other's main court opponent, but still the best of friends," Althea said. The feelings remained mutual. "We got along fine," Fry said recently from her home in Longwood, Florida. "I liked Althea. We had a good time together." But like Doris Hart, Fry noted that Althea had an air of superiority that raised the level of competitiveness among her opponents. "She had an attitude that made a lot of us want to beat her; Maureen Connolly had the same attitude," Fry said. "You don't go up to shake hands and say, 'I'll beat you next time.'"

Fry dominated Althea in most of the tournaments on their Australian tour, although Althea did win two singles titles against Fry in the New South Wales and South Australia tournaments. Will sent her a clip from the latter with the headline, "It Was a Good Day for the Gibsons," a reference to Althea and Neil Gibson of Sydney. Using editing symbols, Will wrote: "I think Darben sounds better. Love you XXXX." One of Althea's worst days in Australia was at the Victoria Women's Tennis Championships. She had a running war with an umpire over foot-fault calls, which had plagued her at a number of tournaments around the world. At one point she told him, "Why don't you stop this, and let's get on with the game?" When rain stopped the match for an hour, she stormed off the court. She had racked up sixteen foot faults and was too mad to conduct any interviews in her dressing room. She was still in a tizzy when play resumed. Once she tallied her twenty-first foot fault, she smacked the ball into the stands. The ball narrowly missed the prime minister's hat, settling about two feet away. Not surprisingly, Fry won 4-6, 9-7, and 8-6.

At the Australian championships in Melbourne, Althea and Fry won the doubles competition. Fry captured the singles crown two days later. "It had been very much her year," Althea said. So much so, that Fry had fallen in love with an American in Australia and extended her stay to get married. She then retired. Althea missed the wedding, since she was headed to Ceylon, where she defended her title in the Asian championship by beating Pat Ward of England. "I was certain now that I was capable of playing on even terms with the best amateurs in the world," Althea said. She was so certain that she made a promise to herself: if 1956 had been Shirley Fry's year, 1957 would be hers.

"After '56, nobody could beat me," Althea said years later. "I had the best serve in women's tennis. I had the best overhead in women's tennis. And I had the most killing volley in women's tennis."

Wimbledon was Althea's primary focus in 1957. She would go in fresh—not overtennised. She would compete in only a few tournaments and only on grass; she wouldn't even defend her French title on the composition courts of Roland Garros Stadium. The ATA gave her a bon voyage party at Birdland, where she hobnobbed with more than three hundred well-wishers, including Sammy Davis Jr., who played around with her on the piano. This time, the USLTA was paying her way to Wimbledon. Sydney Llewellyn drove her to Idlewild airport, and Buddy Walker came along for the ride. Edna Mae Robinson, who met them there, tucked $20 into Althea's hand as they said good-bye. Althea had checked her two bags, but she took her three tennis rackets with her on the Pan American Stratocruiser. "I didn't want anything to happen to them." Angela Buxton, who had invited Althea to stay at her flat in Paddington, was waiting with a friend when the plane landed in England. Buxton wouldn't be Althea's doubles partner at Wimbledon this year since she had sprained her wrist. Instead, she'd be broadcasting the matches on television. With the exception of the Queen's Club Tournament, Althea competed in all the Wimbledon warm-ups, capturing all the singles titles. "I was ruthless on the tennis court. Win at any cost. I became an attacker. If your first serve ain't good, I'll knock it down your throat. It just so happened that I had the talent to win at another level instead of being the meanie on the tennis court.

"You got to know your opponent," she added. "You got to know their strengths, their weaknesses, see how they move, what balls they don't like. Once I know this, they'd only see the ball at their weak points, not their strengths."

Confident that she'd take home the Wimbledon crown, Althea picked out an evening gown for the ball and wrote an acceptance speech. Her opening match at Wimbledon was a tough one against Suzy Kormoczy of Hungary, but she won, 6-4, 6-4. In the semifinals she defeated a local favorite, sixteen-year-old six-footer Christine Truman. "I was pretty excited. It was quite a feeling to be a Wimbledon finalist." Althea didn't let any of the catcalls and jeering faze her. "I'll mess them up on the court, and then the joke will be on them," she responded. In a jubilant mood Althea met up with two friends from the ATA, Katherine Landry and Dorothy Parks, both WAC captains in Germany, who were on leave to support her at the tournament. They reminisced over filet mignon and sherry at Le Couple, a French restaurant that Althea loved to visit when she was in London. She opted against hanging out later with them so that she could rest up for her big day.

July 6, 1957, was shaping up to be a unique day—sultry with heat and all abuzz since Queen Elizabeth II would be making her first visit to Wimbledon. The monarch usually opted for horse races over tennis matches. A spectator took advantage of her presence by approaching the royal box and displaying a banner about protecting the queen from war-mongers. The queen simply smiled as a police officer and referee escorted the woman out of the area.

With the temperature hovering around 100 degrees, Wimbledon set a record for 1,071 fainting spells during the two-week tournament. It was the kind of heat that can make a tennis player have an off day, but Althea welcomed it. "There is something about a hot, still day that brings out the best in your shots," Althea said. "The sweat seems to loosen your muscles and perfect your aim." It appeared to be work-ing, as Althea won the first set, against Darlene Hard, a perky twenty-one-year-old from Montebello, California, who had upset Louise Brough in the quarterfinals. "When I rushed the net, I got the volley. When I stayed in the back-court and Darlene charged the net, I hit past her."

"At last! At last!" Althea exclaimed as play came to an end with the score at 6-3, 6-2. She was officially the queen of ten-nis with a Wimbledon singles title to prove it—the first black champion in the tournament's eighty-year history. As workers unfurled a green carpet, she waited with Hard by the trophy table. The two players stood at attention as the queen and three attendants walked onto the court and then they curt-sied. "My congratulations; it must have been terribly hot out there," Queen Elizabeth said after shaking Althea's hand. "Yes, Your Majesty, but I hope it wasn't as hot in your box," Althea replied. "At least, I was able to stir up a breeze."

The smiling monarch wore a rose-and-white printed silk dress with pearls, gloves, a pale pink hat with a red band, and white open-toe shoes with a matching purse. "The queen had

*At her first Wimbledon
championship.*

a wonderful speaking voice, and she looked exactly as a queen ought to look, except more beautiful than you would expect any real-life queen to look." Althea clenched her jaw to fight back tears as she accepted the twenty-eight-inch gold salver adorned with bas-relief images of women athletes and engraved with the names of past champions. Althea was honored that she was the first Wimbledon winner to receive an award from Queen Elizabeth and one of only a few to have an award presented by any queen. "Shaking hands with the queen of England was a long way from being forced to sit in the colored section of the bus," Althea pointed out.

Alice Marble noted the change in the woman on whose behalf she wrote the scathing open letter to her peers in the tennis community nearly a decade earlier. "It looks as though Althea has more confidence," Marble said. "That was half her battle. She had worlds of ability. But she was scared."

"I have been told that all I have to do to become the greatest woman tennis player in history is to conquer myself," Althea said. "I think I've finally learned how not to beat myself.

"Winning this title is the greatest thrill since I started playing tennis," she added. "I'm not going to be satisfied, however, until I win at Forest Hills." In addition to her singles title at Wimbledon, she won doubles with Hard, 6-1, 6-2, but missed having a triple crown when she and her mixed-doubles partner, Neale Fraser of Australia, lost to Hard and Australian Mervyn Rose, 6-4, 7-5.

When Althea arrived at the ball that night, the crowd on the sidewalk applauded. Those inside stood and did the same as she took her seat at the head table between the duke of Devonshire and her counterpart, Lew Hoad, the men's singles champion from Australia. After Hoad made his speech, she delivered hers, termed a spellbinder by some. She opened the three-and-a-half-page acceptance speech, written in green ink on onionskin paper, and told the crowd: "In the words of your own distinguished Mr. Churchill, this is my finest hour. This is the hour I will remember always as the crowning conclusion to a long and wonderful journey." She noted that her award belonged to many, and she singled out Buddy Walker, Fred Johnson, Doctors Johnson and Eaton, Llewellyn, Buxton, the ATA, and the USLTA. "And finally," she said, "this victory is a sincere thank-you to the many good people in England and around the world whose written and spoken expressions of encouragement, faith and hope, I have tried to justify." She concluded by focusing on the responsibilities of the crown, calling it a "total victory of many nations" and a "collective victory of many champions."

"God grant that I may wear it with dignity, defend it with honor, and when my day is done, relinquish it graciously. I thank you."

As the band played "April Showers," she danced with Hoad and even the duke. Ham and Vic Seixas coaxed her into singing a few numbers, so she obliged with "If I Loved You" and "Around the World." The celebration continued at the Astor Club on the West Side, where Althea repeated the tunes, prompting the manager, Bertie Green, to extend an open invitation and the bandleader to tell her that she was welcome to sing with the group at any time.

On her arrival back on U.S. soil, Althea was kept behind on the Pan Am Clipper as the other passengers disembarked to ensure clear shots of the new queen as she descended the stairs and walked across the red carpet. The three people who bid her bon voyage when she departed on her transatlantic flight had been joined by a throng for her return, which had been delayed by an hour and a half. "Quite a difference from the day I left," she noted. As soon as Althea saw her mother, she exclaimed, "Hi ya, sweetie pie!" and rushed to give her a hug and a kiss. "It made me feel good right down to the tips of my toes to see Mom so happy." Millie, Bubba, Will, and her first coach, Fred Johnson, were there, too. Edna Mae pinned an orchid on her, while Buddy gave her a cigarette lighter that played "La Vie En Rose," symbolizing her love of Paris.

A police escort led Althea and city officials from the airport to a breakfast celebration at Bertram Baker's house and then to her childhood home in Harlem. When the Cadillac pulled in front of her doorstep, her neighbors on 143rd Street cheered as soon as they caught a glimpse of Althea and swarmed around her after she got out of the car. Her father leaned out of their third-floor window, waving and yelling.

During the post-Wimbledon celebration Althea was persuaded to sing a few numbers.

A self-appointed spokesman holding up a black dog told her, "I just want to tell you how grateful we all are and my dog, Blackie, is." Ten-year-old Anthony Hunter's statement drew laughter from the crowd. "It meant a lot to me to have all those people come out of their tired old apartment houses up and down 143rd Street to tell me how glad they were that one of the neighbor's children had gone out into the world and done something big."

It was a big deal all over the world but especially in communities like Harlem. Winning Wimbledon was akin to winning the White House as far as many black Americans were concerned. "Some people just don't know what that means and what it meant to us then," explained L. Garnell Stamps, who used to peek through the fence around Dr. Johnson's tennis court in Lynchburg, Virginia, to watch Althea practice. "That's the world championship of *all* tennis—the greatest tennis player in the *world*, and the Queen of England was there to see it!"

"At that time, we didn't have people who could run for president of the United States," added Stamps, who later interviewed Althea for "Viewpoint," a public affairs program sponsored by the NAACP chapter in Lynchburg. "We did not have many nationally known people. There were a few in the arenas and on the field of play and in other things. We had to look up to those."

So black America insisted on a celebration befitting the newly crowned queen. In fact, James L. Hicks, a prominent columnist for the *New York Amsterdam News*, claimed that his paper worked behind the scenes to push for a ticker-tape parade so that the Queen of Tennis could greet her public. Leaders at the black weekly talked city officials into granting a parade for Althea, Hicks said, after a mayoral aide insisted that only heads of state were worthy of such recognition. The paper refuted the aide's claim by providing records on parades for Charles Lindbergh, General Douglas MacArthur, and others. At that point, the track star Jesse Owens was the only other black American to have been so honored and that was in 1936 when he literally ran down Hitler's claims of Aryan superiority by winning four gold medals at the Olympics in Berlin. Althea's supporters felt it was long past time for another black hero to parade down the Canyon of Champions, and they prevailed in their push for a parade.

At noon the day after Althea's homecoming, mounted police led a ticker-tape parade up Broadway, from the Battery to City Hall. The procession included army, air force, and Coast Guard color guards as well as bands from the fire department and the U.S. Third Naval District. Sitting along the back headrest of an eggshell-colored Imperial convertible was Althea in a silk dress with red-and-blue checks and a white orchid at her shoulder. Over and over again, she exclaimed: "It's amazing! It's wonderful!" as she waved and blew kisses to

The ticker-tape parade after Wimbledon.

the cheering crowd. Bertram Baker of the ATA; Manhattan Borough President Hulan Jack; and Richard Patterson, the commissioner of the Department of Commerce and Public Events, rode with her in the car, while her family followed in vehicles behind them as strips of paper and confetti rained on them. "This is the proudest day of my life," Dush Gibson said. His wife agreed. "I'll never forget that ticker-tape parade up Broadway and the way all those thousands of people cheered our girl," she said. "That was just the most wonderful thing that ever happened."

It was said that the parade was larger than those held for the Prince of Wales, Lindbergh, MacArthur, and Owens. Strangers and kinfolk, like Althea's beaming cousin Mattie Bryant, made it their business to be there, coming from near and far to be a witness to history. "I went downtown," Mattie recalled, "and I remember going around saying, 'That's my cousin! My cousin!'"

At City Hall, Mayor Robert F. Wagner presented Althea with the city's bronze medallion. "She is a great representa-

New York City's mayor Robert F. Wagner with Althea at a reception he gave at the Waldorf-Astoria upon her return home as the Wimbledon champion.

tive of the city and country and if there were more like Miss Gibson we would have a better world today," he said. Later, Wagner repeated the presentation at a luncheon in her honor at the Waldorf-Astoria's Palm Room attended by her family, close friends, politicians, and supporters like Jackie Robinson. The mayor told the gathering that Althea was a wonderful example to "show New York children they can be fine citizens and reach the top in sports or any walk of life."

"I never thought I would ever be in such a place," Althea responded, "with all my people present, receiving a medal from the mayor of New York just for hitting a little ball around."

The celebrations continued with a balloon-festooned block party uptown in Harlem. The telegrams and letters kept coming with all sorts of stamps, on all sorts of paper, in all sorts of languages, from all sorts of people. President Dwight D. Eisenhower wrote in part: "Recognizing the odds you faced, we have applauded your courage, persistence, and energy. We are most proud of you."

Clearly on a roll, Althea won the clay-court championship in Chicago and the Pacific Southwest singles title. She would cap off the year by winning something even sweeter. On the Sunday morning of the finals at Forest Hills, a friend opened her salon on 125th Street to fix her famous customer's hair. Althea then joined Llewellyn and a vice president from the Harry C. Lee company for breakfast at the Vanderbilt Hotel on Park Avenue, where Althea and most of the other players were staying. Lee paid her $75 a month to serve on its advisory board and to hold up its racket covers in her photos. "I was nervous and confident at the same time— nervous about going out there in front of all those people, with so much at stake, and confident that I was going to go out there and win." In the finals she would face Louise Brough again, and by now she had grown accustomed to beating her. There would be no repeat of the near-miss seven years ago when she first came to Forest Hills. Still, both contenders— Althea, who had just celebrated her thirtieth birthday, and Brough, now thirty-four—were described as being taut as racket strings.

As Althea began to close in on victory with a 4-1 lead, tears flowed down Brough's face. Althea's strategy of letting Brough make all the errors paid off, and her dream came true as she won her first national championship with a score of 6-3, 6-2. "It was a marvelous feeling to see that last point go home and know that I had done it," she said. Vice President Richard Nixon presented Althea with a silver vase overflowing with white gladioli and red roses, along with a tray and a gold tennis ball. "Winning at Wimbledon was wonderful, and it meant a lot to me," Althea said. "But there is nothing

Vice President Richard Nixon presents the winner's trophy to Althea when she wins her first championship at Forest Hills. At right is Mal Anderson of Australia, the winner in the men's division.

quite like winning the championship of your own country." And nothing like making history with yet another first. The *New York Times* reported that her acceptance speech drew "the longest hand-clapping heard in the stadium in years." Undefeated since January when she lost Australia's grand slam to Shirley Fry, Althea beat Brough for the fourth time that year at the Pacific Coast championship in Berkeley before heading to Los Angeles for a vacation. And she broke another barrier as the first black player on the U.S. Wightman Cup team, which beat Great Britain 6-1 in its thirty-four-year-old duel.

Althea's boisterous reception in New York, with one hundred thousand people of every race, creed, and color celebrating her triumphs along the Canyon of Champions and then the overpowering ovation at Forest Hills provided a stark contrast to what nine black students were facing in Little Rock, Arkansas. While Althea was being lauded, the students

In 1957 Althea broke another barrier as the first black player on the U.S. Wightman Cup team.

required the intervention of National Guardsmen to protect them from people bent on doing them harm simply because they wanted to get an education—and integrate Central High School in the process. At the same time, Althea knew that she couldn't become too comfortable basking in the glow of her homecoming for she, too, had been subjected to the same type of venom that was being spewed in Little Rock—being called "nigger" or sent hate mail—and she would experience it again and again. In fact, just weeks after being crowned the Queen of Tennis, she was unable to stay at any of the hotels in Oak Park, Illinois, outside of Chicago, when she competed in the clay court championship. Instead, she stayed at a motel miles away from her competitors. And the Ambassador East Hotel in Chicago refused to book its legendary Pump Room for a luncheon in her honor. While Althea often stayed with Angela Buxton when she was in England, she had more freedom moving about Europe and other parts of the world than she did in her own country.

In an editorial questioning Arkansas Governor Faubus's resistance to integrating the high school, *The Evening Star* in Washington wrote: "There will be more setbacks in the South. But in the end, racial discrimination surely will give way before examples of the kind that Miss Gibson is setting." Dean Gordon B. Hancock, a writer for the *Associated Negro Press* in Chicago, said, "The Negro who can vote and does not vote is a traitor to the cause of Negro advance. If the Negro can be Gibson-hearted in his fight for his rights, his triumph is only a matter of time. . . . Long live Althea Gibson, Negro!"

Another downside for Althea was hearing naysayers question her wins, characterizing them as flukes or saying that she lacked strong competition. Sarah Palfrey Cooke who had helped to prepare Althea for her first visit to Forest Hills begged to differ. She felt that Althea had come of age on the court this year and that she had learned to wait for the right ball rather than attempting to kill each one. Althea said she had a new philosophy. "I'm looking at it in a different aspect," she explained. "It's only a game and games are competition. You are out there to compete and if you go out there with the idea of enjoying it, you can become relaxed and you can control it. It won't control you." It was clear to her that she'd have to go out and do it all over again to prove that she was truly worthy of reigning as the queen of tennis. As always, she was up for the challenge.

An additional challenge was the sudden spate of bad press questioning whether success was going to her head. She was accused of snubbing a reporter by refusing an impromptu interview, keeping a radio crew waiting for hours in Paris, asking a photographer to move back six feet because she didn't photograph well in close-ups, and generally being curt, surly, insulting, and an all-around "Bum of the Court." Perplexed, Althea responded that she was misunderstood. "I am amazed at these stories about my treatment of the press," she responded. "I have always treated the reporters with the greatest respect, but I don't stop every time they bark." She noted that some reporters became upset just because she wanted to take a sip of water after a match before answering questions. She felt that she had been gracious in fielding inquiries on whether she was planning to marry (not right now), turning pro (no comment), or representing her race (not intentionally).

If she had any thoughts about turning pro, she was keeping them to herself. She wasn't about to jeopardize her amateur status at this point in her skyrocketing career. She had learned the hard way about saying or doing the wrong thing, even unintentionally, like the time she unwittingly posed for a picture in front of a milk advertisement in Europe. An innocent mistake, yet it could have given the impression that she was endorsing the product when she had no idea what was behind her at the time. Fortunately for Althea, the photographer agreed to destroy the negatives. While Jack Kramer openly expressed his interest in possibly promoting a pro tour with Althea and Maureen Connolly—sidelined after Maureen was in an accident involving her horse and a truck—Althea publicly expressed no interest in or knowledge of his intent. When asked for a comment about Lew Hoad's $125,000 pro contract, she would only say that as his family's breadwinner, he was justified in trying to support them by any means.

As Althea geared up to defend her titles, sports journalists around the country voted her the Associated Press Female Athlete of the Year. She received two trophies, one in memory of the all-around athlete Mildred "Babe" Didrikson Zaharias, who had won the AP award six times. "What makes this such an outstanding honor is that it doesn't represent one sport but all sports," said Althea, who succeeded the Olympic diving champion Pat Keller McCormick as winner and beat out the golfer Patty Berg and the bowler Marion Ladewig. "I hope I may be able to win it again." Althea also became the first black woman to appear on the cover of *Sports Illustrated*, and she also graced the front of *Time* magazine.

Althea's return to London in 1958 was a near repeat of the previous year. She won most of the warm-ups leading to Wimbledon, but she and her teammates lost the United States' twenty-eight-year claim to the Wightman Cup, four matches to three, largely due to the performance of seventeen-year-old Christine Truman of Britain. Truman, who lost to Althea the previous year at Wimbledon, turned the tables in a 2-6, 6-3, 6-4 upset. Two weeks later, Althea entered the finals at Wimbledon with "Centre Court jitters" against Angela Mortimer and was down in the first set at 0-2, 2-4. But she pulled herself together, shooting forehand drives to Mortimer's feet and deadly serves to win 8-6, 6-2 to retain her singles crown. "She was tough," Althea admitted. "I found her ground strokes particularly good. They kept me at the back of the court and prevented me from coming to the net until late in the match." She teamed with Maria Bueno of Brazil to capture the doubles crown against Margaret Osborne DuPont and Margaret Varner. But near exhaustion by the time of the mixed-doubles contest, she missed the opportunity for a triple crown for the second year. Nevertheless, she would be leaving Wimbledon with two back-to-back singles championships and three consecutive doubles titles, each won with three different partners. "I hope to be at Wimbledon again next year, health permitting and God willing," she said.

No ticker-tape parade awaited Althea in New York this time around, but Mayor Wagner proclaimed July 16, 1958, as Tennis Day in her honor during a reception at Gracie Mansion. The questions about her skills continued to pop up with speculation on how she'd fare against an Alice Marble or a Mo Connolly. Some dismissed her as being the best of a bad lot. And Kramer was still making noises about wooing Althea

When Althea won her second championship at Forest Hills, Secretary of State John Foster Dulles (left) presented the cup. At right is her coach, Sydney Llewellyn, who would become her second husband.

to the pro circuit. But he said he would offer her a $25,000 salary only if she regained her national title. Althea planned to remain an amateur until she proved she was the best in the world. "Some people don't think so, and I must teach them that they're wrong."

That's exactly what she did at Forest Hills, lobbing Darlene Hard into submission to hold onto her title, 3-6, 6-1, 6-2. "This was a satisfying tournament for me," Althea said. "I lost to Truman in the Wightman Cup, so I owed her one and paid her. Then I never had beaten Beverly Fleitz before, and I got past her. The Fleitz match was my toughest." Whenever Althea wasn't on the court, she was in bed trying to recover from a cold that left her wheezing and sluggish. In the finals Althea drew gasps from the crowd when she fell trying to return one of Hard's balls and stood around wringing her right hand. She had sprained two fingers, but she continued to play. She was also a bit off after losing to Hard in the first set of the finals. "I was a little nervous after that," Althea said, but she scanned the stands and glanced at Sydney, who inconspicuously put his hand to his chest. "That meant lob. I threw up the most gorgeous lob you would ever want to see. And so after that, I just walked through the third set and defended my title successfully." But the real turning point came after Secretary of State John Foster Dulles presented the awards to Althea and the male champion, Australian Ashley Cooper. "I wish to announce my retirement from the ranks of amateur tennis players," Althea told the stunned crowd. "I am tentatively setting a period of retirement at one year. My titles are now open to anyone."

Chapter 5

Playing New Notes

It was important to me that my singing be accepted for the right reason, that is, simply because it was good and not because it was novel that a champion tennis player could also sing.

THE QUEEN OF TENNIS didn't really know what to do with herself after the back-to-back victories at Wimbledon and the U.S. nationals. Should she stay in amateur tennis? Should she turn pro? Should she sing? Should she act? Should she settle down with Will? She was glad that she had decided on a year of semiretirement to decide. "I don't know if it's a blessing or a curse," she acknowledged, "but I'm flexible, and I believe in building upon all the talents the Lord has endowed me with." At times she worried that she was too flexible. It's not surprising that Althea would try to sing and act professionally. She could spend entire days in movie theaters, and she so loved music that she had lost her favorite job when she was a teenager after admitting to her boss that she had skipped work to catch Sarah Vaughan in concert.

More than a dozen years earlier, in 1943, Althea had come in second place in the Apollo's amateur talent show. From that point on, she said, "I was never without a melody on my lips." Music had always been part of her life, with her mother playing swing music on the piano, everyone dancing around the house or at hot spots like the Savoy, and the sound of doo-wop filtering up from the street to the Gibsons' third-floor railroad flat. Althea loved Billy Eckstine and so did Bubba, who crooned a little like the smooth singer. In the "Negro capital of the world" known as Harlem, there was a reservoir of talent. Rising stars and those already shining brightly were everywhere. The teen sensation Frankie Lymon lived up the street, and the bandleader Buddy Walker had become her mentor through PAL. Jerome Carrington "Fats" Waller, Florence Mills, Edward Kennedy "Duke" Ellington, and Fletcher Henderson had all called Harlem home at some point. Althea saw no reason that she could not add her name to the list, especially since she was not only a singer, but also a saxophonist, or so she thought.

"She was lousy in the beginning," Mary Ann recalled of her aunt's early musicianship. "Lousy, lousy," Bubba added, shaking his head. "She used to come home with her saxophone, trying to show us she could blow a sax. I told her, 'You can't blow nothing girl!' But she did it for pleasure, for her entertainment. It was something she wanted to do." Althea treasured the sax from Sugar Ray. Buddy Walker, who taught her how to play it, felt the sax was overpriced at $135 and said he talked the storeowner who sold it into refunding $25. Walker's lessons had come in handy when Althea moved into the Eatons' home in Wilmington, where she played the sax in the high school band at Williston and sang in the choir for a short time. Quitting the choir over the difficulty in finding a good fit for her deep voice cost her some appearances on radio and at local events in North Carolina. But she made up for it over the years. Arvelia Myers said Althea was the life of the party during their ATA days and beyond. As soon as she walked through the door, dressed to the nines with not a hair out of place, she lit up the room with her smile and drew people to her like a magnet, many of whom talked her into singing a number or two. It was the same during the goodwill tour of Southeast Asia, where her performances included a noontime blues concert in Ceylon. "Everywhere we went to a cocktail party, she sang," Ham Richardson said. "She had a beautiful voice. We liked to sing together." Rather than simply citing an example from her repertoire, he breaks into song: *Love is a many splendored thing . . .*

Althea was good, Richardson acknowledged, but she was no Lena Horne—nor Sarah Vaughan, Gordon Parks added. "I had the basic equipment to be a good singer: a strong but well-controlled voice, a fairly wide vocal range, and an individual style," explained Althea, who had been a singer with a five-piece combo at a nightclub in Jefferson City, Missouri, when she was a teacher at Lincoln University. "What I lacked, however, was extensive training and guidance, so in the fall of 1957 I set out to rectify that shortcoming." She found a vocal coach in James Scott Kennedy, a professor of speech and voice at Long Island University, and Llewellyn, her tennis coach, also became her personal manager. Althea made her official public debut as a singer at a 1957 tribute to the blues legend W. C. Handy at the Waldorf-Astoria Hotel in New York. "My appearance there impressed an executive of Dot Records, who asked me if I wanted to cut a long-playing album for him. I joyfully accepted."

Negotiations began in earnest with the usual back-and-forth on contractual terms. Strips of onionskin paper were stapled all over Althea's contract with typewritten changes suggested by her attorney, Earle Warren Zaidins, who had a law office at 33 West Forty-second Street, off Fifth Avenue. A provision in item thirteen about being a member in good standing of the American Federation of Television and Radio

Artists had been crossed out with a black pen along with item fourteen specifying a contract period of one year. The period was shortened to six months, a change Althea would later come to regret having initialed. Once Dot's legal department approved the contract, signed by Althea and Dot's president Randolph C. Wood at the beginning of 1958, she wound up with royalties on 90 percent of net sales, including 5 percent of the retail list price on 78s, 45s, and extended-play and long-play records, and 2 percent on records sold outside of the United States. She'd also receive $22.50 for each song recorded or for the equivalent in playing time.

Scheduling a recording date that worked for Althea, the musicians, and the production team took some doing. When a date was finally nailed down, Althea had only a week to prepare. "I hastily selected my songs, but seven days left me little time to polish them, let along rehearse them thoroughly with my group," she said. "What was worse, a few days before the session, I came down with the flu. The big day couldn't be postponed, and so I had to climb out of a sickbed to perform." Sounding like a "cow mooing into a megaphone," she lamented, "I wasn't exactly in top condition to launch the voice that would eclipse Ella Fitzgerald's and Peggy Lee's overnight." Relying upon tea, lemon, medicine, and thick sweaters, she did her best. She had no choice, because the entire album had to be recorded in one session. She chose eleven standards plus her signature song, "So Much to Live For," written by Professor Kennedy. The other selections included "I Can't Give You Anything But Love," I'm Just a Prisoner of Love," and "Don't Say No." She was accompanied by the Dole Dickens Quartet, which included a pianist, a bassist, a guitarist, and a drummer. "If any phrase conveys my attitude towards life, no matter what setbacks I undergo, it's 'So Much to Live For,'" she explained. "For as I beheld the future, its promise was almost unbearably exciting!" One exciting bit of news

Althea was sick with the flu when she recorded her album, Althea Gibson Sings, *for Dot Records. Here she poses with an executive from Dot.*

was an invitation from the producers of *The Ed Sullivan Show* to appear during the week her album was released. "Between the time of their invitation and the time of my appearance, I was chirping like a bird."

In April, Tom H. Mack, the director of album repertoire at Dot, sent a letter also expressing his joy and suggesting that Althea send one of her advance album copies to Sullivan. "I am very enthused about the possibility of his introducing it. It would be a wonderful plug." He also informed Althea that "Love Set" would no longer be the title of her album, which contributed to its release being pushed back to June. Althea was scheduled to appear on *The Ed Sullivan Show* on

May 25 and again on July 13 after defending her title at Wimbledon. In a letter to Mack dated April 16, 1958, Zaidins inquired about the album's new title and questioned the choice of the single Dot planned to release first. "Althea was over to my home last night, and both of us carefully went over the record," he wrote. "It seems to me, and I do not propose to tell you your business, that as far as a single release is concerned, it would seem to me that 'So Much to Live For,' from a commercial standpoint, might be a better single release than 'Don't Say No.' The former has two things over the latter, which may make it more commercial. They are (1) a semi-R&B beat and (2) a message. Incidentally, it is my feeling that Sullivan will want to have Althea do 'So Much to Live For' because of its message."

Althea meticulously kept track of carbon copies of letters like these along with correspondence from Dot and her royalty statements. She secured most of them in reverse-date order with a two-hole aluminum fastener inside the top of a manila folder. She jotted notes on some of the letters, for example, indicating that in May a Dot publicist wouldn't accept charges for a person-to-person call that cost $8.47.

At the end of May, Althea walked onto the stage of *The Ed Sullivan Show*. From her debut album, simply titled *Althea Gibson Sings*, she chose "So Much to Live For" as the number she'd perform. "Ed Sullivan was extremely cordial and the audience most warm," she said. "I was keyed up like an overwound watch, but managed to relax myself before going on with the kind of self-administered pep talk I'm used to giving myself before tennis matches." Despite Althea being overpowered by the orchestra, the audience gave her a big round of applause. Even more notoriety surrounded her next visit since she had won her second consecutive singles title at Wimbledon. This time she sang "I Should Care," which was also well received. "I've always had some uneasiness over the

When her record album debuted, Althea was invited to appear on The Ed Sullivan Show.

genuineness of the enthusiasm for my singing which was displayed on those two occasions. It was important to me that my singing be accepted for the right reason, that is, simply because it was good and not because it was novel that a champion tennis player could also sing." The novelty did play somewhat of a role in her reception by Sullivan and many others, Richardson believed. "He was always amazed, as everyone was, at this tall, gangly athlete. When she sang, she really had a very soft and marvelous voice."

But the public wasn't amazed or aware enough to buy her album in record numbers. "The record did not live up to my expectations," Althea said. "In fact, it sank beneath a sea of indifference." In addition, the revision she had initialed shortening her contract from one year to six months had come back to haunt her. On August 5, Zaidins received a telegram ending her relationship with Dot: "Due to general cutbacks in artist roster, we must regretfully forego exercising our option on Althea Gibson. Wish you much success. Regards, Tom Mack." Naturally Zaidins, who had been firing off letters to

Dot all along, had something to say about the company's efforts and asked for an explanation. "Gentlemen: I am in receipt of your royalty statement for Althea Gibson, for the period ending June 30, 1958," he wrote. "Suffice it to say that I am extremely disappointed in the statement. The promotion of *Althea Gibson Sings* by your company has left much to be desired."

Although Dot literature proclaimed that the company produced "The Nation's Best Selling Records," the slogan obviously didn't apply to Althea's album. The athlete-turned-singer didn't make a dime. Any royalties on the 98-cent 45s or the $3.98 LPs were eaten up in expenses, including her $270 advance for recording 12 sides at $22.50 each and $41.25 for each musician at the recording session. Month after month, the royalty earnings statement showed a negative balance. J. N. Bailey, an executive at Dot, said that 1,230 copies of the album had been sold through November and that he expected sales to pick up since Althea's name was always in the news, particularly after she won her second nationals title. But Bailey said that her single, "Around the World," was virtually at a standstill. "The single selection—number 15758—sold what might be termed an unbelievably small quantity—it was actually thirty records," Bailey wrote. "The reason this may sound extremely strange is because of our type of selling. That is, we do not force distributors to buy records. Samples were distributed to all distributors and DJs. If there is a reaction to the record, orders come in. If there is no reaction, of course, nothing happens, which is the case with many records of which this is one."

It was disappointing news for Althea, especially since she could have used the money, but she didn't have time to sulk. She had her memoir coming out, the possibility of a part on Broadway, and a definite role in a real Hollywood movie, with the likes of John Wayne and William Holden. "They were as charming in person as they were on the screen," said the movie addict, who had to control her excitement. John Ford directed the movie, *The Horse Soldiers*, which was set during the Civil War. Althea had the part of a maid to a Southern belle, portrayed by Connie Towers, who feeds and flirts with the Yankees, but is caught spying on them and overhearing their plans to sabotage a key Confederate supply depot in Vicksburg, Mississippi. "While I went along with wearing the authentic costume of that period, right up to the handkerchief on my head, I drew the line at some of the dialogue they put into my mouth," Althea said. "The script called for a grossly heavy Negro dialect replete with 'yassuhs' and 'yassums,' and I found these offensive and unnecessary. Furthermore, they were unnatural to me. I felt I could deliver the dialogue in my own style without betraying the intention of the writers or stepping out of character.

"Though my protest was quiet, I was resolutely determined not to utter lines that reflected so negatively and distortedly the character of a colored woman," Althea stressed. "I felt that my own dignity and the dignity of the American Negro were on the line, and though I realized I was jeopardizing that delicious salary for the sake of a principle, I was prepared to act to that length if necessary to illustrate my sincerity. When the powers that be recognized that I meant what I said, they conceded the point and deleted the obnoxious lines."

With visions of an Oscar dancing in her head, Althea was open to playing the prima donna to make her point and giving folks some real drama. "Though I would have liked to storm off the set and retreat to a mountain hideaway to sulk until the producers begged me to return, I did nothing so histrionic." She was really getting into this acting thing, dropping by the studio on her off days to absorb the atmosphere and watch the goings-on. "It was deeply satisfying even to

Playing a maid to a Southern belle in the movie The Horse Soldiers, *Althea refused to speak in the grossly heavy Negro dialect in the script.*

trip over a cable or bump my head on a boom," she admitted. "On days when they were shooting a scene with me in it, I was required to show up on the lot at seven in the morning, a perfectly obscene hour to be doing anything but hitting the pillow as far as I'm concerned. But I loved Hollywood so much I would bounce in at seven, groggy but ready to involve myself in whatever there was to do, even if it was but to sit still and keep my mouth shut. All throughout the filming, I was never sure if it was stardust in my eyes or just plain exhaustion." The family atmosphere on the set was reassuring for the novice actor, and she appreciated Ford's patience and pointers. After the film wrapped, the cast celebrated at a cocktail party with Gregory Peck and other stars. "It wasn't easy to keep the cocktail from shaking out of my glass."

A *New York Post* ad for the film's run at the Loew's Metropolitan on Fulton Street in Brooklyn late that summer read: "The Horse Soldiers with Althea Gibson." Of course, John Wayne and William Holden had top billing above the title.

The reviews for the movie and the portrayals were mixed but mostly favorable. "For those who like tennis, there is Althea Gibson, women's national champion, who plays a slave," a critic for *Time* magazine wrote without passing judgment on her performance—a road taken by many reviewers. However, the *Reporter* was a little more blunt: "Shortly after Mr. Wayne gets his show on the road, he decides, apparently, that an all-male cast isn't quite what Ulysses S. Grant and United Artists had in mind when they dispatched him, and he stops off at a plantation house where he picks up a young woman with an erratic Dixie accent (Constance Towers) and her Negro maid. (The tennis champion Althea Gibson makes her screen debut in this role. Miss Gibson should stick to her own racket.)"

Reviews for *The Horse Soldiers* coincided with those for her autobiography, *I Always Wanted to Be Somebody*, a rags-without-the-riches story penned with the sportswriter Ed Fitzgerald. "Althea Gibson's book is more than the conventional how-I-did-it story of a sporting champion," Reginald Brace wrote in the *Yorkshire Post*. "It is an account—written in tough, terse terms—of the uphill struggle for recognition of a Negro girl reared in poverty-stricken Harlem surroundings, with little to recommend to the world but a fine ball sense." One reviewer described it as "a story as candid as it is startling." Another noted that it included "incidents that might have caused bitterness to a less sunny, vital nature" and that "even behind sadness runs the golden glint of a natural, childlike humor." *The Saturday Evening Post* and several other publications ran lengthy excerpts of *I Always Wanted to Be Somebody*, which ends prophetically: "I'm Althea Gibson, the tennis champion. I hope it makes me happy."

"I read her book and read it more than once," said Billie Jean King, who still has a copy of *I Always Wanted to Be Somebody*, now out of print, on her bookshelf. King, who now coaches the Fed Cup team, also has the *Althea Gibson Sings* album. "She had a great voice," said King, who would periodically ask Althea to sing. Raised on jazz and the big band sound, King grew up in Long Beach, California, with an appreciation for standards. In King's book, Althea ranks not terribly far behind Ella Fitzgerald musically but at the top of the heap athletically.

While Althea continued to sing and play her sax, no major offers for movie or music projects came in after *The Horse Soldiers* and *Althea Gibson Sings* in the late fifties. While Althea's future remained in a state of flux, she was optimistic about the possibilities and stayed single so that she could freely explore whatever came her way. "I'm not about to throw away everything for love," she said. "I can do without a man if I have to. I've done it for fifteen years, and I guess I can do it for while longer." In fact, her confidence—some say ego—had been strengthened so by her triumphs that she was more relaxed in interviews and quick on the uptake. When someone pressed her about her marriage plans, she quipped "Are you available?"

"Tennis built up my ego, which is part of every athlete," Althea explained. "Tennis helped me. No one had more problems than I did. I thought everybody was against me."

She maintained her involvement in athletics by turning pro, working as a sports commentator, appearing in print and television advertisements, endorsing various products, and becoming more involved in social issues and community activities. Three of her favorite topics for lectures and interviews were education, sports, and fitness. For example, she discussed the issue of high school dropouts on *Speak for Yourself*, a Sunday talk show on WAST-TV, channel 13 in Albany, New York.

One of her print ads was for the Equitable Life Assurance Society of the United States, for which she was paid $200. Prepared by the Foote, Cone & Belding advertising agency, the ad highlighted a recurring fitness theme that would mark Althea's work throughout her life. It featured a black-and-white drawing by Robert Riger of Althea in position for a low backhand with a separate image of a white girl with a high backhand next to a headline that asks "Will She Be as Great a Player as Althea Gibson?" The text reads: "It's a long road from paddle tennis on the streets of New York to the championship at Wimbledon. But Althea Gibson went all the way. . . . Not every youngster can be a champion. In fact, very few even participate in organized sporting events, much less become stars. But every young person—if only a spectator—can be as physically fit as our star athlete."

Chapter 6

Turning Pro

I may be the queen of tennis right now, but I reign over an empty bank account.

AFTER BRINGING THE WORLD to its feet with her sweep of Wimbledon and Forest Hills two years in a row, Althea had left everyone in shock by giving it all up. "It was a terribly difficult decision," she admitted much later, but she had been tired of depending on others for everything—even stamps— and she wanted desperately to support herself. Three major goals were to obtain a place of her own, buy a new place for her family, and start the Althea Gibson Academy to give to young people what she had been given. "I'd like to see my own family more comfortable," she explained. "They never had much. I want them to enjoy the full fruits of whatever success I earn. Their happiness is uppermost in my mind.

"Being a champ is all well and good, but you can't eat a crown," she added. "Nor can you send the Internal Revenue Service a throne clipped to their tax forms. The landlord and grocer and tax collector are funny that way: they like cold cash. I may be the queen of tennis right now, but I reign over an empty bank account, and I'm not going to fill it by playing amateur tennis, even if I remain champ from now until Judgment Day."

Althea was taking a huge risk. She had no firm offers; she didn't even have any firm plans. She was winging it. "I relied heavily on the fame I had achieved and on my faith in myself and in Providence to provide for the future," said Althea, who had been born into a Baptist family but became an Episcopalian like the Eatons and went through confirmation while living in North Carolina. "I have no deep regrets that I didn't look more carefully before I leaped, but if I had to do it again, I might ask Providence to 'put it in writing.'" Althea figured that at the very least, she'd have a year to bask in her glory as well as dabble in this and that. As it turned out, it gave her time to sing, to act, to write her book, and to weigh her options as an athlete. She loved sports too much to give it up for good, but she was clearly leaning more toward being a pro athlete instead of remaining as an amateur. She saw four ways to support herself as a pro:

1. Playing for cash prizes in professional tournaments
2. Joining a country club or tennis club as a teaching pro
3. Touring with other pros
4. Endorsing products for a corporation

Althea ruled out becoming a full-time teaching pro since she knew that she was too much of a perfectionist to give less than her best to students. As a result, her own game would suffer and she'd become too restless. "Furthermore, it was somewhat unrealistic for me to consider becoming a pro at a club because there was the larger question of whether any clubs would consider *me*. Even if I'd had an unquenchable yearning to be a teaching pro, the clubs weren't exactly tripping over themselves to offer me jobs. It was here that the barrier of race slammed in front of my face. To hail my talents in public doesn't cost anything, but to hire a Negro—and a Negro woman at that—to teach white club members called for a bigger expenditure of courage than most club owners were willing to make."

Endorsements were few and far between. Other than promoting Tip-Top bread for the Ward Baking Company or appearing with Karol Fageros in print ads for "The Bat," a wooden tennis racket from Harry C. Lee & Co., nothing of any consequence came her way or to other black tennis players for much of the rest of the twentieth century. (That would, of course, change for Venus and Serena Williams.) Pro tournaments were also not yet plentiful or lucrative. It would be another decade before the debut of open tennis in 1968, which allowed amateurs and professionals to play in the same tournaments, potentially winning tens of thousands of dollars in prize money or even millions. What captured Althea's attention was the prospect of touring with other pros and reports that players like Lew Hoad were raking in $125,000 under the promoter Jack Kramer. If Kramer could run successful tours with men, why couldn't there be a tour with women? To explore this and other options, Althea, Llewellyn, and her attorney formed Althea Gibson Enterprises.

In the interim Althea accepted her second consecutive Female Athlete of the Year award from the Associated Press based on her 1958 world and national titles. She also came out of "retirement" to go on a goodwill tour of Latin America and the Caribbean, visiting Chile, Colombia, Guatemala, Haiti, Peru, and Venezuela in early 1959. Three thousand spectators cheered her victory against the Chilean champion Carmen Ibarra at a stadium in Santiago, while she was a guest of Katherine Dunham in Haiti, where the celebrated choreographer maintained a second home. Althea lost only once during the tour and played primarily against men. When she returned she played in an exhibition that Ham Richardson set up in Washington. They beat Vic Seixas and Shirley Fry in mixed doubles, and she defeated Fry in singles, 6-2, 6-3.

While Althea didn't defend her titles at Wimbledon or Forest Hills, she went to England as a sports correspondent for the *London Evening Standard*. The press and the public missed the excitement Althea brought to competitive play. Izzy Rowe, a columnist for the *Pittsburgh Courier*, suggested that the public finance Althea's participation in amateur tournaments. "Her finesse on the tennis courts has brought great glory to America and the race," Rowe said. "We should sponsor Althea Gibson and keep her in a fashion befitting a girl who walked with kings and queens carrying the proud banner of the common man." Without Althea, women's tennis had become a "yawn" and "ho-hum," wrote Gene Roswell in his "Working Press" column. "It's been dreadfully dull in the USLTA women's championships at Forest Hills this year without a standout player or even, at least, a standout personality," he added. "Althea wasn't the sweetest or most cooperative soul when she first hammered her way into big-time amateur tennis.

"But whatever her social failings," Roswell continued, "the gal did exude drama, excitement, controversy—and how she could powder the ball. If you didn't like her as a person, you had to appreciate her as good, live copy."

Althea provided good and bad copy during the second half of 1959, heating up the summer over a racial incident involving the West Side Tennis Club at Forest Hills and then in September at the Pan American Games in Chicago. The tennis club refused membership to Ralph J. Bunche, a Nobel Peace prizewinner and an undersecretary for Special Political Affairs at the United Nations, along with his fifteen-year-old son. Wilfred Burgland, the club's president, claimed that as many as three hundred members would quit if Jews and blacks

The glamorous Althea.

were granted membership. While a number of politicians and
civic leaders criticized the club—some calling for boycotts,
revocation of any city funds or privileges, and the relocation
of the Davis Cup and national competitions—Althea said she
was still willing to play tennis at Forest Hills. Being able to
compete there or attend matches was enough, Althea felt,
and she had no desire to join the club.

129

"I'm so mad at Althea Gibson I could break one of her best tennis rackets over her head," wrote the *New York Amsterdam News* columnist James Hicks. With all the support Althea had received from blacks, Hicks and others felt that the least she could do was to support another member of her race. "Althea is not proud enough of Ralph Bunche to spit in the face of some bigots who have spat in Bunche's face by barring him from their tennis club—and who would spit in Althea's own mother's face simply because she is a Negro!"

Even members of the West Side Tennis Club publicly supported Bunche, such as Mrs. Leroy Wagstaff who said she was "shocked, disturbed and embarrassed" and called for a poll of the membership to verify Burgland's "bunk" claims. "I think more would be inclined to resign over this attitude than if Dr. Bunche were permitted to become a member," Wagstaff claimed. "I feel like resigning now." The Town Tennis Club on the toney east side of Manhattan, not far from the United Nations, extended an honorary membership to Bunche and his family.

But not everyone was critical of Althea's stance. The *New York Daily News* contended that Althea's comment made her "look a lot better than certain breast-beating politicos who have injected themselves in this hassle for the obvious purpose of making political hay." Bertram Baker of the ATA sent Althea a letter commending her position: "Your forthright statement to the press was a demonstration of courage, clear thinking and an indication of your sense of fairness. . . . You have not only earned your title of World's Tennis Champion but also as a champion of 'Fair Play' in the field of Human Relations."

At the Pan Am Games, Althea's comments and her performance stirred more controversy but to a lesser extent than the Bunche brouhaha. Despite Althea's uneven tennis game as a retiree, she beat Yolanda Ramirez of Mexico, 6-4 and 7-5, in a face-saving singles victory for the United States. But she and Karol Fageros lost in doubles against Ramirez and Rosa Reyes. In addition, she and her mixed-doubles partner, Grant Golden, were beaten by Reyes and Francisco Contreras. During postgame interviews, Althea's comments about potentially playing as a pro reportedly prompted calls from some Pan Am and AAU officials for an investigation with the possibility of sanctions if her remarks warranted them.

The issue was soon moot. Althea announced the following month that she would begin a world tour as a professional. She signed a contract with Abe Saperstein, the promoter of the Harlem Globetrotters, that would pay her nearly $100,000. Her partner on the tour, Karol Fageros, would receive $30,000, making them the highest paid women in tennis. Fageros, the No. 5-ranked U.S. player, had also been part of the State Department tour in Asia a few years earlier. The two women would open for the Globetrotters or play at halftime. Saperstein thought they would be a great addition to the tour with the popular hoopsters and their crowd-pleasing antics. While Fageros had talent, she would also be a draw because of her beauty and flashy outfits. Dubbed the "Golden Goddess," Fageros had blonde hair that prompted Helene Curtis to name her one of the ten best coiffured women in America and she wore gold lamé panties under her tennis outfits. A big deal was made of her 36-25-36 figure and her Hollywood aspirations. The panties were said to have been made with twenty-four-karat gold. Fageros ordered forty-four more at $25 a pair for the tour from a Chicago dressmaker.

On New Year's Eve the tennis players opened for the Globetrotters game against the Baltimore Rockets at Madison Square Garden. The lineup also included a pro basketball game between the New York Knicks and the Minneapolis

Lakers, a "ballet on bicycle," and a brother-and-sister balancing act. In each city, from Boston to Little America, Wyoming, the tennis duo used portable nets, white tape for the baselines, local ball boys, and prominent businessmen or politicians as game officials. Sometimes they were surprised by the condition of the gym or the shadows cast by the balls. "If you lobbed a ball high enough, you could lose it in the lights," Althea said. "On a few occasions, the ball never came down, and the audience roared with laughter as I stood there, racket poised for a murderous slam, while the ball dribbled to rest on a rafter."

The spacious skies, amber waves of grain, and majesty of purple mountains prompted Althea to hum patriotic tunes during seemingly endless road trips. The world she had seen. But she had no idea of how much beauty stretched across America. The downside to seeing all of this beauty was in getting there. "Traveling is more tiring than playing tennis," she said. "I knew it'd be rough, but I didn't know how rough." The tight schedule left little time for movies, parties, or other diversions. Before they knew it, it was time to load up the U-Haul and station wagon and head with their tiny entourage to the next stop.

At some of the stops Althea would warm up with Meadowlark Lemon and other Globetrotters. She amazed them with her layups and dunks but kept them in the dark initially about her basketball experience. "I found them wonderful gentlemen, courteous, sympathetic, and fun-loving," Althea said. "The fact that they were Negroes made my tour a little easier to bear, for it was comforting to have people with me with whom I could completely drop my guard from time to time. It's sad to say so, but no matter how liberal, how well accepted into the white community, no matter how popular or famous, no matter how unprejudiced a Negro may be, most of us have to wear some sort of mask outside our own group, and it's a relief to be able to put that mask down from time to time when we're back with our own kind." She was also comfortable with Fageros after traveling so much of the world with her. "We played as if our lives and honor depended on winning," Althea said. "When she beat me, she beat me magnificently. Whoever won, though, the crowds loved our matches."

"I'm getting a real kick out of it," Fageros said of the tour. "I'm making some money, and we're bringing tennis to people who would never otherwise see it." Althea preferred playing before the Globetrotters' games rather than during halftime when the entertainment was scheduled. "That sort of thing rubbed against the grain because it seemed to classify us as an 'act,' a vaudeville bit rather than a serious display of athletic prowess," she said. "But I didn't let that kind of resentment eat at me. Life is too short." Parksy, as she called Gordon Parks, didn't like the tour, referred to by some as a "pro circus." He felt it was demeaning and beneath Althea. Robert Ryland, ATA men's champion in 1955 and 1956, also wasn't crazy about the tour and felt that Althea turned pro too soon. He felt that she might have gone farther if she had remained an amateur longer, since she was just reaching her peak.

Nevertheless, Althea felt on top when the one hundred-game tour ended in April 1960. She capped off the experience by entering the Pepsi-Cola World Pro Tennis Championships at the Cleveland Arena the next month. Winning the singles and doubles titles in Cleveland gave her the bragging rights to truly be the queen of tennis as both an amateur and a pro. She was also able to realize her dream of moving her family from their Harlem apartment by using some of her tour earnings to put a down payment on a ten-room, single-family house in Queens. "I got myself a beautiful apartment and knew, for the very first time, the satisfaction of having a home of my own. After years on the road, accepting the hospitality of others, I was at last in a position to have a place to come back to, a place where I could return the kindnesses to friends visiting New York." She moved into a two-and-a-half-room apartment at Central Park Terrace, a year-old building at 461 Central Park West with air-conditioning and inside garages. She ordered nearly $1,400 in home furnishings from Interiors by Coronet on St. Nicholas Avenue. Her order included a triple dresser with a shadow mirror, a sectional sofa, an ivory and gold television with remote control, a brass TV cart, and drapery.

Yes, Althea was on top of the world—so much so that she turned down Saperstein's contract extension for an international tour. She and her partners in Althea Gibson Enterprises became "giddy with greed," figuring that if they eliminated the middleman, Saperstein, they could keep all of the profits. All they had to do was line up two basketball teams and book the venues. There was no reason they shouldn't be able to make a go of it with Athea as a headliner. She was one of the "most-publicized tennis players of all time," as Bob Addie of the *Washington Post* put it. *The Sunday Bulletin* in Philadelphia went even further, ranking Althea as one of the most newsworthy women of the fifties, period, right up there with Queen Elizabeth, Golda Meir, Eleanor Roosevelt, and Eva Perón.

What they failed to factor in was the financial risk involved and the strength of the Globetrotter name. Under Saperstein, they got paid whether the tour was a success or a flop. Their tour was a flop. Neither Althea's formidable talent nor Karol's gold lamé panties were enough to fill seats on the tour. After just three months on the road, they had to pack it in. "I was, in effect, ruined," Althea said. The $25,000 in red ink drowned her hopes for a professional tennis career, especially since she had made only $500 playing in the pro tournament in Cleveland. "In the past, title winners had been avalanched with offers to appear in some public exhibition or go on some tour or teach at some club," Althea said. "But the only avalanche that hit me was one of silence, and that much silence can suffocate you.

"The taste of disappointment was distinctly bitter to me," she said. "When I looked around me, I saw that white tennis players, some of whom I had thrashed on the court, were picking up offers and invitations. Suddenly it dawned on me that my triumphs had not destroyed the racial barrier once and for all, as I had—perhaps naively—hoped. Or if I did destroy them, they had been erected behind me again." Althea said that she could have handled the slights better if she had been an unknown. "But once a Negro has established himself and the snubs still come, does he really have any alternative but to believe he is being discriminated against by virtue—or should I say, by vice—of his skin? . . . When it's apparent that the hostility is directed at my color, I boil over with indignation."

The disappointment was so bitter that Althea said she began to lose interest in tennis after playing in the pro tournament in Cleveland. "The world has begun to fill me with a sense of futility, almost disgust," she said. "Of what value is a room full of trophies and a scrapbook full of praise when you have on your tongue the bitter taste of man's inhumanity toward you?"

Dubbed by *Ebony* "the most significant black athlete in America" and considered the first to achieve true global fame, she was at the top of her tennis game with virtually no place to go. And she was dead broke.

"The fact that I did have a run of bad luck helped me to see clearly who among my past acquaintances was most loyal to me," Althea said, and the most loyal of them all was Will Darben. The subject of marriage resurfaced in the early sixties as the two grew closer, but Althea turned Will down yet again just as she had other suitors over the years. In the back of her mind, she always wondered whether they were pursuing "Althea Gibson the champion or Althea Gibson the woman," she explained. "From the 'you just love me because I'm a star' argument, I moved to the opposite pole with the 'you just feel sorry for me; I've got to prove I'm worthy' argument."

What contributed to saving Althea from feeling worthless was her yearlong contract with the Ward Baking Company to travel around the country using her radiant smile and gift of gab to push Tip-Top Bread—"the freshest bread in town."

It was then that she officially decided to join the Ladies Professional Golf Association.

"I wanted to stay in sports a little longer," she said. "I felt that if I was an athlete, I could do something else. Golf seemed the thing I could go into and make a contribution."

Chapter 7

Swing Time

Anything I do, I want to be the best at it.

"THAT GIRL HITS just like a man," Jerry Volpe, the owner and pro at the former Englewood Country Club in northern New Jersey, said of Althea's golf game. With a tailwind, she could drive a ball 325 yards down a course's emerald carpet of grass. "My style of play," Althea explains, "was aggressive, dynamic, and mean."

When she played with men, Althea played by men's rules. Some golfers said they wouldn't have let her hit off the women's tees, because they were closer to the hole and she would have had too much of an advantage over them. This was a startling admission as the fifties gave way to the sixties. Men generally preferred to see women delicately sipping tea—not matching their long drives off a golf tee in those days. However, a handful of white and black men alike encouraged Althea's play, including the boxer Joe Louis, an avid golfer who had also supported her tennis career by financing her first Wimbledon trip and rolling out the red carpet whenever she was in Detroit.

These men weren't simply open-minded enough to skip the "little lady" treatment; they were no fools. They knew better than to give Althea a handicap. Many a man and woman have gone down in flames unable to best her at billiards, bowling, basketball, tennis, paddleball, baseball, football, or boxing. "I could never beat her," says Dr. William Hayling, Althea's gynecologist in New Jersey, and later a good friend who lost to her in everything from pool to tennis. And the thing was, he said, chuckling, "She only played as hard as she had to, to win."

"No sport seems to be beyond her capability," noted the *New York Post* columnist Gene Roswell. "Althea has the muscle and coordination for basketball and baseball, the speed and finesse for tennis, the touch and delicacy of control for pool and Ping-Pong, and the cold aplomb for golf." So it didn't come as a shock when rumors about Althea giving up tennis for golf turned out to be true. Plus, as early as September 1958—just weeks after her second win at Forest Hills— Althea had joked about a possible new athletic career before leaving Spalding's in New York City with a new golf bag, balls, clubs, shoes, and umbrella. "Gentlemen," she boasted, "you now are looking at the next women's golf champ."

Althea had learned to play golf in Tallahassee at Florida A&M, a powerhouse in virtually every sport among historically black colleges and universities. The first time she played a round, she scored 99 and won a match during a trip to Tuskegee Institute in Alabama, the first black college with its own golf course. "I hit a few golf balls with Althea. She beat me at my game, and I was the golf coach," recalls Hansel Tookes, who also coached football at Florida A&M and later became A&M's athletic director. "She just figured she could whip everybody in golf, tennis, and pool," he adds with a laugh. "She was just a natural athlete."

At eighty-one, Tookes is the sole survivor among athletic officials who ruled the invincible Rattlers during the time Althea played on the women's tennis and basketball teams and the men's golf team. "I'm the last of those guys who knew Althea," he says. "All of them are dead now." Tookes and the late Dr. Oscar A. Moore, the baseball coach and chair of the Physical Education Department, also hired Althea to baby-sit their children. "We wanted some of that positivity to rub off on our kids." Who knows if her no-nonsense but encouraging ways had any effect, but her charges certainly have success stories of their own. Hansel E. Tookes II became the president and chief operating officer of the Raytheon Aircraft Company in Lexington, Massachusetts, and Judi Moore Latta, Ph.D., also the goddaughter of the legendary FAMU athletic director Jake Gaither, served as the chair of the acclaimed Department of Radio, Television and Film at Howard University and the acting general manager of WHUT-TV, both in Washington, D.C.

At FAMU, Althea had been a star among stars. "We were kind of kingpins in athletics," Tookes says proudly. "We had the pick of the litter. We got the best of the best." And Althea still stands out as one of the best athletes he encountered during his forty-four years at FAMU, which honored the 1953 alumna as the athlete of the century at the turn of the millennium. "She's one of a kind," says Tookes, who still lives in Tallahassee. "She had the desire, but she had the physical makeup, too. She wasn't fat and funky. She wasn't carrying a lot of baggage." Tookes notes that Althea had the ideal height, weight, and hand-eye coordination beneficial for an athlete in a range of sports. "She's tall, lean, and lanky. That's an asset in tennis as well as golf."

Golf was a sideline for the physical education and health major in those days; Althea's focus then, of course, was on tennis. That focus began to shift, however, after she reached her peak on the courts. With limited opportunities in pro tennis and massive debt from the failed tour, she had no other source of income, no investments, and no savings. "What did I win? I won peanuts," Althea said of the prizes. "In my day, it was for peanuts, for cups, for silverware and not the bread." Women's professional golf wasn't much better financially than tennis in the early sixties, but it was better. While the airlines and other major sponsors opened their coffers primarily to the men, Sealy Posturepedic and Eve Cigarettes were two companies that supported women, sponsoring $50,000 and $53,000 classics, respectively. Winning first place could earn a woman golfer as much as $10,000. True to the times, it was a far cry from the $100,000 to $200,000 of men's tournaments that shelled out up to $60,000 for first place. But women were used to pay inequity then. Many were already "in their place" as housewives and stay-at-home moms. Those who had paying jobs brought home only a small piece of the bacon while men had the full slice—hence the push for an Equal Rights Amendment that would gather steam in the next decade.

As she set out to take on pro golf, qualifying in just three years and becoming the first African American member of the Ladies Professional Golf Association, Althea drew comparisons to Babe Didrikson, who started playing golf professionally at age thirty-six, winning forty-one tournaments. The daughter of Norwegian immigrants, Babe Didrikson was a founding LPGA member and Olympian who excelled at track, baseball, basketball, and golf. "Althea is taller, stronger, and possibly just as gifted as the immortal Babe in coordination, reflexes, speed, and confidence," Roswell wrote at the time.

"It's no secret," Althea pointed out when she took up professional golf. "The Babe always has been an inspiration to me. She was a great all-around athlete who took up golf late.

. . . I have gone as far as I can in tennis. Now I intend to do the same thing in golf."

"I want to be the only woman to be champion in tennis and golf," Althea said on another occasion. "Maybe because I'm a champion. I think like a champion."

Althea also liked a good challenge, and golf provided plenty. "That ball just sits up there daring you to hit it," she said, "and you know, it's no good if you don't hit it right." But her biggest challenge, many felt, was her late start with golf since many of her counterparts turned pro in their early to midtwenties—not at age thirty-three. Althea just shrugged it off, as she did most things. "You're never too old," she countered. "They said I came along too late in tennis, didn't they?" To her way of thinking, the main thing she had to overcome was keeping her tennis techniques out of her golf game. "Anything I do, I want to be the best at it."

Because of her size and power, Althea used longer and heavier clubs than many women at the time. For example, she had 43½-inch woods with an R shaft (medium flexibility) and a 12- to 13½-ounce weight. When swinging, Althea relied upon the same juice she used in tennis to whack the ball across the net at high speeds to the baseline, while her opponent was left bewildered and breathless near the net. But that was a little too much juice for the short game in golf, which requires a more deliberate finesse. Some said she also turned her hand over too quickly at impact when hitting the golf ball.

To prepare for the LPGA, Althea said she spent lots of time at Volpe's club in Englewood "driving for three hours in the morning, playing eighteen holes to thirty-six holes, and then hitting drives again until dark." She listened attentively to the pointers that other golfers shared, one noting that she dropped the club too far behind her on the backswing. "So I shortened up and that ball is really traveling," she said at the time. Althea also picked up tips from Ann Gregory, fifteen years her senior and considered the best black woman golfer. Althea's growth fueled her desire for the game, and she welcomed the exercise. "Just walking after that ball, I come in after eighteen holes much more tired than after tennis. I'm exhausted."

"And she can practice endlessly—for hours and hours," Volpe exclaimed. "I've never seen anyone like her. She gets me tired just watching. This girl will take a wedge and work the same shot over and over again until you think she isn't human. With her will and desire alone, she's got to be great. Althea has everything to be tops. Right now, she can hit as long as any woman ever did."

The Ward Baking Company also supported Althea's golf goals by renewing her $25,000 annual contract as a spokeswoman through its community relations department. The company also agreed to a more flexible schedule to give her time for golf lessons and eventually tournaments. While out on the road making radio and TV appearances or speaking at schools and community events, she squeezed in time on the course.

"Once I had my game together," Althea said, "I entered local amateur contests." In May 1961 she participated in two black competitions, the Harlem Y Tournament at the Lakewood Golf Course in New Jersey and then the Green Ladies Tournament in Philadelphia. She finished twenty strokes ahead in the ninth annual North-South Negro Golf Tournament in Miami on February 23, 1962. She carded 86 with a 254 total. Behind her were two New York women, Myrtle Patterson, who registered a 91 for 274, and Elizabeth Wright, who shot a 94 for 276.

In June, Althea occasionally outdrove Betsy Rawls, a four-time U.S. women's open champion, at a procelebrity preliminary tournament to the next day's J. E. McAuliffe Memorial. "Althea has great potential," Rawls said. Althea almost had three birdies at two par-three holes on the Plainfield Country Club in New Jersey but missed the putts.

"As far as my progress is concerned, I am satisfied," Althea told Lincoln A. Werden, a sportswriter for the *New York Times*. "Actually, I'm never fully satisfied until I reach the next stage. . . . I plan to work hard on my game and develop it."

To qualify for the LPGA, Althea needed to finish in the top 80 percent in three out of four consecutive tournaments. Her first tournament after applying for her card was at the Kenwood Country Club in Cincinnati in early 1963. She was still averaging 84.5 strokes, while other golfers were around 74. At one point, she dropped seven strokes to 77 and hit the top 80 percent in two tournaments in a row. Her game, she said, was getting its "groove." With just one more win, Althea could get her playing card. But there was drama at the next stop. She couldn't use the clubhouse to shower, change clothes, or even eat. Rather than being unnerved or making a scene over what she called "silliness," she took her "I'll-show-them" attitude out on the links. And did she ever. Althea came in ahead of almost half of the other golfers and earned the coveted card.

During her first year on the LPGA tour, she competed in six events. The next year, she played in seventeen tournaments, winning $561.50. (By comparison, the LPGA leader Mickey Wright took home $29,800.) Althea was a formidable presence on the golf course. She not only stood out because of her skin color and height, she was also a bona fide star with an international following. She dressed the part, too, in her coordinated outfits usually with long shorts and often topped with a slouch hat, a cap, or a stylish tam with a pompom. But with the heat in some places, it wasn't unusual to see her with a white towel draping her shoulders.

With her caddy on the professional golf tour.

Standing out was a mixed blessing in October 1964 at the Arizona Biltmore Country Club in Phoenix. Althea had her best score ever—69 in the first round, which put her in the lead of the Thunderbird Open. But the high was short-lived. She miscalculated her score the following day and was disqualified. Instead, Ruth Jessen ended up winning the $1,350 first prize at the tournament with a score of 289, and Wright came in second.

For the first six years, Althea competed in every LPGA tournament, which could be scheduled at far-flung regions of the country from one week to the next. She traveled anywhere and everywhere she could under all sorts of conditions. "You have to be a trouper," Althea points out. "It's a grueling pace when you're living out of a suitcase."

She had to kick out roughly $250 a week for meals, lodging, and transportation—more if she flew by plane. So she usually drove in car caravans with other golfers on the tour to save money, sometimes in the Oldsmobiles donated to the LPGA. The low tournament prizes in women's golf and the sponsorship from Dunlop sporting goods in 1964 barely offset her expenses, and she lost the Tip-Top contract once her golfing schedule went into overdrive. Fortunately, she had the backup of Will Darben, who was now a manager at a doughnut plant in Newark.

"Although I didn't realize it fully for a long time, I was coming to depend on him," Althea admitted. "He was like a part of me but not so much a limb you consciously use; he was more like a vital organ whose existence keeps you alive but which you usually take for granted." Althea also admired Will's character and devotion to his family, particularly when his sister had to quit her job to care for their mother. "He worked himself almost ill to bring in extra money to support the household and pay for his mother's medical expenses," she said. "I've seen men run away from their responsibilities under similar conditions." Will's persistence and patience paid off, as Althea's dependence and admiration transformed into something much stronger.

"My love for Will grew beyond manageable proportions," Althea explained. "We decided to stop fighting the inevitable." During a long-distance phone call in October of 1965, Will agreed to meet Althea in Las Vegas where they would marry in a private ceremony and enjoy a short honeymoon. Then they were off to Phoenix for Althea's golf tournament. "Although Will had watched me play in many matches," Althea said, "I felt almost childishly nervous to know that my *husband* was in the gallery that day."

The newlyweds were inseparable—touchy-feely with public displays of affection whether they were touring Hoover Dam or gazing into each other's eyes as they held hands over a checkerboard tablecloth at a club in Harlem. Friends literally called Will her "knight in shining armor." He was her protector, once defending her honor by jumping in the face of a man who was cursing in his wife's presence at a bar. "Althea was right there behind me," he later joked. "I knew she had my back."

Althea said that they made music together—literally—he playing the piano she bought him as a wedding present and she the saxophone if she wasn't singing during their duets. They cooked together in the kitchen, making waffles with sausage and Bloody Marys for themselves and a menu of other dishes for their guests. He was the one who could burn in the kitchen; she was a recipe cook. They played bid whist, poker, and other card games into the wee hours of the night. They also played doubles, mostly with Will standing at the ready with his tennis racket as Althea ran around the court hitting the balls.

In addition to Will's support, friends would send her checks while she was on the road, and a jewelry company executive once gave her $250 a week, sponsoring her for about three months.

Althea's progress made the investments seem worthwhile. In 1966, for example, she broke the course record at the Pleasant Valley Country Club in Sutton, Massachusetts, with a 68 during the Lady Carling Open. She competed in twenty-five events the next year, averaging 75.82 and taking in $5,567.50—her highest annual earnings in golf. In April she set a women's course record at Lake Venice with a score of 68. Her stroke total of 217 was within 4 strokes of the top golfer Kathy Whitworth's winning score. Althea also tied for third place in the Pacific Golf Classic, held that September at the Shadow Hills Country Club in Eugene, Oregon.

The sportswriter Jim Obert described Althea as "a rare type of female athlete who happens along only once in a while. She virtually explodes with energy. Her desire to excel is insatiable."

They made music together, literally and in all other ways. Will and Althea with her trophies in their East Orange, New Jersey, apartment.

To help Althea continue to progress, Dr. Hayling talked Dr. William Cassio into joining him in sponsoring Althea's tour in 1967 and 1968. He asked his friend, the former New York mayor David N. Dinkins, whose children he had delivered, to draw up a contract whereby each physician would put up $500 a year. "It was a mutual thing where Cassio and I got together to help Althea. It was difficult getting sponsorship in those days," explained Dr. Hayling, who now lives in Murietta, California, near San Diego. "We were good friends and saw her through some tough days on the golf course." Dr. Hayling added that Althea had also approached Maggie Hathaway, the president of the Beverly Hills NAACP and an avid golfer, about sponsoring her golf tour, but the chapter was having money woes of its own and couldn't support her financially. Open to all options, Althea did whatever it took to make ends meet. She secured bank loans against future winnings and later took on a day job as a recreation supervisor for the Essex County Parks Commission in New Jersey, delighting giggly children in Montclair and other areas who stood in line to try to beat her in Ping-Pong, only to fall one by one like dominoes.

Work, marriage, and the lack of sponsorship gradually limited the number of tournaments Althea entered. She didn't feel like playing much when her father died in May 1967. "It came as a terrible shock to me," recalled Althea, who said that her father's unfulfilled dream had been to live out his days back home on a farm in Silver, South Carolina. "It left me deeply, infinitely sad. I can only console myself with the realization that he lived long enough to see me make something out of myself and to receive a few of the humble benefits of my success."

Althea's tournament participation dwindled down to seven events in 1970. That year she won $3,653.75 and had her best performance on the tour. During the $20,000 Len Immke Buick Open at the Raymond Memorial Golf Course from June 25 to 28 in Columbus, Ohio, she was in a three-way playoff for first place. "It was pretty exciting," recalls PGA and LPGA member Renee Powell, who gathered with other players to watch and cheer Althea on. As it turned out, Sandra Haynie and Althea ended up tying for second place. While Mary Mills took home the first prize of $3,000, Althea earned $2,032—more than she sometimes won in an entire year of play and nearly four times her annual golf prizes when she started on the tour. She came close to exceeding that amount by being a contender for the $2,250 first prize at the Lady Carling Open in Massachusetts. Off to a strong start after breaking the course record the previous day, she blew her lead by being too slow and drawing a two-stroke penalty.

"She was very methodical and tried to get all her ducks in a row before she made a move to take a swing," explained Marlene Hagge-Vossler, a co-founder of the LPGA and a member of the tournament committee charged with enforcing "absolutes," rules that could not be appealed. "She was really upset. She said, 'Marlene, you're my friend!' I said, 'Althea, I am your friend, but you were the slow player in the group.'" Always a good sport, Hagge-Vossler believed, Althea cooled down after about an hour, apologized, and sucked up the loss to Whitworth, who eventually became the first LPGA member to amass $1 million in career earnings.

Despite having thrown her share of tennis rackets and slammed balls into the stands, Althea managed to avoid the absolute on throwing golf clubs. The fines started at $25, which doubled and tripled with each offense, causing some players to make comical dives to catch an errant club after realizing the error of their ways. Althea also avoided the $50 fines for being late. Unlike some of her tennis days, Althea remained on good behavior. At golf tournaments, she would swing from being intensely focused to playfully animated, as she was when, with a few twists and kicks, she did a little dance to coax the ball into the cup on the final green of the Sealy Posturepedic Pro-Amateur Classic. At that tournament, held at the Desert Inn Country Club near the Strip in Las Vegas, May 13 to 16 in 1971, she tied for thirteenth place, walking away with $800 of the $50,000 in prize money.

"She got really good in such a short period of time," Whitworth said. "She'd already paved the way in tennis. For her to make that move again showed a lot of courage. It was just a terrific thing."

"Althea is not a role model for just people of color," stated Powell, who joined the LPGA tour at the age of twenty-one in 1967, four years after Althea. "Althea Gibson is a role model for women, because she came along at a time when women were breaking a lot of barriers." Althea's style of play, for example, helped to dispel stereotypes about women's abilities, says Powell, now the senior golf professional at the Clearview Golf Club in East Canton, Ohio, built by her father,

William, in 1946, and still the only golf course designed and owned by African Americans.

"People always had a stigma that women couldn't do things aggressively," explained Powell, who has a photo of her with Althea hanging in the clubhouse of the historic landmark. "Althea showed that you can be a female and excel. And excel with power and grace."

During the height of Althea's golfing career, she demonstrated both as she shared the links with a number of notables, from the baseball pioneer Jackie Robinson to Lee Elders, the first African American to qualify for the Masters, the golf world's most prestigious event. Althea and Elders also trained under the legendary black golfer Theodore Rhodes, known as "Rags" for his dapper attire on and off the course.

"Althea was a good player," said Elders, who qualified for six Masters, making the cut in three. "She could really hit." Althea hit so well that she beat Roland Brown, a member of the Guardians who was considered unbeatable, Dr. Hayling says. They played in Scotch Plains, New Jersey, at the Shady Rest Golf and Country Club, formerly known as Westfield until it was sold to the Progressive Realty Corporation in 1921, becoming the first black-owned club. "It was a social mecca for blacks," Dr. Hayling says.

Even though her performance on the golf course was no match for her feats in tennis, Althea was still making history, following in the steps of some of the earliest known black golfers, such as John Matthew Shippen Jr. and Dr. George Franklin Grant. Shippen was the first black golfer to play in the U.S. Open, shooting a 78 in the first round for a five-way tie for first place in 1896. He ended up with a combined score of 159 in a tie for fifth place. The native Washingtonian, who won $10 at the Open, is also considered the first U.S.-born professional golfer. He played in four more opens and ended his career working at Shady Rest, where Althea beat Brown. Dr. Grant, who graduated with honors from Harvard's dental school in 1870, invented the first golf tee. His invention, which was issued patent number 638,920 on December 12, 1899, made it possible for golfers to end the annoying practice of reaching into a box or bucket for a handful of damp sand to shape into a mound on which to tee up their balls. However, it is assumed that slaves in the United States were first introduced to golf when Englishmen and Scotsmen founded the South Carolina Golf Club in Charleston in 1786, according to Calvin H. Sinnette, a golf addict and the author of *Forbidden Fairways: African-Americans and the Game of Golf*. The slaves were thought to have served as caddies and "finders" who marked holes since there were no greens and yelled "fore."

It's unknown when the first black women started playing golf, but photos exist of young girls and boys holding make-shift clubs as early as 1905. Women entered the national championship of the United Golf Association (UGA), similar to the ATA, for the first time in 1930, with Marie Thompson of Chicago as the winner followed by Lucy Williams of Indianapolis. Nine years later, two women successfully pressed for membership in the UGA. Ironically, the men weren't exactly crazy about the idea of women members—even though the UGA was organized in 1925 because whites weren't crazy about the idea of blacks as members in their groups: the U.S. Golf Association (USGA), established in 1894, and the Professional Golfers' Association of America (PGA), founded in 1916.

One of Althea's golfing mentors, Ann Gregory, is still hailed as the "Queen of Negro Golf Women" and had so many awards that she and her husband built an addition onto their home in Gary, Indiana, to house them. A seven-time UGA women's champion, Gregory won more than one hundred events and was the first African American woman to participate in a tournament sponsored by the USGA in 1956. This was a result of the Chicago Women's Golf Club becoming a USGA affiliate to help Gregory branch out beyond the black golf world. In fact, Gregory was destined to become the first black LPGA member in Althea's stead. Approached as early as 1950 about turning pro, she declined so that her game wouldn't take her away from her little girl and husband more than it already had. Ethel Funches, Gregory's closest competitor and a five-time UGA women's champion, was also encouraged to join the LPGA, but she didn't want to deal with the drama that came with playing in an overwhelmingly white environment. Althea, on the other hand, had no qualms about being a pioneer or a token, and she was still single when she joined the LPGA, since she had rebuffed Darben's wedding proposals for years, finally saying yes in 1965.

While some debate who was the stronger player among the three—Althea, Gregory, or Funches—Powell likened Althea's athletic career to that of Michael Jordan. "He's a good basketball player and he's a good baseball player, but he wasn't a great baseball player." When Powell thinks of Althea, three words immediately come to mind followed by laughter: "Aggressive! Confident! Determined!

"If Althea had been able to finesse her game and had a better short game—which she had worked at a lot—it would have allowed her to get farther," Powell explains. "It's touch and feel when it comes to the short game. That's where you have to save a lot of your strokes. . . . Most of the people had it over Althea in that department, because they had worked at it longer. Her strength was in the long game. She had terrific mental strengths, too."

Judy Rankin, a former LPGA star and a TV analyst, agrees. "She might have been a real player of consequence had she started when she was young," Rankin said. "She came along during a difficult time in golf, gained the support of a lot of people, and quietly made a difference."

The difference she made endures today, notes Dinkins, a close friend who met Althea in the late forties along with Dr. Hayling at Shady Rest, the black-owned country club in New Jersey, where she was playing Ping-Pong when they first laid eyes on her. "If a black person achieves in any discipline, it assists the rest of us," Dinkins stresses. "Althea is not only a role model for black boys and girls, she's also a role model for others."

On the links, Althea was certainly a role model for Powell and even today for golfers like Tiger Woods. Powell compared Althea's role to that of Robinson, Louis, and the Olympic track star Jesse Owens. "She came with a great name, had done so many things, and was an American hero," Powell said. But even with all that fame, Althea faced far more formidable odds than simply her age.

"Being a minority, being an African American in the field of golf, which at one time was a lily-white sport, certainly you're going to run up against many obstacles and many prejudices," Powell explained. "So no matter what your name is, if you happen to be black and everyone else happens to be white, you're going to run into problems. She had so many battles." Powell and Althea were the only two black golfers on the tour among roughly seventy-five LPGA members.

"If my being out here and playing golf can be of some stimulation to other young ladies of my race to play golf, then I feel I've made a contribution," Althea said. "In everything, there has got to be a beginning."

After Althea applied for her LPGA card in 1963, she singlehandedly integrated courses in St. Petersburg, Florida, with her written request to play at the Lakewood Country Club in the local women's open, later known as the Orange Blossom Classic.

As the golf columnist Bob LeNoir put it, who would have had the nerve to turn down the queen of the sports world, who had also been so warmly received by England's royal family? Althea was granted entry denied the golf pioneer Charlie Sifford just a year earlier. Sifford was relegated to simply watching the St. Petersburg Men's Open in 1962 rather than playing. But that was nothing; he once found human feces in the cup of the first green when attempting to qualify for the Phoenix Open with Joe Louis, Rags, and other black golfers. And that was *after* being banned from the locker room. They waited for the excrement to be removed, and things stood still for almost an hour.

"When Althea came out, there were some reservations with some of the girls about her because they didn't know how she was going to be received by some of our sponsors," said Lenny Wirtz, who served as the LPGA's first commissioner from 1961 to 1969. "Well, it worked out exactly as they had perceived it and I had perceived it."

Like other members of black golf's finest, Althea faced similar slights. "There were a lot of tournaments that wouldn't accept me," she said. Country club officials throughout the Deep South—and some in the North, for that matter—had no qualms about turning her down for tournaments. She was shut out of a wide swath of tournaments, stretching from South Carolina to Texas. "I don't know if they thought I was going to eat the grass," she quips. "All I wanted to do was hit the ball off it." On the occasions when Althea was deemed worthy of stepping foot onto the greens, she often had to change clothes and shoes in a car, because she, too, was banned from coming inside the club. She also continued to have problems staying in some hotels.

Shortly after Hagge-Vossler met Althea, she walked into a motel in Columbus, Ohio, around midnight just as a desk clerk was arguing with Althea over her reservation. "He was giving her a really hard time," Hagge-Vossler recalled. "He was telling her she didn't have a reservation or anything. Althea is very precise, very meticulous, very organized, and she has this confirmation slip and everything.

"Obviously when he made the reservation, he didn't realize she was black. So I said, 'Althea, I'll take care of it. Let me register, and I'll talk to you in a minute.' So she kind of got the message. So I registered and everything and I said, 'Althea, come on and bunk in with me.' And the guy just glared at me. He gave me the most awful look."

Wirtz recalled a similar incident at another motel when he happened to be in the lobby as Althea and Sandra Palmer were attempting to check in. "I'm walking away as I hear this desk clerk tell Althea they don't have a reservation for her, and she told me she made one," Wirtz explained. "So I went over to the guy and I said, 'What's this, you don't know?' He said, 'My God, I don't know what happened! We don't have it, and we're sold out now. There's nothing I can do. There's no room available.' I said, 'Wait a minute! *Just* a minute!'"

After asking Palmer to give up her single and to stay with another golfer, Wirtz turned to the desk clerk: "'Put Miss Gibson in Miss Palmer's room; she's not going to stay there.' And then of course I had this guy, 'cause I was gonna go after him. And he gave her the room." Wirtz, who had long interacted with black people, growing up in Cincinnati and being a referee for collegiate and pro basketball, was dismayed to see Althea subjected to such treatment over and over again. When sponsors didn't want her to attend receptions and dinners, he'd tell that he wouldn't be attending either and he'd take Althea out to eat. When waitresses would take forever to take their orders, he'd complain and take her elsewhere.

"You could see that that type of thing probably went on with black people in a lot of places that white people don't understand," Wirtz said. "It always bothered me when anything came up."

One of the most novel strategies was when organizers began labeling their tournaments "invitational" in order to invite whom they pleased. The LPGA encountered this tactic as it tried to expand the tour by playing on courses at new housing communities. Real-estate developers didn't want to turn off potential white buyers with the likes of an Althea or a Powell, so they just didn't "invite" them. However, Wirtz told the sponsors, "We all play, or we all stay away."

FAMU's Tookes turned somber as he recalled the "For Colored Only" signs and the tribulations of athletes like Althea during the Jim Crow era. "You had to eat behind a curtain or sit in a different place, and you just got off a plane where you were fully integrated," he recalls. "Even in New Jersey—I'll never forget this—you'd try to go to a hamburger joint and they'd say, 'We don't serve you people.' It was terrible, I'm telling you.

"That mentality still exists—although the law won't let them do what they would like to do," he pointed out. "Right here in Perry, Florida, people still have to buy their drinks from the back door."

Remarkably, and much to the chagrin of many race-conscious men and women, Althea publicly shrugged off such incidents. Rather than making a fuss, she held her head high and tried to beat Jim Crow with her golf clubs as she had with her tennis racket. "Althea went through a lot more of that than I did," according to Powell. "She has a great sense of humor. She could laugh about a lot of things."

The reception and support that Althea got from some white people gave her hope that things could change. Just as Alice Marble had chastised her white peers in tennis, calling them "sanctimonious hypocrites" for blocking Althea's entry into key tournaments, Volpe, Wirtz, and her fellow LPGA members showed the bigots of golf the error of their ways. In addition to giving Althea pointers early in her golfing career, Volpe made her an honorary member of his previously all-white country club in Englewood, New Jersey. Golfers like Hagge-Vossler would invite Althea to share their rooms when her hotel reservations would mysteriously disappear. And by challenging the invitational tournaments, Althea says that Wirtz "made a big contribution to this perpetual motion."

Wirtz's stance was "If you take one girl, you take 'em all. That's it—no ifs, ands or buts." However, he and other LPGA leaders acknowledge that it was tough getting to this point initially with such a fledgling organization and one that tended to book sponsors at least a year in advance. "Back in the sixties, people weren't standing in line to put on ladies professional golf tournaments," Wirtz said. The LPGA had been in existence only since 1950, and it was still very much a grassroots organization. "Our headquarters was pretty much out of the back end of the car," said Whitworth, a three-time LPGA president. "The press room was the parking lot." Until the women were able to hire a field staff, she added, they made their own pairings, marked the golf course, set tees, kept score, and governed themselves, often a sticky situation with the "absolutes."

At the height of the civil rights movement, the LPGA was in a catch-22. Althea was a marquee player who gave the LPGA much-needed visibility and drew spectators to the galleries. Many members liked her and wanted to take a stronger stand against bigoted sponsors. But at the same time, they wanted to survive. "If the tour folded," Whitworth asked, "what would we have accomplished? Not a whole lot."

"I hated to cancel a tournament at that stage over one player," Wirtz admitted. "The other girls would, I thought, just resent her if they couldn't play golf a week because of her." So Wirtz asked Althea to be patient and give him time to replace the sponsors. He also implored her to avoid making a scene or being confrontational. She agreed.

"I gave her my word, and I told her it could cost me my job, but I'm gonna get rid of 'em," said Wirtz, who replaced at least three sponsors over their racial stance. "Some of our girls didn't understand it when some of these sponsors weren't on the tour anymore, and they kind of ripped me up. But I never did tell them the reason why. And if they weren't smart enough to figure it out, then that's tough. But Althea knew." "We did get some of those issues resolved," Whitworth added, "but it took a while and she was good about that 'cause she had every right to just shut us down."

The PGA leadership, on the other hand, didn't have a history of acting as forcefully as Wirtz & Company. Dewey Brown, a fair-skinned black golfer, pulled a fast one on the PGA by joining in 1928. But in 1934, when the PGA figured out that Brown was "light" not "white," he was expelled without notice. In 1943 the PGA adopted its infamous "Caucasian clause," which banned black golfers from becoming members. (The LPGA voted early on against such a clause.) Sifford became the first black golfer on the PGA tour in 1960, but getting his playing card didn't mean he could play everywhere. "It didn't mean anything," he told Pete McDaniel, a writer for *Golf Digest* and the author of *Uneven Lies: The Heroic Story of African-Americans in Golf.* "It didn't get me past those big ol' guards with those big ol' .45s." The PGA removed the "Caucasian clause" from its constitution the next year in 1961, but it took some doing. Various factions within the PGA routinely blocked any change, and when California's Attorney General Stanley Mosk said that the PGA wouldn't be able to use the state's public courses if it banned black golfers, the organization replied that it would simply use private courses. After Mosk contacted attorneys general in a number of states, the PGA realized that he wouldn't give up and scrapped the clause. But by that time, golfers like Rags, who played in sixty-nine PGA events, had seen their best days come and go.

The PGA's hand was forced again in the nineties. Officials swiftly implemented a policy to bypass clubs that discriminated on the basis of race, religion, sex, or national origin to distance the PGA from racist comments made in June 1990 by Hall Thompson, the founder of Shoal Creek, a private club in Birmingham, Alabama. "We don't discriminate in any other area except the blacks," Thompson told a reporter in defending his club's vanilla roster. "We have the right to associate or not associate with whomever we choose. The country club is our home, and we pick and choose who we want." With the Shoal Creek fiasco rocking the golf world, the PGA of America championship was relocated from the club and held elsewhere.

Even today, there are clubs that do not welcome African Americans or women with open arms. The lawyer, author, and socialite Lawrence Otis Graham confirmed that when he recently went undercover as a busboy and caddy at country clubs in Connecticut. And Tiger Woods, a favorite of Althea's, who handles race similar to the way in which she did, has also endured his share of slights—his phenomenal fame, talent, and "Cablinasian" roots notwithstanding. In his first television commercial Woods criticized golf courses that shunned players of color. But after receiving so much heat for his comments, the triple Masters champion backed off from speaking out. He also drew heat for not speaking out against Augusta's exclusion of women.

"I knew what it would be like," Althea explained. "I accepted the adversity. I was trying to get my player's card, and back then you could only get it by playing in so many tournaments."

Although some saw her as a sellout when it came to pressing the race issue, others saw her as a class act, especially her

Golfing in the late 1970s.

friends. "She was an outstanding athlete who carried herself with dignity," Dr. Hayling says.

Althea struck a balance in her private life through her somewhat blissful marriage and also found release by singing and socializing with friends. She could be a loner out on the road, but she'd occasionally entertain the other golfers during cookouts at Wirtz's house in Cincinnati, play cards, watch movies, or go out to dinner. Once, the golfers cancelled a tournament round, with the sponsor's approval, because the temperature soared higher than 100 degrees in San Diego. Instead, they cooled off at a beach party.

"She may have had a lot of social pressures coming on the tour, but she handled them gracefully," said Marilynn Smith, a three-time LPGA president and co-founder. "She was friendly to all of us, and we just felt like she was one of us. She molded right in with the group. We didn't see her as an outsider. She's a very special lady."

"I always enjoyed Althea," Whitworth said, "and I still get a smile on my face when I think of her."

After participating in 171 tournaments, Althea stepped off the tour in 1977 but continued to play for pleasure. "I haven't been giving my all to golf because of other commitments," she explained. In recent years, she had also limited her participation to tournaments on the East Coast since she lacked sponsorship. Although she was one of the LPGA's top fifty winners for roughly five years and had won a car in a Dinah Shore tournament, her lifetime earnings in golf never exceeded a total of $25,000. Her highest ranking was twenty-seventh in 1966, and her best tourney was the 1970 Immke Buick Open in which she tied for second. "I was born too soon," Althea noted.

"Even though she didn't win, she was competitive," Smith said. "She added to the tour."

Dave Anderson, a sports columnist at the *New York Times*, agreed. "It's pretty phenomenal for a person starting late," he said of Althea's golfing career. "Her ability to play on the golf tour at such an advanced age showed that this woman was a remarkable athlete."

Chapter 8

The Comeback Kid

*As long as God has given me the strength and good
health, the rest has got to be up to me.*

WITH THE DEBUT of open tennis in 1968, professionals and
amateurs could compete together for the first time. Competition was greater and so were the financial rewards. As a
Christmas present to herself, Althea decided to make a comeback—at the age of forty-one. "I want at least one more
crack at Wimbledon as a professional," she said, adding that
she also hoped to attract contracts. "Tennis is my first love,
and that's where the money is." Her earnings in just one tennis victory could eclipse what she made the entire year in
golf, which amounted to $2,764.50 for nineteen tournaments. "When I was playing tennis, I wasn't making a living,"
she said. "I have some regrets I retired and here came open
tennis.

"I feel great," Althea told the sportswriter Murray Janoff.
"It isn't a matter of age at all. It's a matter of how we feel and
the outlook we have on life itself. As long as God has given
me the strength and good health, the rest has got to be up
to me."

"The important thing to understand is that I'm not coming back to knock the world off its feet," she added. "The big thing is that I feel I can contribute something. And I know it's going to be a struggle. But I'm willing to accept it." She was right. It was a struggle playing in her forties, but she continued to make a contribution and set an example for younger players—particularly African Americans and women. One of Althea's biggest fans, Billie Jean King, and her then husband, Larry, who was in law school at the time, had an ambitious plan to hold a tournament at the Oakland Coliseum. The plan was to invite four men and four women. "We had five thousand dollars to our name," recalled King, who describes her friendship with Althea as one of the most important ones in her life. "We wanted Althea to come." King was thrilled when Althea, one of her childhood idols, agreed to participate. Althea practiced five hours a day to prepare for the Oakland Pro Invitational in February 1969. It would be her first tournament since 1960, and she'd be competing against pros half her age. Technically, Althea had remained the world professional champion in the years that it took for open tennis to become a reality. It was a meaningless title in many respects, as she had no competition, there was no market for women's professional tennis, and she had abandoned the sport for golf. Now past her prime, she didn't win the tournament in Oakland, but she held her own.

"My hands aren't as strong as they used to be, and my muscles are sore because they aren't quite as supple," Althea admitted after the tournament. "But I've been through the hard knocks before, and I think I can do it. A friend told me, 'If anyone can do it, you can!'" She still needed to make believers in the tennis community. While she had previously faced obstacles based on race and gender, she had the added burden of age. The three factors formed a formidable barrier at times. "It seems a little strange that after being a world champion I haven't been offered a teaching position at any club," Althea said. She was also having trouble landing television commercials and finding an agent to represent her. "It's almost as if they're saying I'm a has-been."

Althea didn't let the naysayers stop her and played in a number of tournaments. "Everyone always forgets that experience comes with age and is more than useful on the tennis court," she countered. And you couldn't tell her anything once Sydney Llewellyn's protégé Art Carrington helped her land a position as the program director at the Valley View Racquet Club in Northvale, New Jersey, where she also acquired a 5 percent stake in the business. As the head pro, she had unlimited access to the six courts at the indoor club not only to teach but also to shore up her own game. She wanted to offer encouragement to other black women through her example. "There are a lot of black women players who have the ability," she said. "I made it in tennis when things were a lot harder, and I want to show them that they can certainly make it now. The door is wide open for black tennis players, both men and women."

The thing that annoyed Althea was being asked to qualify to play at Forest Hills and in other tournaments. "Why should a former world champion have to do that? Why should I have to play some lesser person just to get in the main draw? No way. I know I could beat them, and they probably know it, too.

"I don't think I'm fooling myself about what I can do," she continued, "but I feel like I can beat almost half of the pros out there now."

Althea plowed ahead, teaming up with Arthur Ashe for mixed doubles at the U.S. Open in 1973 and stepping in to play Chris Evert at the finals of the S&H Classic in Fort Lauderdale, Florida, the following year after Evert's opponent, the Australian Kerry Melville, stubbed her toe. "Althea played well, but time has robbed the great black woman athlete of the slashing strokes and great court mobility that earned her the U.S. and Wimbledon championships in the late 1950s," wrote Al Picker in his "Match Point" column in *The Star-Ledger*. "Even so, the crowd loved it. For the record, the score was 6-1, 6-2 for Chris." When Picker asked Althea about climbing back to the top at forty-seven, she said, "Any time they agree to let me play in the championship round without having to qualify, I'm ready."

Nothing was off limits for Althea. In early 1976 she had made it to the finals of *Superstars* on ABC, winning the basketball shooting and bowling competitions and coming in second throwing softballs, but pulling a muscle in the fifty-yard dash.

A return to the top of the tennis ranks, however, was never to be. That added to an ongoing series of disappointments, slights, and setbacks, stoking an underlying bitterness in Althea that some found off-putting. To make matters worse, Althea and Will had separated. Rosemary attributes her best friend and brother's split to Althea's travel schedule. It was one of the main reasons it had taken them so long to marry in the first place, she said. But Althea's brother, Bubba, said that Will was a "womanizer," and others privately added that Althea might have had affairs, too. Even if Will had been stepping out on Althea, they said, who could blame him? She lived on the road.

"He worked hard and had a nice apartment, but he was there by himself," Rosemary said of Will. "He was a good-looking guy—a nice guy—and ladies liked him. So he figured, 'Why should I live this lonely life?' That's how I think it went down." When Althea filed papers, they simply cited a separation of more than eighteen months as the grounds for divorce. The Darbens' divorce became final in August 1976, and Althea returned to using her maiden name.

Althea tried to avoid discussions about her marriage and shrugged off the divorce. "The fact that it didn't work out had nothing to do with my career," she told Kay Gilman, a writer for *The Star-Ledger* in Newark. "With understanding and sincere concern, a couple can make it no matter what their careers are or where they have to go. . . . We just didn't make it, that's all, and we didn't have any children, thank goodness."

Out there on her own without a safety net, Althea was even more determined to make a decent living. "To my surprise, she vented her bitterness about not making any money," recalled Evelyn Cunningham, who covered Althea on occasion as a news and sports reporter for the *Pittsburgh Courier* and bonded with her to some degree over their similar height and experiences being coached by Fred Johnson at the Cosmopolitan. "I always felt so sorry for her. I still do. As full of grace as she was on the tennis court and generally in interviews, the basic human grace was not there. The anger was there."

Describing Althea's behavior as "the feeling-sorry-for-oneself syndrome," Cunningham expressed frustration that she was unable to do more to make Althea happy and that she was at times hesitant for fear that Althea's bitterness might do her more harm than good if her sentiments spread any more than they already had. "On occasion when I might have been some help in getting someone important involved in giving money, I felt a little uncertain about how she would handle the person," explained Cunningham, who is well connected and well regarded in Harlem and throughout the New York area among people of all backgrounds. "She expressed it openly to many people—her anger about not making money. It always bothered me and embarrassed me, because I knew it could turn people off."

But, Cunningham noted, "I never heard her blame it on her race." While Althea wasn't one to play the race card, she did at various times note the impact that her color and gender had on her fortunes—or lack thereof. "I was born too early," she'd often say. And just as often, she'd add that "I can't cry over spilt milk."

Toward the end of her golfing career, she opened up to the *New York Post* columnist Gene Roswell on her beliefs that race limited her endorsements. "When I came out of tennis as the world champ and turned pro in golf in '63, I was a big name in sports," Althea said. "It would have seemed good business to put my name on a tennis racket or a golf club or even to have used me for endorsements."

"I think it's color—because I'm black," she added. "I've reached the point where I can't understand why the white man is so unkind to the black man."

Still, she tried to let her determination win over her frustrations and forged ahead, attempting professional comebacks not only in tennis but also in golf in her fifties and even her sixties. "Everybody I play with seems to think I'm still quite good," Althea said, justifying a return to the links. "I feel the inclination to try to win one before my time is up. . . . I think I have the game, and the only way to get it all out is to play. I still want to prove to myself that I can be successful in golf."

At fifty, she was shooting in her 70s but missed the cut at key tournaments including the Bent Tree Classic in Sarasota, Florida, in February 1978 and the American Defender Golf Classic in Raleigh, North Carolina, in April. Still, she was committed to playing in as many tournaments as "my physical being would let me." Althea claimed she had "good everything"—coordination, legs, eyesight, overall physical shape. "With all these attributes, or God-given talent, whatever we should call them, why, it could be unforgivable not to exercise those skills," she insisted. And LPGA officials, players, fans, and sports pundits were thrilled to see Althea exercising her skills. "Naturally, it makes me feel good to have the public like me," she said. Meanwhile, she also explored the possibility of joining the United States Golf Association as an amateur. In a letter to the New Jersey executive director verifying Althea's fifteen years as a touring pro, the LPGA commissioner Ray Volpe closed by writing: "On a personal note, Althea is charming, intelligent, personable, and very motivating in many of the speaking engagements I have been fortunate enough to attend. On any level, in any atmosphere, on any court or field, Althea Gibson, at least to this writer, is a champion."

In July 1987 Althea shot for 83 at the Futures Golf Tour's $15,000 Jerry Weiner Memorial in Jamesburg, New Jersey. Three years later at the age of sixty-three, she was one of 195 women trying to earn LPGA playing cards at a qualifying tournament in Venice, Florida, in September 1990. But shooting at 86, she came in last place. "I don't want to talk about it," she told a *Sports Illustrated* writer. "I'm mad at my game." Being such a competitive athlete all her life, however, she was not mad enough to stop. In typical fashion she set her sights on the fifty-four-hole sectional qualifier in August at the Plantation Golf and Country Club in Sarasota and a September qualifying event in Rancho Mirage, California. The final shot would be in October at the Indigo Lakes Resort in Daytona Beach, Florida.

"I want to get back my LPGA tour card so I can have the privilege of playing when I want to," said Althea, vying to become the oldest active member on the tour. "I'm playing as much as I possibly can, mostly with gentlemen. They make me tee off from the men's tees. I can still outdrive a lot of them."

Althea never regained her card, but that didn't keep her off the links. In 1991 she played in the PGA's Doral-Ryder Open Golf Tournament in Miami along with the former NBA star Julius "Dr. J" Erving, the late tennis champion Arthur Ashe, and the Cincinnati Reds Hall of Famer Johnny Bench. On the ninth hole of the Doral's Blue Monster course, noted the Ryder System chairman M. Anthony Burns, "she putted it in for a birdie, like she did it every day."

The third area in which Althea attempted a comeback was marriage in 1983. Husband number two was Sydney Llewellyn, the tennis coach under whose guidance she won Wimbledon and her partner in Althea Gibson Enterprises. With all the time that they had spent together, it wasn't a surprise that they had become closer. In fact, there had been rumors of an affair. But it was the type of closeness reserved for good friends or business associates—not husband and wife. Whether they loved Llewellyn, hated him, or were indifferent, Althea's family and friends saw no sparks between him and Althea and scratch their heads to this day over the attraction. "They were a mismatch," Bubba said, hesitant to elaborate on his true feelings. "He was a nice man. He wasn't mean or anything like that, but their life together wasn't meant to be. I'll just put it that way."

His admirers recall his joie de vivre, his skill on the tennis court, and his chutzpah. Gordon Parks recalled that Sydney would go up to anyone, whether he knew him or not, and offer his opinion—like the time he stopped the tennis champion Pancho Gonzales and gave him unsolicited pointers on his game. "Llewellyn was an inspirationalist," said Art Carrington, who began taking lessons from him when he was nine years old and remained close to him through the years. Sydney's detractors saw him as an opportunist who felt that he "made" Althea and that he should reap the benefits. They felt that he wasn't husband material and that a man in his seventies was much too old for Althea, who was in her fifties. Althea ignored them.

Her friends didn't trust her new husband. They warned Althea that he was too controlling, demanding, and materialistic. Llewellyn, who called himself "Dapper Dan," loved clothes and especially the powder-blue Mercedes that his new wife gave him. He wanted 15 percent of everything she earned, before and after their marriage. He also wanted her to invest in his various ventures, such as his invention for an exercise machine.

"I never liked Sydney," Rosemary admitted. "Sydney wasn't really for Althea; he was for Sydney. Sydney was the opposite of my brother. . . . He was a gentleman and Sydney was not. Sydney was for everything he could get out of Althea money-wise and probably that was one of Althea's downfalls."

Over time, Althea began to see her husband as her friends saw him. She became increasingly cautious with her finances. Once, when she was hospitalized for tests of her gastro-intestinal system, she refused to give him her purse to take home for safekeeping. Instead, she stood on the hospital bed, retrieved her purse from the panels in the ceiling over her bed, and gave it to a friend. Llewellyn was infuriated and repeatedly questioned her actions. Without missing a beat in her conversation, she kept talking as if he didn't exist.

The second-to-the-last straw was when he struck her in the face. Surprisingly, she did nothing—even though she had the boxing skills to knock him squarely on his behind. The last straw was when she found soiled towels behind their bed. Meticulous herself, Althea would have never put them there: she considered this concrete evidence of Llewellyn's long-suspected affairs. Soon marriage number two became divorce number two in less than three years. "He was a player," Car-rington said jokingly.

Eventually, Althea and Will Darben reunited. They toyed with the idea of remarrying and met regularly at the Harris Diner, which was equidistant between her apartment and his at a senior citizen's center in East Orange, New Jersey. Some-times he invited her over for lamb chops, since he cooked better than she did.

And he resumed his job as the official turkey carver at the Gibsons' home in Queens, where everyone was glad to see them back together. "We liked Will," Althea's nieces, Sandra Givens and Mary Ann Drayton, said in unison. "He loved all of us, and we loved him," Sandra added, reminiscing about him teaching her how to ride a bike.

"He was always fun and jolly," Mary Ann explained. "He was easy to talk to, get along with, and be around. Althea was a different story. We could be around Will and felt okay. Althea? Whew!" Although their Aunt Althea doted on them as children, Sandra and Mary Ann would sometimes hide from her or avoid rooms in which they detected her signature fragrance, Shalimar. They aren't sure why they hid, perhaps childishness, they said, or maybe just to avoid saying or doing the wrong thing in her presence. "She was a mild-mannered person," Mary Ann said. "Until you pushed her," Sandra added, completing her sister's sentence.

"She could talk to you in a way that would make you cry," Mary Ann continued. "You would have to listen hard, because she'd whisper. She'd just put the fear in you from talking to you, looking at you." But Will knew how to keep Althea light-hearted and could make her laugh.

Althea cried for two days after he went into a diabetic coma and died in the late nineties. Instead of attending his funeral, she went to the crematorium in nearby Montclair, New Jersey, and watched as his body was reduced to ashes. Althea, who retrieved his wedding band, decided then that she also wanted her funeral held at Trinity Episcopal Church, the church they attended in downtown Newark, and for her ashes to be entombed near his, at a cemetery not far from the Darben family home at 69 Pleasant Way, where they had lived as newlyweds.

Chapter 9

Ambassador for Excellence

I had help, and now I want to use my talents to help others.

"I love to get high," Althea once confided. "But I do it differently. I do it on the tennis court or the golf course." That's the message she shared with pupils at Woodbridge Middle School in New Jersey as the supervisor of the Governor's Council on Physical Fitness and Sports. Althea visited the school in April 1991 in response to a successful letter-writing campaign by students in a special-education class. The students had been learning about persuasive writing, and their powers of persuasion had paid off in luring Althea to the school. They had been drawn to stories of her struggles in school when she was their age and how she managed to turn her life around.

During her visit Althea captivated the seventh and eighth graders with her pleas to "always play to win" and by autographing tennis balls. She closed with a rendition of her signature song, "So Much to Live For." Her message got through to Christina Martin. "I'm going to set my goals like you said

*Working for the Governor's
Council on Physical Fitness
and Sports in New Jersey.*

and do it," she wrote in a thank-you letter. "I want to be just like you when I get older. You're my idol."

Those are the kind of moments that fueled Althea during her serial retirements from tennis and golf through the seventies and early nineties. She positioned herself as an ambassador for excellence who still had a lot to offer in helping others reach their potential. Althea worked with everyone from schoolchildren to amateur and professional athletes attempting to step into her sneakers. Her position on New Jersey's fitness council alone kept her busy speaking at more than three hundred schools and senior citizen centers a year. "If you have a little bit of talent for any kind of sport, do it," she'd tell students. "Look what sports did for me." The elderly got that message, too, as she encouraged them to exercise, eat healthy meals, remain active in their communities, and consider participating in the state's senior games.

With all Althea had been through in her life, she was the perfect ambassador for excellence, having overcome obstacles of race, class, and gender.

Althea inspired both young and old. Here she speaks to senior citizens.

She was the perfect advocate for education. After all, she was a dropout who went back to school and graduated tenth in her class at the late age of twenty-one. Then she completed college and became an educator herself at Lincoln University.

She was the perfect example of how to clean up one's act. Here was a truant who came close to being sent to a reformatory and bounced from one odd job to another. But she rose above it all and became an international symbol of success.

She was also the perfect role model for keeping one's cool. A self-described hothead, she showed incredible patience and restraint while enduring subtle slights as well as overt oppression during her athletic career. Nothing that her protégés endured could compare to being relegated to the back of the bus, shut out of tournaments, forbidden from using water fountains and lunch counters, banned from bowling alleys, forced to change clothes in cars outside segregated country clubs, and denied not only lodging but also a mere reservation at a hotel for a luncheon in her honor.

"I just let all of that roll off my back like water and put my game together the best I could," Althea would say.

Her new game off the tennis court and golf course took her in a number of directions. At the start of the seventies, she directed women's sports and recreation for the Essex County Park Commission in New Jersey; ran Pepsi-Cola's national mobile tennis project; and gave tennis lessons and clinics and conducted special events and other programs at the Valley View Racquet Club in Northvale. "I'm motivated to try to help develop young people in tennis because of the way I came up," Althea said in a 1972 interview with Barbara Kukla for the *The Star-Ledger* in Newark. "I had help, and now I want to use my talents to help others." While she hoped to groom future champions, she encouraged young and old to play tennis just for the fun of it. "Not everyone is born to be an athlete, but everyone needs recreation and diversions," she would tell her audiences. "Tennis is a fantastic game for the release of tension and for sheer pleasure."

The mobile tennis program brought portable nets and other equipment to several cities, including Atlanta, Boston, Detroit, Newark, New York, and Philadelphia. "I learned how to play tennis with a paddle in the streets and so can you," she told children at Weequahic Park, one of Pepsi's seven sites in Newark. "If you don't hit the ball the first time as well as you want, don't give up. That's why your instructors are here—to help you." Hands shot up in the air when she asked for volunteers to try out moves and clapped when she urged applause for a job well done.

"This program provides constructive competition, better use of leisure time, and a sense of achievement and enjoyment to youngsters who have never had an opportunity or even considered the possibilities of playing tennis or entering tournaments before," Althea said at the time. Harking back to her own experience, she believed that tennis could make the difference between keeping children "on the court rather than in the courts."

Teaching a tennis clinic for youngsters.

It also gave her the opportunity to share her philosophy on being a winner: "The loser is always a part of the problem; the winner is always a part of the answer. The loser always has an excuse; the winner always has a program. The loser says it may be *possible*, but it's difficult; the winner says it may be *difficult*, but it's possible."

The opportunity to be the program director and a shareholder at Valley View brought Althea closer to her dream of running an academy to give back to younger players what she had been given. While she was delighted to hold the position, she still couldn't forget how difficult it had been to obtain such roles despite having been the number-one tennis player in the world. And this one came through Art Carrington, Sydney Llewellyn's protégé. "I've been playing tennis for twenty-some years, and it's taken me this long to obtain a position in my particular field," she said. "It didn't bother me, though. I felt it was their loss, not mine. . . . Things are better now, but not completely."

It wasn't as if opportunities never came, but Althea felt that they flowed to her peers while they trickled to her. Still, Althea took her smile and skills wherever she was invited to lend her name in support of various causes or occasions, whether it was for the American Heart Association or Family Tennis Week at Abercrombie & Fitch. In October 1971 Althea joined a reunion of fellow ATA players from the Cosmopolitan and Ideal tennis clubs at Lane Park for a dedication ceremony renaming the playground at 150th Street and Seventh Avenue after the one-armed coaching legend, Fred Johnson, who died in 1963 at the age of seventy-two. "I can truthfully say that he started me on my way to become the champion that I became," she said. As part of the ceremony, Johnson's widow, Justine, unveiled a granite monument and eleven-year-old standout Garris Brown challenged Althea on the court. In a more even pairing she was invited to Shirley Fry Irvin's hometown in March 1973 to join her in an exhibition match to promote the Akron Open Tennis Tournament in Ohio. Althea played in a number of celebrity benefits with the comedian Bill Cosby; the former New York mayor David N. Dinkins; the basketball greats Julius "Dr. J" Erving and Dave DeBusschere; the actors Charlton Heston and Sidney Poitier; the 1960 Olympic track star Rafer Johnson; the New Jersey governor Brendan T. Byrne; the photographer Gordon Parks; and Dr. Bill Hayling, her ob-gyn and the president of the Coalition of 100 Black Men in New Jersey.

To maximize her appearances and responsibilities at Valley View, Althea also teamed up with her manager, Gil Fuller, and athletes David Stallworth and Wilma Rudolph in 1974 to form Vanguard Sports, a personal management and sports equipment firm in Newark. Vanguard billed itself as a gateway to tennis, basketball, football, baseball, and soccer for urban youths. It would also help pro athletes branch out into business, public relations, radio and television commercials, and public speaking. In addition the company would develop, manufacture, and distribute sporting goods. "Our aim is to discover and develop potential talent," Althea explained. "We will be based in Newark, and our search will include Y's, schools, and neighborhood clubs."

Vanguard was an issue for Althea and Will, who repeatedly warned Althea to watch out for people trying to separate her from what little money she had with the business venture of the moment. Fuller was one of those people, as far as Will was concerned, but Althea didn't see it. She was excited about Vanguard and okay with loaning money to Fuller.

As it turned out, Vanguard became just another seemingly sure bet that went nowhere, just like the plans to film Althea's life story or to operate a hotel in Newark. "William told me that he didn't like what was going on," Rosemary said. "They were divorced, but she would discuss things with him. The bad part about the whole thing is my brother was very smart and all she had to do was ask him. He wasn't out for her money or anything or notoriety. But people make mistakes in life.

"He knew that he wasn't good for her, but Althea was a very determined person—in other words, bull-headed," Rosemary said, recalling her brother's opinion of Fuller. "I remember him telling me he told Althea, 'Watch what you're doing. There are a lot of people out here who would get you involved in all kinds of deals.' So she didn't listen; so what's he going to do?"

A year after the divorce, Governor Byrne nominated Althea to succeed Abe J. Greene of Patterson, New Jersey, as the state's athletic commissioner. "I'm flabbergasted," Althea said of her nomination. "What can I say? I'll have to think about it first." State legislators didn't have to think too long in confirming the appointment, making Althea the first woman in the country to hold such a role. Althea took over the $7,000-a-year, part-time post at a time when it seemed to be growing in stature with the impending debut of the Meadowlands Sports Complex and the sanctioning of such high-profile sporting events as Mike Tyson's heavyweight bouts. But the role didn't have as much clout as Althea would have liked and was limited to the regulation of boxing and wrestling.

When Althea was sworn in that November, she told the gathering, "I will do everything in my power to bring, improve, and promote professional, collegiate, and amateur sports in the State of New Jersey." Expanding her responsibilities would help create more job opportunities, bring in more revenue, and raise the excitement level for sports. "Why should people have to travel into New York or Philadelphia to see a football or basketball game?" she asked in an interview. "Why shouldn't Newark or Camden have professional teams of their own?" The new commissioner also wanted to strengthen youth athletic programs, build more bike paths, and lure more residents out into parks.

A perfectionist, Althea immersed herself in the new job and planned to deliver on her promise "to be one of the best athletic commissioners that New Jersey has ever had." With her street savvy and acquired social graces, she was comfortable with society types, movers and shakers in politics, pushy promoters, and shady characters alike. "What can I do for you, babe?" she'd ask, while jotting their wish lists on a notepad that she kept at the ready. By Christmas, Althea had sent a three-page memo to Governor Byrne, which opened by noting that the position's part-time status made the commission and its role in developing sports "a dubious entity and operation." She complained that the commission lacked autonomy, budgetary oversight, and adequate funding. To make New

Jersey "the new mecca for professional sports in the eastern United States," she listed a number of other recommendations:

- Making the commissioner an automatic member of all bodies dealing with sports
- Expanding the position to full time with an increase in salary
- Involving the commissioner in construction of any sports facilities
- Providing immediate funds for the commission to develop a master plan for pro sports as well as more office space

State senator Frank J. Dodd, a Democrat from Essex County and a sponsor of the Comprehensive Boxing and Wrestling Act, had an ongoing debate with Althea about what should be done and by whom. But Althea grew weary of all the political posturing and red tape. Noting that Althea had brought "new excitement" to the position of athletic commissioner, Governor Byrne accepted her resignation "with regret" in January 1977. "I don't wish to be a figurehead," Althea said after barely a year in the job. Hamilton Richardson recalls that Althea was upset that the job didn't fit its lofty title and that she was limited in carrying out her vision to provide athletic opportunities for young people.

Despite her frustration with bureaucracy, three months later she announced that she was crossing over to the other side, attempting to make the move from voter to vote-seeker, from appointee to an elected official in the New Jersey State Senate. In the Democratic primary in June she'd take on Dodd and Assemblyman Eldridge Hawkins, also from Essex County. "I had to be persuaded; I never thought I would be in politics," said Althea, who was following in the footsteps of Paul Robeson, a Renaissance man who also tried to bridge

Running for state senator in New Jersey.

athletics, entertainment, and politics. "I thought about what I had read about crooked politicians, the kind not concerned with people, but then I finally thought, maybe this was my chance to do something for a number of people."

Beneath an illustration of her swinging a racket on her campaign brochure is the slogan "Our platform and issues as we see it!" Althea's promises included unifying communities in Essex County, fighting for more funding for community projects and jobs, and pushing for "equity in taxation." She hit the stump hard, going on walking tours of towns like Hackensack, talking enough politics to make her hoarse, and even "starring" in a concert and political rally behind her apartment building in East Orange, dressed in a green dashiki and white bell-bottom pants accompanied by a multicultural R&B band in which musicians wore everything from huge afros to gold lamé pants.

"I have to look back on my competitive tennis days," she explained. "I go at politics vigorously. I go out to win, not to be just a participant." But all of the photo ops, handshakes, and champagne breakfasts were not enough to get her elected.

She came in second to Dodd in the primary but didn't rule out another run for office. It never happened.

However, she still gravitated toward public service, eventually becoming the manager of neighborhood facilities and then the manager of the Department of Recreation in East Orange, an appointee of Mayor Tom Cooke with whom she had campaigned on the same slate. She also served on the State Athletic Control Board and became the supervisor of the Governor's Council on Physical Fitness and Sports. One of the most unusual aspects of her job on the council was taking on Bobby Riggs in the "Battle of the Senior Sexes" as a highlight of the Senior Games in September 1987. This was Riggs's third time in such an event, but this time the stakes involved no money nor bragging rights. Previously, the "Happy Hustler" had beaten Margaret Court but lost against Billie Jean King in a virtual media war over gender superiority. True to form, Althea, then sixty, announced that she would trounce the sixty-nine-year-old Riggs, but she caught the flu and wasn't herself. While giving play-by-play accounts from the court, Riggs won 8-5. However, the overall goal of the Senior Games was successful in attracting seven hundred participants who competed in everything from cycling and swimming to table tennis and horseshoe tosses.

Named employee of the month by the New Jersey Department of Community Affairs in May 1990, Althea was touted as "our very own superstar" in the department's newsletter, *DC Action*. But she was "just another employee" on the elevators and in the hallways. "I like being treated like an ordinary citizen," she told her coworkers at the awards ceremony. "I am so full in my heart to be so honored." Little did she know how prophetic her words would be someday. Despite her international acclaim and effectiveness in preaching the gospel of fitness, she was unceremoniously dumped from her position due to budget cuts. She was truly being treated like an ordinary citizen and just another employee. She was given just one-day notice of her termination. In a letter dated June 29, 1992, the director of human resources wrote: "For economic reasons, effective with the close of business Tuesday, June 30, 1992, your continued employment with the Governor's Council, Fitness and Sports, will no longer be possible." While Althea continued to hold her head high, she was deeply hurt and disappointed. This was no way to treat a queen.

There were those, however, who recognized that once a queen, always a queen. They honored Althea's reign of excellence, giving her some, but not all, of what she felt was her due. In the years since she put down her racket and golf clubs professionally, she had received eight honorary degrees and been inducted into the National Lawn Tennis Hall of Fame, the Florida Sports Hall of Fame, the Black Athletes Hall of Fame, and the New Jersey Sports Writers Association Hall of Fame.

As one of the first six inductees into the International Women's Hall of Fame, Althea was placed on par with such pioneers as the aviator Amelia Earhart and her idol, Babe Didrikson Zaharias, who excelled in golf, track, and other sports. It was part of the first annual "Salute to Women in Sports," a black-tie event sponsored by the Women's Sports Foundation on September 16, 1980, at the Plaza Hotel in New York City. Cheryl Tiegs reviewed women's sports clothes from 1850 to 1930, while the singer and avid golfer Dinah Shore was among the entertainers. Althea was presented with a portrait, which was later displayed at the U.S. Open in 2002 for the forty-fifth anniversary celebration of her back-to-back national and international singles championships.

In January 1991 Althea became the first woman to receive the Theodore Roosevelt Award, the highest honor from the National Collegiate Athletic Association. She was cited for "symbolizing the best qualities of competitive excellence and

As part of its first annual "Salute to Women in Sports," in 1980 the Women's Sports Foundation presented Althea with a portrait of herself.

good sportsmanship, and for her significant contributions to expanding opportunities for women and minorities through sports." President Dwight Eisenhower had been the NCAA's first honoree in 1967. Other Roosevelt awardees have included Presidents Ronald Reagan, George Bush, and Gerald Ford; the Olympic track star Jesse Owens; the golfer Arnold Palmer; the former Los Angeles mayor Tom Bradley; and the comedian Bill Cosby, all of whom were varsity athletes in college.

Althea gave away many of her awards to friends who helped her over the years, but she presented her five Wimbledon trophies to the Smithsonian Institution National Museum of American History in 1988. "Who could have imagined? Who could have thought?" Althea said during the presentation. "Here stands before you a Negro woman, raised in Harlem, who went on to become a tennis player . . . and finally wind up being a world champion, in fact, the first black woman champion of this world. And believe it or not, I still am."

Although not the highest honor, one close to her heart had come during her first trip back to Florida A&M. Her visit during the convocation in May 1976 moved her to tears. It came twenty-three years after her graduation and included several receptions in her honor as well as a press conference at which she was presented with the keys to the city of Tallahassee. Many members of her FAMU family greeted her at the airport, much like the throng that had awaited her at the train station when she returned to campus after a tournament as a student. A police escort led a motorcade of more than two dozen vehicles to FAMU, where she addressed the topic "Blacks Honoring Black Professionals and Other Achievers" before a standing-room-only crowd at Lee Hall Auditorium. She discussed the challenges of dealing with discrimination while trying to excel and the essential qualities for success: "stick-to-itiveness, hard work, determination, patience, self-discipline, and the intelligence to benefit from one's own mistakes."

Encouraging students to use these qualities to reach their full potential in all areas, she'd make such pronouncements as "You don't get to be an AKA without hard work!" As she recognized other sororities, fraternities, and organizations in a call-and-response, she drew cheers and brought the crowd to its feet, with some members of the audience standing on chairs. Afterward, she pledged $500 to start a scholarship fund in her name and concluded with an a capella rendition of "So Much to Live For" to hearty applause.

Chapter 10

Revolutionizing the Sports World

Preparation implies hard work and diligence whether or not you are an athlete, astronaut, actress, head of a corporation or a family.

"You play like a girl!"

Those were once fighting words. Today, playing like a girl is not such a bad thing—especially if that girl is Althea Gibson. She is one of the key women who turned this once-derisive put-down into a compliment. She made it okay to be a girl, okay to be a girl who has a clue about sports, and okay to be a girl who's got game.

Althea was much more than a double threat or even a triple threat. Beautiful, smart, witty, and immensely talented, she excelled at every sport she tried. But back in the day, it wasn't okay for a girl to have so much athletic talent. "All the girls thought I was the worst tomboy they'd ever seen," said Althea, who was captain of the girls' basketball team in high school. "That wasn't enough athletic action to keep me happy, so I used to go out to the field during football and baseball

186

practice and play with the varsity boys. It used to hurt me real bad to hear the girls talking about me when they saw me doing that."

It's now the golden age of women's sports, thanks to the trailblazing of women like Althea and to gender-equalizing initiatives like Title IX, which is intended to reduce the disparities in education and athletics between girls and boys at high schools and colleges. No longer needing to ask themselves "Could I? Should I?" girls and women are comfortable playing almost any sport, including boxing, football, or even bobsledding. The number of girls playing high school sports increased from 1 out of 27 in 1971, to 1 out of 2.5 in 1998. The involvement of girls on school teams increased 31 percent in the 1990s, compared to just 9 percent for boys.

"It is the change in psychological atmosphere towards the woman in sports that has made all the difference," Althea insisted. "In the past, she was discouraged. In the present, she is encouraged. Today, it is no longer considered unfeminine to be in sports, and it is known to be good for your health." Based on her own experience, she thought it was good for girls to beat boys every now and then. Girls who have the chance to play competitively with boys gain "a better sense of equality," Althea believed. "By competing at this early age, she learns not to sit back and be pushed aside by men as inferior, nor that to compete is unladylike. So she develops the desire to succeed that will carry over into her business and professional life." The key, she stressed, is to get a good education and be prepared to grab opportunities as they arise. "Preparation implies hard work and diligence whether or not you are an athlete, astronaut, actress, head of a corporation or a family."

Althea also helped revolutionize the entire universe of sports—making strides that have benefited everyone from Billie Jean King in tennis to Lisa Leslie in basketball to Mia Hamm in soccer to Tiger Woods in golf. She championed good sportsmanship and conduct, fought for greater pay equity between men and women athletes, pushed to ensure that Title IX and other measures do in fact create more opportunities and scholarships, advocated for competition between amateurs and professionals in a variety of sports, and emphasized the need for improved facilities and resources for athletes as well as for the general public. For African Americans, she was not only "a credit to her race," but she also deftly used her racket and golf clubs to smash the color barrier in two elite sports. In addition she co-founded the Althea Gibson Foundation with Frances Clayton Gray to continue her legacy with training and resources for children interested in golf and tennis.

Early on, she predicted that women would be able to make a good living in team sports such as pro basketball or softball. Had the Women's National Basketball Association been in existence earlier in her life, she would have attempted a third pro career.

"To anyone, she was an inspiration, because of what she was able to do at a time when it was enormously difficult to play tennis at all if you were black," David Dinkins said. "I believe if anybody does well in engineering or architecture, or medicine or dentistry, or law or sports, it helps the rest of us."

"She just meant so much to me," added the former U.S. Open and Wimbledon champion Billie Jean King, also noting that Althea's contributions transcend race, gender, and athletics. "I've always felt connected to her and thankful and grateful for what she's done for people of color and for me." King, a founder of the Women's Sports Foundation, first saw Althea play at the Pacific Southwest Tennis Center in California when she was about thirteen years old. She became entranced by her style and modeled her own game after Althea's. They also shared a passion for advancing the cause of women and athletes of color, joining forces on a number of occasions over the years.

"The courage and determination of great American women athletes like Althea Gibson, Earlene Brown, and Wilma Rudolph, to name a few, helped not only black women but also played an important part in breaking down color and gender barriers in society," said Cheryl Miller, an NBA broadcaster who won a gold medal as a member of the 1984 U.S. Olympic basketball team. "I realized that their journey is one of the reasons I am where I am today."

Miller, who has experienced a number of challenges since trying to join a boys' basketball team at thirteen, was also the former coach and general manager of the WNBA's Phoenix Mercury and the former coach of the women's basketball team at the University of Southern California, her alma mater. She and her brother, Reggie Miller, the shooting guard for the Indiana Pacers, are familiar with the kind of obstacles that Althea faced. They grew up listening to the experiences of their parents, Carrie and Saul Miller Sr. "My mother played on an all-black basketball team and was not allowed to play with the white teams," Cheryl Miller said. "My father had the size and talent to play in the National Basketball Association but was confined to the Negro Basketball leagues and never got a chance at the big prize." The Millers gave their five children the same message that Buddy Walker, Sugar Ray Robinson, and Drs. Eaton and Johnson emphasized to Althea: do your best and always believe in yourself.

"It was during high school that I started getting interested in the struggles of black women athletes who had persevered and triumphed over cruel hardships," Miller said. "I remember reading an article about Althea Gibson. I was impressed and inspired because she always maintained that she was a tennis player, not a Negro tennis player. Her triumphs as the first black winner, male or female, of the U.S.

Open and Wimbledon led many to compare her with Jackie Robinson. And what I remember today about her was that she refused to see herself as a Negro who made it in sports but as a human being whose talent, skill, and determination were at the core of her athletic success."

Miller is grateful to athletes like Althea. "They lived in a time when women were second-class citizens," she said. "They pushed, they persevered, and whether they knew it or not, they were opening doors that will never be closed again."

Cynthia Cooper, who led the Houston Comets to several WNBA championships, has also been impressed by Althea's accomplishments and wrote a play in honor of Althea and other sports heroines. Her one-act play, *How She Played the Game*, was featured in "Women Heroes: In Praise of Exceptional Women" off Broadway in the mid-1980s. The same is true for Mocha Lee, the winner of several fitness competitions and a former track athlete. "She is so awesome," said Lee, who did extensive research on Althea and portrayed her in a play called *She's Got Game*.

Before his death, Arthur Ashe always credited Althea with paving the way for him and attributed the tremendous increase in the number of African Americans trying tennis to her participation at Wimbledon, Forest Hills, and other key tournaments. One of these African Americans is Zina Garrison, who described her feelings about being the first black woman since Althea to be ranked in the top ten and the first to reach the Wimbledon finals in thirty-two years. "I was fine until Althea walked on the court during one of my warm-up sessions. Just seeing her and thinking about what she had achieved on this same court caused me to sweat."

"Althea Gibson and Arthur Ashe, the first black players to win Grand Slam titles, made my journey less difficult," said Garrison, the first African American captain of the U.S. Fed Cup team and the coach of the 2004 U.S. Olympic team.

"Their trailblazing careers gave me something to aim for; their guidance gave me something to cherish."

It took twelve years for another black man or woman to win a Grand Slam after Althea's 1956 victory in France. It was Ashe who followed suit at the first U.S. Open in 1968, in Australia in 1970, and at Wimbledon in 1975. Yannick Noah won the French Open in 1983, and then Serena Williams took the U.S. Open in 1999—not long after faxing a letter and list of questions to Althea for a school project. Big sister Venus, of course, won back-to-back titles at Wimbledon and the U.S. Open in 2000 and 2001. That feat was achieved more than four decades after Althea's.

"It's really a privilege for me to win this Wimbledon while she's still alive," Venus said after her first Wimbledon victory. Althea was proud of the Williams sisters and glad that she was no longer the lone stranger. Someone had finally caught up to her record.

"Their time is now," Althea said. "They have worked very hard to get to this point and position. They have the talent and the availability of resources to attain a greater record." Althea was thrilled to watch the evolution of this rare sister act and would periodically pass on pointers to Venus and Serena as they captured one crown after another. She congratulated them "for accomplishing this historic achievement."

Many youngsters, weekend players, and rising stars like Garrison and Leslie Allen improved their game under Althea's tutelage. "She was a born coach," says Benny Sims, Chanda Rubin's coach and the former director of the Sportsman's Tennis Club in Dorchester, Massachusetts, who had invited Althea to run a tennis camp there in the early 1980s. "But people weren't utilizing her, which is the story of her life."

Garrison says she was in awe of Althea when she invited her to a camp she was running for pros in Boston. It was the summer of 1980, and Garrison was just sixteen. "She had an

With her students, including Zina Garrison (far left) and Leslie Allen (second from right).

air of royalty about her," Garrison wrote in her memoir, *Zina: My Life in Women's Tennis.* "She walked with her shoulders squared and her head held high, her deep, booming voice demanding respect."

"She pushed me as if I were a pro, not a junior," Garrison said. "I owe the opportunity I received to her.

"It was to the point where I was either going to play tennis or not play tennis," she explained recently. "She actually told me if I was going to play tennis that I had to work harder. She tried to get me to understand that I needed to be stronger mentally. All I remember more than anything is working harder than I've ever worked in my whole tennis career.

"She wouldn't let me be a wimp when being a wimp was all I wanted to be."

Then as now—and especially in Althea's day—wimps could not survive as tennis players. "You must be a tiger consistently on the tennis court," Althea said, in addition to having a good serve and solid ground strokes. In an interview for *The Indianapolis Recorder* in the early eighties, Althea the coach agreed with Arthur Ashe's prediction that there would be no "monstrous breakthrough" by black tennis players unless, she pointed out, they were "killers" on the court and knew how to play each and every opponent. Besides Allen and Garrison, other potential tigers included Renee Blount, Dianna Morrison, Kim Sands, and Andrea Whitmore. "It's hard to say who may break through," Althea said at the time. "They all seem to have determination and class."

History, it seems, has proven Althea and Ashe right. The list of breakthrough black players is short. It starts with Althea's protégés, Leslie Allen and Zina Garrison; and Ashe's discovery, Yannick Noah; later followed by Lori McNeil, Chanda Rubin, Malivai Washington, James Blake, and, most dramatically, the Williams sisters.

Allen, who attended the same camp with Garrison and two other players, says that being coached by a legendary world champion like Althea was a turning point in her tennis career. "It was the most amazing experience for a lot of reasons," she recalled. "To be able to have a forum where we're at a black facility, we're getting coaching from black folk, and we're black girls training in a meaningful way was sort of like a dream." Althea altered Allen's belief system, complimented her game, and boosted her confidence to such an extent that she began making it into the main draw of major tournaments and winning. Her international ranking immediately jumped from No. 152 to No. 39, eventually rising to No. 17. In 1981 she became the first black woman to win a major tournament in twenty-three years, when she captured the Avon Championships of Detroit and took home $125,000. Allen, who runs the Win for Life program through her Leslie Allen Foundation, has also competed in all the Grand Slams.

"It was more of her presence and being very assured with everything and anything," Allen said of Althea. "She transferred that to us: 'You have to be very confident. You have to be assured. You have to have lots of intent, lots of purpose—not just happy to be in the game. Try and win the game!'

"There was her overall philosophy of what it took to be a champion and how to think like a champion and approach picking up the ball like a champion or bouncing the ball when you're getting ready to serve like a champion—as opposed to 'I hope I do well here.'"

Althea, who continued to coach Allen in New Jersey and accompanied her on tournaments, took the old adage "each one, teach one" to heart. She was always willing to give younger players a boost, especially those participating in paddle tennis or other programs in Harlem where she grew up. Although her own resources were limited, she'd give what she could to help someone in need. When Sylvia Hooks quit her teaching job to play on the Virginia Slims tennis tour in 1973, for example, Althea donated a few hundred dollars toward her expenses. "What I've accomplished has been through the efforts of people who believed in me, people who felt I had something to give," Althea explained. "This is where it all began. If it wasn't for members of the American Tennis Association and the two doctors who sponsored me and accepted me as part of their families, I don't know if I would have made it. Everybody needs help or words of support."

In a historical assessment of women in sports for *Ebony*, William C. Rhoden wrote that "Althea Gibson and Wilma Rudolph are, without question, the most significant athletic forces among black women in sports history." While Rudolph's triumphs brought more *visibility* to black women as athletes—since television delivered to living rooms throughout the world images of her setting records and capturing three gold medals at the 1960 Olympics in Rome—Althea's accomplishments were more *revolutionary* because of the "psycho-social impact on black America," said Rhoden, now a sports columnist for the *New York Times* who was a consultant on *The Journey of the African-American Athlete*, a critically acclaimed HBO documentary. "Even to those blacks who hadn't the slightest idea of where or what Wimbledon was, her victory, like Jackie Robinson's in baseball and Jack Johnson's in boxing, proved again that blacks, when given an opportunity, could compete at any level in American society."

Rhoden described Althea as a "sports iconoclast who was thrust into a war simply because her race, her Harlem upbringing and her desire to succeed, placed her in direct opposition to the formerly lily-white tennis establishment. She was resented by a significant portion of that establishment, because she represented a threat to its basic foundation."

In many of her speeches Billie Jean King asks her audience to imagine excelling amid the type of bigotry that Althea endured. "She used to enter a tournament and they would cancel a tournament because she was in it. Can you imagine that you enter a tournament and because of your color that then it's cancelled? Can you imagine putting up with that? That's just ridiculous!" Leslie Allen agrees. "Nothing that any of us—me, Zina, Venus, or Serena—have *ever* experienced compares to what Althea experienced on a regular, regular, regular basis."

"I just let all of that roll off my back like water and put my game together the best I could," Althea explained time after time.

"She bit her lip and kept going; she was unusual in that sense," her close friend and physician Dr. Bill Hayling recalls. "Althea just went about her business and ignored the racism. She had pretty thick skin."

Keenly aware of the hue of the skin she was in, Althea made a conscious decision not to be a crusader even though she hated the double standard she endured when she ventured outside the more liberal and multicolored New York City. Bill Davis, who has known Althea since their childhood at Harlem's Cosmopolitan Tennis Club, says that she never wanted to dwell on racism so that it wouldn't shift her focus away from winning on the links and on the court, where she could make her strongest contributions. It was Althea's way of keeping her "eyes on the prize," as civil rights leaders were fond of singing. And Davis emphasizes that part of Althea's legacy was in showing how one could quietly make an impact, allowing her actions to speak louder than her words.

"She just smiled and said, 'Here I am baby,'" Gordon Parks said, chuckling and throwing up his hands for emphasis. "Everybody was encouraging to her, and I think that helped her attitude." Parks believes that Althea took the right approach in dealing with the racism. "I don't think she was wrong in not being more forceful in her attitude," Parks said. "She let her racket do the speaking. There are enough people out there who protest—the Urban League and on and on and on. They weren't out there on the court where she was." Using his own experience as an analogy, Parks said he wouldn't have been as effective or successful as a photographer if he had dwelled too much on race when he was trying to break into such magazines as *Vogue*, *Life*, and *Harper's Bazaar*. "I knew a barrier was there, and I knew that I could break it down only by doing the kind of work that they look for—and surprising them."

Yet, some people still find it remarkable that Althea didn't "go off" more given her strong personality and considering all that she was up against—especially once she made the transition to golf. At least with tennis, she could run off any feelings of aggression to calm the agony of defeat or the rage of racism. Golf moved much more slowly, and you couldn't simply powder the ball when you felt like it depending where you were on the course. Charlie Sifford said keeping cool was often the best strategy for black golfers back in the day, even though he didn't always pull it off himself. "If I didn't act like a professional, if I did something crazy, there might never be any blacks playing," he explained. "I toughed it out, and I'm proud of it."

Renee Powell agrees with his sentiment—and she quickly acknowledges that she endured far less in the way of racism than Althea, Sifford, and other golfers despite the threats on her life, attempts to run her off the road, and repeated requests for credentials at tournaments. "You try to ignore what you can ignore," said Powell, adding that she was lucky to have had the support of her parents, Althea, and other LPGA players. "You never noticed a reaction from Althea. I don't think either of us reacted, because a lot of times it makes it worse. If there are only two of you, it's different than if there's a dozen." She also speculates that Althea's fiercely independent nature made her tough and allowed her to shut out things around her. "I remember Althea told me she was on her own at the age of fourteen," Powell recalls. "It didn't matter to her, I don't think, what anybody thought or how they felt."

It was true. Althea played by her own rules in life. "Someone once wrote that the difference between me and Jackie Robinson is that he thrived on his role as a Negro battling for equality whereas I shy away from it," she said. "That man read me correctly."

While she refused to step on a soapbox, she wasn't totally silent. She'd discuss race when asked, work quietly behind the scenes, and comment on what she saw on occasion. For example, during the period in which she was making the transition to pro golf, she questioned the segregated seating at a 1959 exhibition tennis match with Karol Fageros in Nor-folk, Virginia. "What's this?" she asked. "I don't like it. I didn't know this sort of thing still existed."

"There's only one difference between us—our color."

Although Althea's comments were widely disseminated by Associated Press and cast a brighter spotlight on the prob-lem, it was a spontaneous move and not as calculated as the efforts of some golfers. Her lack of awareness that "this sort of thing still existed" was a curious claim, and perhaps she said it for effect, for heightened incredulity. After all, the event was held below the Mason-Dixon Line, and segrega-tion was well entrenched nationwide. Yes, Althea's comment had to be for effect; her subtle way of drawing attention to the problem of prejudice.

Race-conscious men and women wished that Althea would have allowed her stubborn streak to surface more often and that she had channeled her righteous indignation in more overt ways, like the golfers who were attacking racism by fil-ing lawsuits or using police escorts to play on public courses supported by their tax dollars. They wanted to see in Althea more of the activism of a Rosa Parks, Fannie Lou Hamer, Ella Baker, Martin Luther King Jr., or even Malcolm X. Like many black people, then and now, they took seriously the adage "to whom much is given, much is expected," based on the bibli-cal passage in Luke 12:48. With the in-your-face protests of Freedom Riders, Black Panthers, and track-and-field medal-ists with gloved fists held high in Black Power salutes at the Mexico Olympics, Althea seemed much too passive.

"I wasn't fighting any cause," Althea explained. "I was out there trying to do a good job for myself and if it was worthy enough to be good for my people, beautiful." Althea's low-key stance was more effective in dealing with racism in the golf world, believes Marlene Hagge-Vossler, the LPGA co-founder, who shared her hotel rooms with Althea. "It made it easier for everyone, and it made us want to help her even more," she explained. "I can be as nasty and rotten as the next guy, but sometimes you're hurting yourself. You've gotta know when to hold and know when to fold." As time went on, however, Althea felt freer to take stronger stances on race publicly, emphasizing that "a strong black America equals a strong America."

Just as it took four decades for Venus Williams to match Althea's back-to-back world and national tennis titles, there's still lots of room for catching up to her example in women's golf. In the half century since the LPGA's founding, only three African American women have played on the tour: Althea Gibson; Renee Powell, from 1967 to 1980; and LaRee Sugg, from 1995 to 1996 and 2000 to 2001. "Look at history and see what was happening to people of color and see why we are not further along," Powell notes. "The LPGA has an open door, but the courses did not."

With the phenomenal interest in golf among African Americans, that should change in time. Although involvement is picking up, economics is today's key barrier since golf is an expensive game, according to Rhonda Glenn, a USGA official and the author of *The Illustrated History of Women's Golf*. The golf writer Pete McDaniels also points out that the decline in caddie programs coupled with the rise in golf-cart usage have also had a major impact, virtually eliminating a natural feeder system that historically introduced many black golfers to the game. Sugg feels that the governing bodies need to do more to diversify their ranks. In 1997 the LPGA started a First Tee Program to introduce young people from various racial and ethnic backgrounds to golf and also runs the LPGA Girls Golf Club. Individuals like Althea, Powell, Peete, Elder, and Woods, along with various community groups around the country, have also started an assortment of programs and clinics. "The First Tee Program is great in introducing kids to golf and character-building skills, but it can only take you so far," Sugg explains. "The industry is not putting its money where its mouth is."

Althea said she hoped that newcomers keep coming and that they have an easier go of it than she did. (In any event, they can make more money with purses now averaging $2 million.) "Just knowing that people have come before helps to be able to show that you can do anything that you set out to do—if you want to do it, if you are determined enough to do it," says Powell, who saw Althea play tennis as a teenager and finally had the thrill of meeting the legend when they were paired at a United Golf Association tournament in Canton, Massachusetts. "It's like if you open a door and it's pitch black outside, you're not as sure that you wanna go out that door. But if you know that someone has walked out that door before you, then you have a little bit more confidence that you can do it, too.

"If it weren't for the Althea Gibsons and the Arthur Ashes, then people might say, 'Oh gee, well I don't know,'" Powell adds. "You have to have a history. History is so important because it teaches our past, and our past teaches us what we can do in the present and what we can do in the future.

"If there hadn't been a Dr. Martin Luther King, where would we be?"

Chapter 11

A Private Life, A Public Legacy

I'm not complaining; I'm just explaining.

ALTHEA GIBSON WAS a queen without a castle. She lived modestly in the same brick duplex apartment that she had called home in East Orange, New Jersey, since the late seventies with virtually the same decor. The primary exception was that a hospital bed replaced the black-and-white herringbone sofa, which had been relocated to the dining room. The end tables remained in place, instead flanking the bed but still holding reminders of her reign—custom lamps fashioned from the 1957 and 1958 Associated Press Female of the Year trophies with the eagles now perched on top of the octagonal, beige shades. From the black leather La-Z Boy recliner on good days or from the hospital bed on bad ones, Althea spent her final days reading newspapers from cover to cover, enjoying CDs like *The Art of Jazz Saxophone*, listening to the Reverend Fred Price on Sunday mornings, and watching protégés on TV. She still relished a good competition whether it was a dog race, a tennis match, or a presidential election. And she particularly enjoyed tracking Tiger Woods's monumental moves on the golf course. She was comfortable, but she had uncomfortable moments.

A private person even as a public figure, Althea lived alone and wanted to be left alone. She decided in her later years that she'd rather inspire and be admired from afar. She wanted to be remembered as she was in her prime. She gave so much at the start of her career that she felt she had little left to give. The world, however, disagrees. Many of her admirers consider her a legend who has given gifts that keep on giving. She worked hard. She played hard. She swung hard against Jim Crow with her racket and golf clubs. But the effort wore her out.

While she closed the door to the world and went inside to live out her life in seclusion, people continued to knock. Althea couldn't respond to all the invitations, inquiries, and interviews even if she had wanted to. She'd always been inundated with requests throughout her career, and the deluge hadn't subsided in recent years, especially once the Williams sisters began nipping at the heels of her sneakers some four decades later.

With all of her accomplishments, Althea was hard-pressed to pinpoint exactly what made her most proud when looking back over her career shortly before her death. She paused to contemplate the question and then softly responded, "I can't really say." But despite the goals she reached, the records she had set, the doors she had knocked down, the very history she made, Althea was happy that one of her biggest dreams had come true. She had successfully created a foundation in her name to give back what was given to her—the opportunity to transform one's life through sports. Through athletics, Althea gained confidence, greater self-esteem, friendships, and love. She gained an education, the most coveted victories, and the awards to go along with them.

The accolades and awards never stopped coming. She received honorary degrees and endless inductions, the most recent being the International Scholar-Athlete Hall of Fame and the International Women's Hall of Fame. Her name graces tennis courts at Manning High School, not far from her birthplace in Silver, South Carolina; the Family Circle Tennis Center in Charleston; Florida A&M University, her alma mater in Tallahassee; and Branch Brook Park in the heart of Newark. Citing her "powerful serve, pinpoint volleys and thundering overhead," *Sports Illustrated for Women* named Althea to its list of the "100 Greatest Female Athletes." Wheaties put her on its cereal box. There's now an Althea Gibson Senior Cup tournament. And she is still the only woman to receive the Theodore Roosevelt Award, the NCAA's highest honor.

With nearly one hundred titles, it's not surprising. But she came along too early to have the monetary awards to go along with her talent. There was no prize money when Althea won Wimbledon. Venus Williams, on the other hand, took home $650,000. Just since 1973, prize money for the women's tour has grown from $900,000 to $50 million today. The most Althea ever made playing tennis was $100,000 during the year that she turned pro—and that was before expenses. In fact, she has said that others made more off her name than she had. Meanwhile, players like Monica Seles and the Williams sisters have career earnings in the tens of millions of dollars, plus lucrative endorsements.

"It's one of the many injustices in life that Althea's greatness was not perceived by enough people early enough and how she never really made any money at this sport as she should have," Dinkins lamented. "But those were tough times. One appreciates the fact that she was not only black, but a black woman—and those were pre–civil rights days when she was accomplishing all this greatness."

When responding to questions about such disparities, Althea frequently said, "I'm not complaining; I'm just explaining." However, she admitted that "I do have regrets that it didn't all happen in my day." If it had, perhaps her downward spiral, which gained momentum in the early nineties, could have been averted. Althea's ouster from the Governor's Commission on Physical Fitness left her devastated. It didn't matter whether it was due to budget cuts or whatever, the bottom line was that she, Althea Gibson, had been dumped. With roughly $3,000 in savings and Social Security as her primary sources of income, she worried about her future. As the bills piled up, she moved closer and closer to bankruptcy. She was also shaken up from a stroke she suffered during a speaking engagement, and she couldn't bear to watch a body built for action slowed down by the ailments that often accompany age.

All of these things, along with the death of her beloved Will in the late nineties, combined to push her into a deep black hole where suicidal thoughts would drift in and out of her head. And she nursed these thoughts with one jigger of vodka after another. She wasn't necessarily living in a drunken stupor, since the vodka was cut with plenty of orange juice and each glass would last her for hours. But alcohol is alcohol, and too much of anything can do a body harm. As she shared her thoughts, her caretakers, Carol Lorraine Gaither and Frances Gray, took steps to intervene, especially since she owned two guns. When she received medical attention, she was diagnosed with depression and given medication to lift her spirits. But what really did the job was the outpouring of love from her community of friends and fans, who raised money on her behalf, spurred on by an appeal from her doubles partner and friend Angela Buxton. Donations ranged from $5,000 from Billie Jean King down to $10 and $15 checks paper-clipped to heartfelt notes in the rattly script of

Subject to applicable tariffs and conditions of use.

EXPIRES   11/30/00
0242102996   455041

For Customer Service, call 212-638-7622; outside NYC: 1-800-METROCARD

MEMBER SINCE 83

ARE YOU A CARDMEMBER?

American Express is the Official Card of the U.S. Open

In 2000 Althea appeared on the New York City Metropolitan Transit Authority's Metrocard, in conjunction with the U.S. Open.

elderly supporters who remembered when. Bill Hayling and Billy Davis joined forces to raise $25,000 at a benefit in Marina del Ray, California. Hayling's daughter sponsored a similar one in Atlanta, as did the tennis pro Pat Balskower in northern California. A group called the Friends of Althea Gibson and the Eastern section of the USTA each raised about $35,000. Combined with the efforts of David Dinkins, Jeanne Moustoussamy-Ashe, and Florida A&M, Althea's supporters raised enough to ease her worries about paying her rent with nearly $40,000 leftover for her foundation after she died.

Nevertheless, Althea remained a recluse, her moods ebbing and flowing depending on whether she took her medications. When she was stubborn, her pills had to be surreptitiously dissolved into her food. But in her move-a-mountain moments, she'd say: "I don't need any medication; I can do this on my own." And she did. No more jiggers of vodka, but she'd still puff on her cigarettes or talk a nurse's aide into picking up pancakes or eggs, sausage and homefries from McDonald's.

The seeds of Althea's discontent had been sown long ago—long before she shut her door. Ironically, they took root when Althea was at her highest heights. Caught up in the excitement of her back-to-back victories at Forest Hills and Wimbledon, she didn't really see it at the time. All she saw were possibilities, not limitations, and any obstacles in her way were kicked to the curb as she had grown so accustomed to doing. A decade later, she gave voice to her disappointments in her 1968 memoir, *So Much to Live For*, long since out of print. She noted the lack of endorsements, the lack of offers to teach or tour, the lack of pros to play, the lack of money from seemingly good business ventures gone bad. Most of all, she noted that any barriers she had destroyed had been erected behind her again. Arthur Ashe pointed out that it took him years to understand "the emotional toll of repressing anger and natural frustration." And he, far more so than Althea, was acknowledged to have been proactive and outspoken in venting his feelings on racism.

"She must have felt like there were so many roadblocks in her path," Billie Jean King said. "She didn't get her due. She was pretty upset with people, so when they tried to help her she always said, 'No.'" King speculates that Althea might have been heralded to a greater extent and retained more visibility had her triumphs occurred after the debut of open tennis in 1968, as was the case with Ashe. "I really tried to include her in anything I was involved in or had control over."

But Leslie Allen, who traveled with Althea in Europe and Africa, pointed out that she saw a difference in how Althea was treated inside and outside the United States. In particular she recalled a ten-day trip to Benin City, Nigeria. Allen competed in a tournament there, and Althea played in the exhibition match during the opening ceremonies. "It was amazing to see her treated like absolute royalty," Allen said. "They knew who she was and so she got her due respect. I had been with her to a couple of events in the U.S.—some of them big events—and it was a sort of perfunctory or cursory acknowledgment of presence."

The last time Althea visited the U.S. Open, she tried to treat an old tennis buddy to lunch. However, she didn't have a reservation. She didn't get a seat. She wasn't asked to wait. She wasn't recognized as one of its own, a two-time champion and Hall of Famer. Althea stormed out, incensed and embarrassed, vowing never to return.

Over the years Althea's bitterness brewed beneath the surface under a thick layer of pride. Arvelia Myers and others noted that Althea was so meticulous about her dress and appearance—never wanting even a hair out of place—that it would make sense that she'd revolt at the idea of being seen less than perfect in public. Slimmer than ever with salt-and-pepper hair, Althea looked better than she thought and far less the worse for wear than some of her peers—many of whom are now weak in the knees, undergoing hip replacements, suffering from memory loss, or dealing with other ailments. Life happens. But from Althea's perspective, she was still a household name far beyond tennis and golf circles. She couldn't be seen looking just any old way. Those of her fans who realized that she was still alive didn't care. But she did. "The reason I don't let anyone in here is because I don't want them to see me this way," Althea explained. "And people gossip so much."

In *Esquire*'s cover story of Muhammad Ali for the magazine's seventieth anniversary, Cal Fussman detailed the great pains taken to prevent the legendary boxer from being seen in a wheelchair as he navigated his way into place for the opening ceremonies at the 1996 Olympics in Atlanta. "If one television camera was to capture the image of 'poor old Ali' confined to a wheelchair," Fussman wrote, "it would be replayed over and over until it was quite obvious to everyone who saw

Like Muhammad Ali, Althea didn't want her physical condition out in the open as she aged. Here they are together when Ali was training to fight Joe Frazier.

it that this was, in fact, what had become of poor old Ali." Never mind that the world has already seen Ali trembling from Parkinson's disease. Everyone also knows that the shakes can leave him just as quickly as they come and that he still has the power to take someone out with his fists. While some cite Ali's visible challenges with Parkinson's as an example of why Althea could have, and should have come back out, it was all the more reason that she wouldn't. For someone who had been so physically strong and vibrant, who had attempted so many comebacks for so long, the last thing she wanted was to be described as "poor old Althea." If you didn't know for sure what had become of her, you'd just have to keep guessing.

Even Althea's friends and family were guessing to a certain extent. All they knew is that she had some nondescript "illness"; they didn't know how bad it was, what it was, or whether it even existed. They fiercely protected her privacy, whether they understood or agreed with her wishes; whether her preferences left them pissed off, hurt, or indifferent. "They were puzzled," said her cousin and childhood playmate Mattie Bryant of Brooklyn, New York, attempting to explain the sentiment of Althea's extended family, who no longer saw her at holiday dinners, reunions, weddings, or funerals—even those for her mother and two of her sisters. "Her sickness is such a deep, dark secret that they don't know what to say. They're afraid if they say the wrong thing, they'll get sued for it. . . . So they just use the word 'sickness' and let it go like that."

"She didn't like talking about her sickness," said Althea's niece Mary Ann Drayton of Petersburg, Virginia, who grew up in the Gibson home in Harlem and then Queens. "She just kept that to herself. She didn't want anybody worrying about her." Drayton's sister, Sandra Givens, noted that "sometimes she would just cut you off and that was it, if she didn't want to talk."

"She was very private; very private," Althea's brother, Bubba, added. " 'Well, there's nothing you can do. Don't call me. Don't bother me,' she'd tell you. Then after a while, she would realize what she said, and she'd start changing and talking a little mellow. It all depends on who she's talking to."

"I would have liked to have seen her more," Gordon Parks said. "I would have liked the public to have been in contact with her more during the last years. . . . She seemed to be ashamed of the way she looked, so she deteriorated, healthwise. She needn't be, I thought."

Out of respect, Dr. Hayling didn't visit Althea, even though he was her physician as well as her friend. "She had a lot of pride," he said. "Being a doctor, I know how people feel when they go through illnesses. That's part of the depression, too, and becoming more or less reclusive." Billie Jean King would plead with her: "'Althea, let us baby you a little!' Sometimes she would soften up." Her buddy Mayor Dinkins would eat up the tape on her voice mail, talking about "Champ, this" and "Champ, that" until she'd cave in and pick up the phone. And Zina Garrison finally just dropped in on her unannounced for literally one last visit, which they both enjoyed immensely.

Althea slipped away on September 28, 2003, barely two weeks after Garrison's visit and a month after her seventy-sixth birthday. She succumbed to complications following respiratory and bladder infections. A few months earlier, she had survived a heart attack that had landed her in the intensive care unit at East Orange General Hospital after her blood pressure had spiked. "I'm tired of hospitals, and I'm tired of being sick," she said upon her release.

She had been so reclusive that some people thought she was already dead when she died, a situation she sensed in her 1968 book, *So Much to Live For*: "I awoke one morning and knew the chilling loneliness of one who foresees that he will be forgotten." But many remembered.

Her body lay in state at the Newark Museum as countless friends, strangers, and loved ones filed past her casket to pay their respects and watched with interest as her sorority, Alpha Kappa Alpha, bid her farewell in its special way. The next morning, her immediate family gathered privately downtown at Trinity and St. Philips Cathedral to view her body, dressed in all white, including her blazer, sweater, and pants. "She looked like Auntie!" a niece replied to questioners asking what, to her, seemed obvious. Althea looked so good, in fact, that those entrusted with her last wishes were momentarily tempted to let the world have a peek.

The cathedral overflowed with people on the main floor, in the balcony, and outside on Broad Street. TV crews, pho-

The pallbearers at Althea's funeral.

tographers, and reporters with skinny notepads or micro-
phones milled about for one last take on the Althea Gibson
story. As the Reverend C. David Williams got the service
underway, he pointed out that the secret to Althea's success
was that she had Jesus as her doubles partner to count on in
the game of life and to turn to when the game grew ugly.
"She knew the victory through him who loved her." With
Althea's ability to play the tenor saxophone and "sing in a
sultry sassy tone," he expressed his sympathy for the angel
Gabriel. And he noted that Althea's part of a new athletic
board in heaven made up of Jesse Owens, Jackie Robinson,
and Joe Louis. "They happen to be right now on the other
side of this table in glory, and I'll bet she's convinced them in
all glory she should be president," Williams added, coaxing
smiles from somber and misty-eyed faces. Althea had once
compared winning her first Wimbledon championship to what
she imagined it felt like to be in heaven. "Only I don't expect
as much cheering and backslapping when I *do* get to heaven,"

she said, jokingly. "Matter of fact, *if* I get to heaven, I'll be happy to hear one whisper, 'Oh, it's her.'"

Calling Althea a trailblazer who "was climbing the rough side of the mountain," the Newark mayor, Sharpe James, said that "she dreamed great dreams and had the courage and conviction to chase those dreams and to make them come true." Zina Garrison said she cherished the opportunity to see Althea smile one last time. She thanked Althea for breaking down the door for herself and others. Denise Jordan, the executive director of the eastern section of the USTA, told the congregation that they were inextricably entwined by Althea's legacy and that she served as a reminder of life's endless possibilities. "There's a slew of us out here doing good things, because Althea was our lantern in the dark."

Leslie Allen implored everyone to share Althea's legacy with young people, not simply pointing out that she was the first this or the first that but explaining what she called the *largesse* of her legacy. This means, Allen and Dinkins explained, putting Althea's accomplishments into the context of the times and delving into the climate of lynchings, sit-ins, separate but unequal facilities and opportunities, and societal limitations on women.

"It was the quiet dignity with which Althea carried herself during the turbulent days of the 1950s that was truly remarkable," said Alan Schwartz, the president of the U.S. Tennis Association, which dropped "lawn" from its name in 1976. "Much progress in combating intolerance has been made in the fifty-three years since the door was pried open, but much remains to be done. As the USTA president, one of my goals is to be a current-day Alice Marble, challenging the USTA to face the fact that the door of intolerance that Althea pried open needs to be torn completely from its hinges.

"Althea could have chosen any number of career paths in her later years; she chose to become a community activist,"

Schwartz noted. "Althea's legacy, therefore, lives on not only in the stadiums of professional tournaments, but also in schools and parks throughout the nation. Every time a black child or a Hispanic child or an Islamic child picks up a tennis racket for the first time, Althea touches another life. When she began playing, less than five percent of tennis newcomers were minorities. Today, some 30 percent are minorities, two-thirds of whom are African American. This is her legacy."

David Dinkins said that "Althea built many bridges over her seventy-six years on this earth to ease our crossing" and that her service for her place on earth was paid in full. "Let her not look down and find any of us in arrears," he added. "She fought the good fight, she finished her course, she kept her faith, and now she can rest—game, set, and match."

As Althea's cortege slowly wended its way through Newark and East Orange, New Jerseyans trickled out of West Indian restaurants, cleaners, gas stations, doughnut shops, corner stores, playgrounds, massive frame houses, and brick apartments. With nearly a dozen officers on motorcycles and so many stretch limousines, they knew that this was no ordinary procession for an ordinary person. They were watching royalty roll by. But this was a down-to-earth queen who considered herself one of their own. She was the people's champ, and she lived around the way like any other sister. Who knew? Many didn't. Althea was heading "home" to be with Will, in heaven and ashes to ashes in the same plot at the Rosedale Crematory in Orange, which happens to be right across the street from the Darbens' old home on Pleasant Way.

After her death, the Satchel Paige theory was bandied about on whether she was really "the one." Howie Evans, a sportswriter for *The Amsterdam News*, for example, said that other women could have been in Althea's breakthrough role and that she just happened to be the lucky one. Similar arguments were made about Paige and other players in the Negro

Baseball League when Jackie Robinson made it to the Dodgers. "There was no player, at that time, who could match Althea Gibson," Parks said. "Take my word for it." Robert Ryland, another ATA player and the first black man to turn pro, agreed. "She was one of the greatest players who ever lived," said Ryland, who competes in senior tournaments. "Martina couldn't touch her. I think she'd beat the Williams sisters," added Ryland, who once coached the superstar siblings.

In one of his dream matches Sam Lacy, who covered sports into his nineties for the *Afro-American* newspaper chain, paired Althea against the eight-time ATA champion Ora Washington. He picked Althea to win.

"She was very sincere, very real, dedicated and determined at trying to do her best the whole time," Ham Richardson said, his words trailing off as he choked back tears and his gaze shifted toward his wraparound view of the East River between Queens and Manhattan.

Despite her ups and downs, Althea felt that she had a thrill overall.

"It has been a bewildering, challenging exhilarating experience—often more painful than pleasurable, more sad than happy, but I wouldn't have missed it for the world!" she said, reflecting back on her career.

"People thought I was ruthless. I was. I didn't give a darn who was on the other side of the net. I'd knock you down if you got in the way. I just wanted to play my best."

Althea Gibson didn't just play her best. She *was* the best. She was born to win.

Epilogue

In my travels, I have encountered people who do not understand Althea Gibson's legacy or love for working-class people. She was a dropout who became an educated, strong citizen of the world. Althea was one of the first international champions who insisted on being known as an "athlete" and not as a "Negro athlete." Like Martin Luther King Jr., she believed we should be judged by the content of our character, not the color of our skin. She bought the Military Park Hotel in Newark, insisting that the city needed a performing arts center. Ironically, the New Jersey Performing Arts Center stands on that site. As the "people's champion" and a public servant, she also supported such issues as affordable housing.

Upon examining her letters and personal effects, I see that she was assigned to go here, do this, say that. Then in her golden years, she came to an unceremonious end—dismissed from the State of New Jersey with a day's notice in 1992. We were unable to help her escape from the ensuing depression. It was only after people the world over sent life-sustaining donations that she realized how much she was loved.

This book shows the true Althea Gibson—fun loving, easygoing, approachable, and, yes, very competitive. She cared about children and applauded younger athletes reaching new heights. She would say, "Fran, records are made to be broken." Her mandate to me was: "Educate the children. It's okay to expose children to tennis or golf, but concentrate on raising money to educate them." She tried to rescue as many children and families as she could—just as she had been rescued.

—Frances Clayton Gray

Afterword

When my sister Serena and I were younger, we didn't always think about the historic steps we were following in or even making ourselves. We were out on the court to get the job done and hopefully have fun along the way. Over time, it became clear that we had graduated to a different level with some of the greats. One of the greatest, of course, is Althea Gibson, and it's been an honor to be mentioned in the same breath with such a legend.

Although some of the challenges that she faced still exist, it's much easier for all of us who have come after her. I am grateful to Althea Gibson for having the strength and courage to break through the racial barriers in tennis. She knocked down walls, which gave us more freedom to concentrate on the game. She was the first African American woman to rank No. 1 and win Wimbledon; I had the opportunity to follow in her footsteps as the second.

Several times during that tournament, I thought about Althea and the difficulties that she faced back in the fifties. It had to be hard because people were unable to see past color. At times, they still aren't. I also thought of Arthur Ashe, who won Wimbledon in 1975 and remains the only black man to do so. And, of course, I thought of Zina Garrison, who inspired me at age ten when she made the 1990 women's final at Wimbledon.

It's still a little unbelievable that it took so long for these accomplishments to occur and that it took more than forty years for someone to match Althea's back-to-back championships at Wimbledon and in the United States in 1957

216

and 1958. Althea always wanted to see someone repeat those victories during her lifetime. I'm glad that I was the first black woman to do that in 2000 and 2001. She also had a chance to witness Serena winning the U.S. Open in 1999 and the French Open and Wimbledon in 2002.

In fact, Althea saw lots of our singles and doubles matches, especially the Grand Slams. It was always nice to know that she regularly watched Serena and me on TV and that she'd take the time to congratulate us or pass on tennis tips through Zina. She considered us "two of the greatest tennis athletes in the world." Unfortunately, I never had the pleasure of meeting Althea, but we spoke on the phone once. I was so starstruck that I was almost unable to say anything. It was like talking with history!

Many people compare my game to Althea's, because of our power, reach, and height. The more I learn about her, the more I see similarities in our backgrounds, competitiveness, growth, and resilience—especially when the odds have been against us. No matter what was going on around us, we tried to maintain our focus and grace under pressure.

And like Althea, I, too, feel a need to be a role model. We all need to do more to expose people of all backgrounds to our sport. Althea's accomplishments set the stage for my success, but she also made a difference for people of all backgrounds in all areas. Through beneficiaries like me, Serena, and many others to come, her legacy will live on.

—Venus Williams

Career Achievements

Selected Awards

Associated Press Woman Athlete of the Year (1957–1958)
Babe Zaharias Outstanding Woman Athlete (1957–1958)
Black Athletes Hall of Fame
First Ladies Salute First Women Award
Florida A&M Athlete of the Century
Florida Sports Hall of Fame
Florida Women's Hall of Fame
International Scholar-Athletes Hall of Fame
International Tennis Hall of Fame
International Women's Sports Hall of Fame
National Lawn Tennis Hall of Fame
National Women's Hall of Fame
NCAA Theodore Roosevelt Award
New Jersey Sports Hall of Fame
South Carolina Hall of Fame
Sports Illustrated Top 100 Greatest Female Athletes
Sports Writers Association Hall of Fame

Grand Slam Record

1957–1958	Wimbledon Singles Championship
1956–1958	Wimbledon Doubles Championship
1956–1958	Wimbledon Mixed-Doubles Finalist
1957–1958	USLTA Singles Championship
1957	USLTA Mixed-Doubles Championship
1957–1958	USLTA Doubles Finalist
1956	USLTA Singles Finalist
1957	Australian Doubles Championship
1957	Australian Singles Finalist
1956	French Singles Championship
1956	French Doubles Championship

Other Key Tournaments

1960	Pepsi Cola World Pro Tennis Singles and Doubles Championships
1959	Pan-American Singles Championship
1957–1958	U.S. Wightman Cup Team
1957–1958	Caribbean Championship
1957	USLTA Clay Court Singles and Doubles Championships
1956–1957	Pacific Southwest International Championship
1947–1957	American Tennis Association Women's Singles Championship
1956	Italian Singles Championship
1956, 1958	71st Pennsylvania Lawn Tennis Championship
1956	All-India Championship
1956	German Indoor Championship
1956	French Indoor Championship
1956	Surrey Grass Court Championship
1956	West of England Lawn Tennis
1956	International Championship, Lyons, France
1956	International Championship, Cannes, France
1956	International Championship, Monte Carlo, Monaco
1956	Eastern Grass Court Championship
1955	Rose Taubele Memorial Championship
1954–1955	New York State Championship
1953–1954	Red Rose Championship
1951	International Championship, Dortmund, Germany
1951	Frinton-by-the-Sea Championship
1950	Good Neighbor Championship
1950	Eastern Indoor Championship
1950	Caribbean Championship

For more information, please contact:

Althea Gibson Foundation
17 Academy Street, Suite 608
Newark, NJ 07102
(973) 596-0333
www.altheagibson.com
agibsonfoundatio@aol.com

Notes

All information is from Althea Gibson, her personal papers, or Frances Clayton Gray unless otherwise indicated. Where necessary for clarity, the following abbreviations will be used to cite information from Ms. Gibson, historical archives, or other sources used repeatedly:

AG Althea Gibson
AGF Althea Gibson Foundation
AGC Althea Gibson Collection
ATA American Tennis Association
CCA Clarendon County Archives, Manning, S.C.
HU/MS Howard University, Moorland-Spingarn Research Center,
    Washington, D.C.
LPGA Ladies Professional Golf Association
SCDAH South Carolina Department of Archives and History, Columbia, S.C.
SCRBC Schomburg Center for Research in Black Culture, New York
USTA United States Tennis Association

Chapter 1. "A Traveling Girl"

1 Opening quotation "My friends and I . . .": "That Gibson Girl," *Time*, August 26, 1957, p. 45.

2 "We'd climb over the fence . . .": Ibid.
 "My parents were doing their best . . .": Brian Lanker, *I Dream a World* (New York: Stewart, Tabori, & Chang, 1989), p. 47.

3 Interview with Mary "Minnie" McFadden, aunt, 2003.
 John S. Silver: Tom Johnson, "Fragments of a Fallen Flag: One Man's Search for the Northwestern Railroad of South Carolina," Clarendon County Archives, Manning, S.C. (CCA), 2000.
 "While we were courting . . .": Althea Gibson with Ed Fitzgerald, *I Always Wanted to Be Somebody* (New York: Noble and Noble, 1958), pp. 8–9.
 Interview with Daniel "Bubba" Gibson Jr., brother, 2003–2004.
 Interview with Thelmer Bethune, cousin, 2003.
 Gibson/Washington Genealogy: Family trees, AGC. U.S. Census records, 1860–1930; Census return for Clarendon County, S.C., 1869, CCA.

4 W. J. Gibson: 1860 slave schedule for Clarendon County, S.C., CCA; 1860 free schedule for Clarendon County, S.C., CCA.

5 Mount Zero Missionary Baptist Church history, Paxville, S.C.

6 January Gibson's holdings: 1898 Clarendon County tax record, CCA. *Briggs v. Elliott*, CCA.

8 Logging and lumber operations: Thomas Fetters, *Logging Railroads of South Carolina* (Forest Park, Ill: Heimburger House Publishing Company, 1990), pp. 106–111, CCA; Johnson, "Fragments of a Fallen Flag," CCA.
Interview with Mattie Bryant, cousin, 2003.
Bootleggers: Walter Edgar, *South Carolina: A History* (Columbia: University of South Carolina Press, 1998), p. 483.
Interview with Agnes "Aggie" Green, cousin, 2003.

9 Demise of railroad: Johnson, "Fragments of a Fallen Flag," CCA.
Cotton industry: Fetters, *Logging Railroads of South Carolina*, pp. 480–485.

10 "The depression hit Silver . . .": Ted Poston, "The Story of Althea Gibson," Article I, *New York Post*, August 26, 1957, p. M2.

11 "Ten-cent cotton . . .": Edgar, *South Carolina: A History*, p. 485.
Exodus: Ibid.
"Those were the draining years . . .": Ibid.

12 Migration of South Carolinians to Harlem: Gilbert Osofsky, *Harlem: The Making of a Ghetto: Negro New York, 1890–1930* (New York: Harper & Row, 1963), p. 129.
"I bought me a cheap blue suit . . .": Gibson, *I Always Wanted to Be Somebody*, p. 10.
Discussion about Junius and Dush: Interview with Mary Ann Drayton, niece, 2003.
Discussion about Junius and Dush: Interview with Sandra Givens, niece, 2003.

13 "I got me a job right away . . .": Gibson, *I Always Wanted to Be Somebody*, p. 11.

14 Harlem history: Howard Dodson, Christopher Moore, and Roberta Yancy, *The Black New Yorkers: The Schomburg Illustrated Chronology* (New York: John Wiley & Sons, 2000); David Levering Lewis, *When Harlem Was in Vogue* (New York: Vintage Books/Random House, 1979).
"There was always lots of food . . .": Gibson, *I Always Wanted to Be Somebody*, p. 11.

15 "When the car pulled up . . .": Ibid., p. 14.
"I was a traveling girl . . .": Ibid.

16 "I guess about the worst thing we did . . .": Ibid., pp. 18–19.
"I remember you could get fish-and-chips for fifteen cents": "That Gibson Girl." *Time*, August 26, 1957, p. 45.

17 Harlem's median family income: Lewis, *When Harlem Was in Vogue*, p. 241.
Harlem rents: Ibid.

20 "That's my uncle . . .": Althea Gibson, "I Wanted to Be Somebody," *Saturday Evening Post*, August 23, 1958, p. 69.
"If Daddy hadn't shown me . . .": Gibson, *I Always Wanted to Be Somebody*, p. 18.

21 Women's boxing history: International Women's Boxing Federation.

21 "There was no way for me to know . . .": Poston, Article I, *New York Post*, August 26, 1957, p. M2.
"At night, we used to go to the school gymnasium . . .": Gibson, *I Always Wanted to Be Somebody*, p. 20.

22 "I would go to the police station . . .": Gibson, "I Wanted to Be Somebody," *Saturday Evening Post*, p. 69.

23 "We used to have to drag her back in the house": "That Gibson Girl," *Time*, p. 45.
"Mom says she used to walk the streets . . .": Gibson, *I Always Wanted to Be Somebody*, p. 23.

Chapter 2. Holding Court

24 Opening quotation "I knew that I was an unusual talented girl . . .": Lanker, *I Dream a World*. New York: Stewart, Tabori, & Chang.
Interview with Daniel "Bubba" Gibson Jr.

25 "The fellows in the block . . .": AGC.
Softball and paddleball awards: AGC.
"Her aggressive strokes . . .": Poston, Article II, *New York Post*, p. M2.

26 Van Houton: "That Gibson Girl," *Time*.
"After about ten minutes . . .": Poston, Article II, *New York Post*, p. M2.
Fred Johnson: Ibid.
"They all said she was a natural athlete, but I was skeptical": Ibid.
American Tennis Association: ATA and HU/MS.

27 Tennis statistics: AGC.

28 "I really wasn't the tennis type": Gibson, *I Always Wanted to Be Somebody*, p. 32.
"I was the first woman she ever played tennis with . . .": Poston, Article II, *New York Post*, p. M2.

29 "I went for a couple of weeks": Gibson, *I Always Wanted to Be Somebody*, pp. 24–25.

30 Interview with Gordon Parks, friend and tennis player, 2003.
"Those days . . .": Gibson, *I Always Wanted to Be Somebody*, p. 32.

31 Interview with Billy Davis, friend and tennis player, 2001–2004.
"I got a regular schedule . . .": Gibson, *I Always Wanted to Be Somebody*, p. 31.

32 "Althea was a very crude creature": Gibson, *I Always Wanted to Be Somebody*, p. 36. "That Gibson Girl," *Time*, p. 45.
"I was able to run my own life": Gibson, *I Always Wanted to Be Somebody*, p. 36.

33 Training camp at Greenwood Lake, N.Y.: Gibson, *I Always Wanted to Be Somebody*, pp. 37–38; Arthur R. Ashe Jr., *A Hard Road to Glory: A History of the African-American Athlete*, 3 vols. (New York: Amistad/ Warner Books, 1988), 3:86.

34 "Althea used to come over . . .": "That Gibson Girl," *Time*, p. 45.
"My New York supporters . . .": Gibson, *I Always Wanted to Be Somebody*, p. 36.
Tuskegee Institute: ATA, HU/MS; Ashe, *A Hard Road to Glory*, 2:63.

34 Roumania and Margaret Peters: ATA, HU/MS.
    "She really worked on me": Gibson, *I Always Wanted to Be Somebody*,
    p. 36.
35 "She should have won": Poston, Article III, *New York Post*, August 28,
    1957, p. M2.
37 "You'll never amount to anything . . .": Gibson, *I Always Wanted to Be
    Somebody*, p. 36.
    "It didn't even leave me time to change my mind": Ibid.
    Arrival in Wilmington, S.C.: Ibid.
    Saxophone: AGC.
    "She hugged me . . .": Gibson, *I Always Wanted to Be Somebody*, p. 36.
38 "At first, she didn't get along too well": Poston, Article III, *New York
    Post*, August 28, 1957, p. M2.
    Interview with Robert Johnson Jr., friend, summer host, and tennis
    player, 2004.
39 "I used to have to make them get off the court": Poston, Article III,
    New York Post, August 28, 1957, p. M2.
40 Interview with Arvelia Myers, friend and tennis player, 2003.
    Interview with Mary Etta Fine, ATA competitor, 2004.
    Interview with Eva Bracy, ATA competitor, 2004.
    Interview with Leo Fine, ATA competitor, 2004.
    Interview with Rosemary Darben, sister-in-law, best friend, and tennis
    player, 2003.
41 "We had wanted for years . . .": Poston, Article IV, *New York Post*,
    August 29, 1957, p. M2.
42 Origins of tennis: ATA; "Negro History," Part 1-1, *The Philadelphia
    Independent*, July 5 and 12, 1958, HU/MS; Ashe, *A Hard Road to
    Glory*, 2:59.
43 ATA history: Ashe, *A Hard Road to Glory*, 2:45, 59–64, 67, 68, 3:150,
    160–169, 211.
    Black tennis clubs: Ibid., 2:59–64, 3:160–169.
    Shady Rest: ATA; HU/MS; Ashe, *A Hard Road to Glory*, 2:66–67.
    "It was very much a family affair": "Playing Tennis on the ATA Tour,"
    Black Enterprise, September 1997, p. 144.
44 Reginald Weir: ATA; Ashe, *A Hard Road to Glory*, 2:61, 62, 64, 3:167.
    Oscar Johnson: ATA; Ashe, *A Hard Road to Glory*, 2:64, 3:160–161, 170.
    Integration of baseball, football, and basketball: Ashe, *A Hard Road to
    Glory*, 2:36–42, 44–58, 98, 3:7–13, 50–52, 64–67, 128–131.
    Armed forces: Schomburg Center for Research in Black Culture: The
    New York Public Library, *African-American Desk Reference* (New
    York: John Wiley & Sons, 1999), pp. 15–16.
45 "It was an especially good break . . .": Gibson, *I Always Wanted to Be
    Somebody*, p. 55.
46 "I'm glad I lasted as long as I did": Ibid., p. 56.
    "I was made to feel right at home . . .": Ibid.
47 Grades: AGC.
    Interview with Edwin M. Thorpe Sr., retired registrar and director of
    admissions at Florida A&M, 2004.

47 "We played on clay courts . . .": "Althea Gibson: FAMU's Pioneer in Women's Sports," *On Target: Building for the Future, The Tallahassee Democrat* supplement, March 16, 1981, p. 11.

"I first played against her . . .": D.C. Collington, "Around Her Alma Mater, They Are Wild About Althea," undated article, AGC.

48 "There weren't many places . . .": Gibson, *I Always Wanted to Be Somebody*, p. 58.

49 Interview with Annette Thorpe, former Florida A&M English professor, 2004.

Interview with Edwina Martin, FAMU basketball teammate, 2004.

Interview with Elizabeth McElveen, a.k.a. Maggie Swilley, FAMU basketball teammate, 2004.

52 "You would have thought for sure I had won . . .": Gibson, *I Always Wanted to Be Somebody*, p. 60.

"We would have waited another year . . .": Poston, Article IV, *New York Post*, p. M2.

Alice Marble: Ashe, *A Hard Road to Glory*, 3:163–165.

"Two days later . . .": "The New Gibson Girl," *Sports Illustrated*, pp. 20, 60–61.

54 Charles Hare: ATA; AGC; Ibid.

55 Telegram from Robert Johnson: AGC.

"Your unafraid declaration . . .": ATA; AGC.

56 "We are somewhat surprised . . .": Ibid.

"She stepped off the court . . .": Poston, Article IV, *New York Post*, August 29, 1957, p. M2.

57 "the entry of Miss Althea Gibson": "New York Negro Girl Will Enter National Tennis Championship," *New York Times*, August 16, 1950.

"Although USLTA announced it . . .": Gibson, *I Always Wanted to Be Somebody*, p. 61.

"the beginning of a new era . . .": Ashe, *A Hard Road to Glory*, 3:165.

58 "the most talked-about women's singles tennis player in America": Undated newspaper article, AGC.

"implied quota": Ashe, *A Hard Road to Glory*, 3:166.

"No Negro player . . .": Lester Rodney, "On the Scoreboard: Miss Gibson Plays at Forest Hills," *Daily Worker*. August 24, 1950.

Chapter 3. "Champion of Nothing"

59 Opening quotation "I made a vow to myself . . .": Lanker, *I Dream a World*, p. 47.

"Just playing with Sarah . . .": Gibson, *I Always Wanted to Be Somebody*, p. 62.

61 Rhoda Smith: Ibid; Poston, Article II, *New York Post*, p. M2; Ashe, *A Hard Road to Glory*, 3:165.

"It was only a short walk . . .": Gibson, *I Always Wanted to Be Somebody*, p. 62.

62 "Have courage": AGC.

62　Significance of the moment: "The New Gibson Girl," *Sports Illustrated*, p. 61.

　　Ginger Rogers: Poston, Article V, *New York Post*, p. M2.

　　"Contrary to all custom . . .": Ibid.

　　"I can't think of a specific time . . .": Milton Gross, "Speaking Out," *New York Post*, June 12, 1956.

　　"The truth is . . .": Poston, Article V, *New York Post*, p. M2.

63　"I would have liked to have gone to a movie . . .": Gibson, *I Always Wanted to Be Somebody*, pp. 63–64.

　　"Nearly 2,000 spectators . . .": "The New Gibson Girl," *Sports Illustrated*, p. 61.

　　Interview with Rosemary Darben.

65　"Louise was one of the big guns . . .": Gibson, *I Always Wanted to Be Somebody*, p. 64.

　　"Miss Gibson was terribly nervous . . .": "The New Gibson Girl," *Sports Illustrated*, July 2, 1956, p. 61.

　　Interview with Louise Brough, opponent at Forest Hills debut, 2004.

　　"I have sat in on many dramatic moments . . .": "The New Gibson Girl," *Sports Illustrated*, p. 61.

66　"The delay was the worst thing . . .": Gibson, *I Always Wanted to Be Somebody*, p. 64.

　　"She won three straight games . . .": "The New Gibson Girl," *Sports Illustrated*, p. 61.

　　"Althea Gibson did not come through the tournament . . .": *New York Herald Tribune*, undated editorial, AGC.

67　ATA/USLTA meeting: Gibson, *I Always Wanted to Be Somebody*, p. 65.

　　Letter to Alice Marble: AGC.

68　Caribbean Tennis Championships: "Americans Sweeping Tennis Championships," *The Daily Gleaner*, February 12, 1951; "Althea Gibson Bows to Chaffee in Title Play," *The Courier*, March 3, 1951.

　　"beat herself": "Althea Gibson Bows to Chaffee in Title Play," *The Courier*.

　　"Miss Gibson tried to smash her way to victory . . .": Ibid.

69　"Every sports-minded person . . .": "Detroiters to Send Ace Abroad: Joe Louis Spurs Drive to Raise Necessary Funds," undated newspaper article, AGC.

　　"What a guy": Gibson, *I Always Wanted to Be Somebody*, p. 66.

　　Detroit donations: Ibid. "Detroiters to Send Ace Abroad."

70　"the city of Detroit takes great pride . . .": Bill Matney, "Jumpin' the Gun," *Michigan Chronicle*, undated.

　　"I never worked so hard in my life": George Puscas, "Althea Praised for Net Game," undated Detroit newspaper article, AGC.

　　"Probably her greatest fault . . .": Ibid.

　　"a revolution is developing . . .": Ibid.

　　"I felt rich": Gibson, *I Always Wanted to Be Somebody*, p. 67.

　　London headlines: AGC.

71　"Harlem's Tomboy Cinderella": John Walters, "Harlem Girl Is a Big Hit," undated London newspaper article, AGC.

71 "There is one splendid thing about Wimbledon": Bernard McElwaine, "They Travel the World for Love of a Racket," undated London newspaper article, AGC.

"Let me make it quite clear . . .": undated London newspaper article, AGC.

72 Comments on courts and weather: "The Gibson Girl Finds a Hot Spot," undated London article, AGC.

Northern Lawn Tennis Club: "Northern Meeting Begins," *The Manchester Guardian*, June 5, 1951; Ben Phlegar, "Althea Gibson Says Net Play Tough in England," Associated Press, undated; "Althea's Ace Service," undated; "Starts With Easy Win," undated, AGC.

"Yes, sir. It's tough over here": Phlegar, "Althea Gibson Says Net Play Tough in England."

Queens Club: Lance Tinghay, "Kay Tuckey Wins Tennis—Now for Semi-Final," *The Evening Standard*, undated; "Miss Patridge Defeated," undated, AGC.

"passing craze . . .": Roy McKelvie, "Mrs. Dupont Is a Title Choice: Wimbledon Hopes," *The Star*, undated, AGC.

"Latest Wimbledon Fashions": "London Laughs" comic strip, *The Evening Sun*, June 25, 1951.

"Breakfast Cartoon": Comic strip, undated, AGC.

73 "Let us hope . . .": McElwaine, "They Travel the World for Love of a Racket."

"When I play . . .": "White-Hat Day for Onlookers," *The Evening Standard*, undated, AGC; "It Was an Evening of Grace—and Spills," *News Chronicle*, June 27, 1951.

"No Gorgeous Gussie frills . . .": undated London article, AGC.

"No woman player . . .": McKelvie, "Mrs. Dupont Is a Title Choice."

74 "swell kid from my neighbourhood": "The Gibson Girl Finds a Hot Spot."

Competing against Pat Ward: John Olliff, "Exquisite Volleying Mrs. W. DuPoint: Miss Pat Ward's Encouraging Display," undated London newspaper article; Frank Rostron, "Althea Storms Net to Win," *Daily Express*, undated; Gerald Walter, "Shocks for U.S.A. Stars: Nancy Chaffee Is Taken to Three Hard Sets; Pat Ward Misses Her Chance," *News Chronicle*, undated, AGC.

Match against Beverly Baker: Frank Rostron, "Sedgman Crushes Italian; Beverly Power-Drives Sweep Althea Out," *Daily Express*, undated; Steve Roberts, "Beverly and Doris Win Easily," undated, AGC.

"Even Althea's service . . .": Laurie Pignon, "Young Fausto Is Crushed by Devil Sedgman: Althea Goes Out," *Daily Graphic*, June 30, 1951.

75 "Drobs . . .": Fred Perry, "Frank Sedgman at His Best: No. 1 'Seed' First in Last Eight," *The Evening Standard*, June 29, 1951.

Frinton: "Few Tennis Upsets at Frinton," undated newspaper article, AGC.

Dortmund: "Scores Easily Over Former Czech Star," *The Afro-American*, July 10, 1951.

"All I got was more experience": Gibson, *I Always Wanted to Be Somebody*, p. 67.

75 Impotent backhand: "Althea Gibson Beaten in Forest Hills Play, *The Afro-American*, September 8, 1951.
Althea Gibson Day: AGC.
76 "Her opponent was running . . .": James Edmund Boyack, "Althea Misses Chance for Tournament Upset," undated newspaper article, AGC.
"I have no excuse": Ibid.
Interview with Doris Hart, tennis opponent, 2004.
77 "Here is a young star . . .": Boyack, "Althea Misses Chance for Tournament Upset."
Bertram Baker: Ibid.
79 "Will had taken a shine to me . . .": Gibson, *So Much to Live For,* p. 113.
Interview with Sandra Givens.
81 "wingding of a time": Gibson, *I Always Wanted to Be Somebody,* p. 69.
"The Biggest Disappointment in Tennis": Ibid., p. 68.
"He insisted I could go all the way to the top": Ibid.
82 "I was tired of never having any money": Ibid., p. 70.

Chapter 4. "At Last! At Last!"

85 Opening quotation "I had the best serve in women's tennis . . .": Lanker, *I Dream a World,* p. 47.
Interview with Hamilton Richardson, friend and team member on Asian tour, 2004.
"We Indians . . .": AGC.
87 Social events in Asia: AGC.
Pressure on goodwill tour: Gibson, *I Always Wanted to Be Somebody,* p. 86.
Boxer Archie Moore: "The Champ Says It With Flowers," *Daily Mirror,* undated London article, AGC.
French Open: Lance Tingay, "Miss Mortimer Fails to Find Her Accuracy; Miss Gibson Worthy Champion; Miss Buxton Shares Doubles Win," *London Daily Telegraph,* undated, AGC.
88 "Though it was funny . . .": Frank Rostron, "U.S. Girl Warned: No More Walking Off the Court," *Daily Express,* May 25, 1956.
"I'm going to insist . . .": Ibid.
89 "I think this is my best yet": Frank Rostron, "Harlem Hustle Wins 2 Titles," *Daily Express,* undated, AGC.
"hot as an exploded A-bomb": "Althea Gibson's Net Stock Zooms Higher," *Pittsburgh Courier,* June 16, 1956.
"The crowds came out to see this girl . . .": Arthur Massalo, *New York Times,* undated, AGC.
"We are fortunate . . .": "A Good Envoy," *New York Times,* undated editorial, AGC.
90 Harold E. Howland's letter from the State Department: AGC.
"On current form . . .": Tingay, *The London Daily Telegraph.*
"Maybe my game was off . . .": "Althea Gibson Given Official Welcome Home by New York," *Associated Press,* July 12, 1956.

90   "scared tennis": Milton Gross, "Speaking Out," *New York Post*, July 8, 1957.

91   "I am just another tennis player . . .": Kenneth Love, "Althea Is at Home Abroad on Tennis Court," *New York Times*, June 24, 1956.

"It is my personal feeling": Arthur Massolo, "Althea, From W. 123d St. to Wimbledon," *New York Times*, July 22, 1956.

"overtennised": AGC.

92   "They were the only two sets I lost . . .": Gibson, *I Always Wanted to Be Somebody*, p. 92.

Will Darben letter: AGC.

93   "We are each other's main court opponent . . .": "Your Court's Great," undated newspaper article, AGC.

Interview with Shirley Fry, friend and tennis player, 2004.

Doubles on Australian tour: "Miss Gibson's Duo Scores in Sydney," *New York Times*, November 11, 1956.

AG singles victories: "Miss Fry Beaten by Althea Gibson," *New York Times*, November 10, 1956; Ron Brock, "World Tennis Champion Beaten: Women's Title to Althea Gibson," *The News*, December 1, 1956; Gordon Schwartz, "Negress Defeats Rival for Title," *The Advertiser*, December 3, 1956; "Althea Gibson Wins Exhibition Games," *The Examiner*, December 21, 1956; Ron Brock, "It Was a Good Day for the Gibsons," *The News*, undated.

Will Darben letter: AGC.

"Why don't you stop this?": "Miss Gibson Shows Temper 'Down Under,'" *The Courier*, December 22, 1956.

94   "It had been very much her year": Gibson, *I Always Wanted to Be Somebody*, p. 96.

"After '56, nobody could beat me": Lanker, *I Dream a World*, p. 47.

Farewell at Idlewild Airport: Gibson, *I Always Wanted to Be Somebody*, pp. 97–98.

95   "I was ruthless on the tennis court": Lanker, *I Dream a World*, p. 47.

"You got to know your opponent": Ibid.

Wimbledon: Tom Ochiltree, "Althea Gibson Defeats Hard," *Times Herald*, July 7, 1957; Gibson, *I Always Wanted to Be Somebody*, pp. 99–110.

"I was pretty excited": Gibson, *I Always Wanted to Be Somebody*, p. 101.

Celebrating with ATA friends: Ibid., pp. 101–102.

96   Queen Elizabeth II at Wimbledon: Ibid., pp. 103–105. "Althea Scores Double, Misses Mixed Crown," *The Sunday Star*, July 7, 1957; "Sign Carrier Is Ousted; Tennis Isn't Her Racket," *New York Times*, July 6, 1957.

Wimbledon heat: Ibid. "Record of 1,071 Faint at Wimbledon," *Reuters*, July 6, 1957.

"There is something about a hot, still day . . .": Gibson, *I Always Wanted to Be Somebody*, p. 103.

"When I rushed the net . . .": Ibid., p. 104.

Accepting Wimbledon award from the queen: Ibid., pp. 104–105.

Queen's attire: Ibid., p. 105; "Miss Gibson Wins Wimbledon Title," *New York Times*, July 7, 1957.

96 "The Queen had a wonderful speaking voice . . .": Gibson, *I Always Wanted to Be Somebody*, p. 105.
97 "Shaking hands with the Queen of England . . .": Ibid., p. 109.
Alice Marble, AGC.
98 "I have been told": "Tennis Queen From Harlem; Althea's Biggest Problem: Conquering Herself," undated newspaper article, AGC.
"I think I've finally learned how not to beat myself": "Althea Conquers Wimbledon, Next Is Forest Hills," undated newspaper article, AGC.
Arrival at Wimbledon ball: Gibson, *I Always Wanted to Be Somebody*, pp. 107–108.
Acceptance speech: AGC
99 Wimbledon dance and renditions: Michael Bamberger, "Inside the White Lines," *Sports Illustrated*, November 29, 1999, p. 114.
Post-ball celebration: Gibson, *I Always Wanted to Be Somebody*, p. 109; "Althea Makes Hit at London Club," *New York Post*, July 9, 1957.
Return to U.S.: Evelyn Cunningham, "Althea Learning That It's Tough Wearing a Crown: Her Responsibility Is Great," *Pittsburgh Courier*, undated, AGC; Murrain, Edward, "Althea Returns Triumphant," undated newspaper article, AGC.
Police escort: "Miss Althea Gibson Comes Home to a Hero's Welcome," *Associated Negro Press*, undated article, AGC.
Homecoming: Cunningham, "Althea Learning That It's Tough Wearing a Crown."
101 From a comment during an interview with Althea: L. Garnell Stamps, host/producer, "Viewpoint, Lynchburg NAACP," Cablevision, Channel 6, Lynchburg, Va., May 8, 1986.
Ticker-tape parade: "100,000 Hail Althea Gibson in Broadway Ticker Parade," *The Washington Afro-American*, July 16, 1957; Barner, George, "Althea's Homecoming Was as Tough as Wimbledon," undated article, AGC; Cunningham, "Althea Learning That It's Tough Wearing a Crown"; James Hicks, "New York Gives Althea Finest Hour," undated newspaper article, AGC.
102 "This is the proudest day of my life": George Barner, "Not Going Pro, 'Not Engaged,'" undated newspaper article, AGC.
Parents: George Barner, "Things Normal Again at Home of Gibsons," undated article, AGC.
"She is a great representative . . .": George Barner, "Althea's Homecoming Was as Tough as Wimbledon."
103 Mayoral luncheon: "Her Finest Hour," *Newsweek*, July 22, 1957.
"I never thought I would ever be in such a place": Ibid.
Another celebration in Harlem: "New York City Pays Tribute to Althea Gibson," undated newspaper article, AGC; Barner, "Things Normal Again at Home of Gibsons."
Letters: AGC.
104 Preparing for Forest Hills: "Althea Gibson Advances at River Forest," undated newspaper article, AGC; "Althea Gibson Wins Clay Courts Title," undated, AGC; "Althea Has Little Trouble Winning Clay Court Title," undated, AGC.

104 "I was nervous and confident at the same time . . .": Gibson, *I Always Wanted to Be Somebody*, p. 117.

Forest Hills: Gene Ward, "2 Aussies in Men's Final; Althea, Louise for Title," *Daily News*, September 8, 1957.

Match with Louise Brough: Ibid., pp. 116–117. "Althea's Dream Is Complete—3rd Crown Won," *Daily Worker*, September 9, 1957.

Vice President Richard Nixon: Gibson, *I Always Wanted to Be Somebody*, p. 118.

"Winning at Wimbledon was wonderful . . .": Ibid.

105 Pacific Coast match with Louise Brough: Edith Austin, "Althea, the World's Greatest," undated article, AGC; "Althea Grabs West Coast Net Crown," undated, AGC.

107 "There will be more setbacks in the South": *The Evening Star*.

"The Negro who can vote . . .": Dean Gordon B. Hancock, "Between the Lines," *Associated Negro Press*, undated newspaper article, AGC.

Sarah Palfrey Cooke: Emma Harrison, "Althea, Pride of One West Side, Becomes the Queen of Another," *New York Times*, September 9, 1957.

"I'm looking at it in a different aspect." Ibid.

Bad press: Ibid.; "Writers Ask: Has Success Gone to Althea's Head?" undated newspaper article, AGC; Wendell Smith, "Has Net Queen Althea Gibson Gone High Hat?" *Pittsburgh Courier*, undated, AGC; "Althea 'Flabbergasted' by 'Prima Donna' Barb," undated, AGC.

108 Rumors of marriage to Will: "Althea Parries Talk of Marriage," undated newspaper article, AGC; "Althea Resting in Montclair, N.J., Her Fiance's Home," undated, AGC.

Posing in front of milk advertisement in Europe: Bob Pennington, "Rival Accuses Althea of Gamesmanship," undated, AGC.

Maureen Connolly's injury: "Wimbledon Winner Proves Value of Tenacity," *New York Times*, July 7, 1957.

Lew Hoad's contract: George Barner, "Not Going Pro, 'Not Engaged.'"

"What makes this such an outstanding honor . . .": "Althea Gibson 'Top Woman Athlete,'" *Christian Science Monitor*, May 22, 1958; "Althea Gibson Voted Top Woman Athlete," *Associated Press*, January 12, 1958.

109 Wightman Cup: "Miss Gibson Bitter in Cup Score," undated newspaper article, AGC.

"Centre Court jitters": "Althea Repeats at Wimbledon: Adds Duo Crown, 'Triple' Bid Fails," *Associated Press*, July 5, 1958.

"She was tough": "Althea May Go for 3d Net Crown," *Associated Press*, July 5, 1958.

"I hope to be at Wimbledon again next year . . .": "Althea Eyes '59 Defense," *Associated Press*, July 5, 1958.

Tennis Day: "Mayor Cites Althea Gibson at 'Tennis Day' Reception," *New York Times*, July 17, 1958.

Jack Kramer's offer: Ed Fitzgerald, "Little Mo vs. Althea Gibson," *American Weekly*, May 4, 1958.

110 "Some people don't think so . . .": Milton Gross, "Speaking Out," *New York Post*, July 8, 1958.

110 "This was a satisfying tournament . . .": "Althea Gibson May Quit Tennis," *Christian Science Monitor*, September 8, 1958.

111 Signal from Llewellyn: *Magic Year in Sports*.
     "I wish to announce my retirement . . .": Ibid.

Chapter 5. Playing New Notes

112 Opening quotation "It was important to me": Althea Gibson with Richard Curtis, *So Much to Live For* (New York: G. P. Putnam's Sons, 1968), p. 33.
     "I don't know if it's a blessing . . .": Ibid., p. 21.
     The Apollo: Ibid., p. 22.

113 Interview with Daniel "Bubba" Gibson Jr.
     Harlem talent: Dodson et al., *The Black New Yorkers*; Lewis, *When Harlem Was in Vogue*.
     Interview with Mary Ann Drayton.
     Buddy Walker: Poston, Article III, *New York Post*, p. M2.
     Interview with Arvelia Myers.

114 Interview with Hamilton Richardson.
     Interview with Gordon Parks.
     "I had the basic equipment . . .": Gibson, *So Much to Live For*, p. 22.
     "What I lacked . . .": Ibid.
     W. C. Handy: Ibid., p. 23, AGC.

115 Dot Records contract: AGC.
     Dot royalty statements: AGC.
     "I hastily selected my songs . . .": Gibson, *So Much to Live For*, p. 30.

116 Correspondence with Dot: AGC.

117 "Ed Sullivan was extremely cordial . . .": Gibson, *So Much to Live For*, p. 32.
     Ed Sullivan appearance: Ibid., pp. 32–33.

118 "The record did not live up to my expectations": Ibid., p. 34.

120 "They were as charming . . .": Gibson, *So Much to Live For*, p. 35.

121 "The Horse Soldiers" ad: *New York Post*, August 11, 1959, AGC.

122 "For those who like tennis . . .": "The New Pictures," *Time*, July 20, 1959, AGC.
     "Shortly after Mr. Wayne . . .": *Reporter*, July 9, 1959, AGC.
     "Althea Gibson's book . . .": Reginald Brace, "Althea Gibson's Story," *Yorkshire Post*, June 8, 1959.
     "A story as candid as it is startling . . .": Alan Random newsletter, June 20, 1959, AGC.
     Incidents: E. Fitzgerald, "A Gripping Novel of the Sea," *Bradford Telegraph and Argus*, June 12, 1959.
     Interview with Billie Jean King, friend and tennis partner.

123 "I'm not about to throw away everything for love": John Barkham, "Keeping Up With the New Books," *Journal Standard*, March 26, 1959.

123 "Are you available?": George Minot, "Althea May Defend Her Wimbledon Title," *New York Post*, March 15, 1959.

Chapter 6. Turning Pro

125 Opening quotation "I may be the Queen of Tennis right now": Gibson, *So Much to Live For*, p. 15.
"I'd like to see my own family more comfortable": Jimmy Powers, "The Power House," *New York Daily News*, July 7, 1957.
"Being a champ is all well and good . . .": Gibson, *So Much to Live For*, p. 15.

126 Supporting herself as a pro: "Olmedo and Gibson Win World Pro Titles at Cleveland," *World Tennis*, July 1960.

127 Endorsements: AGC.
Goodwill tour: AGC.

128 Defeating Shirley Fry Irving in Washington: "Althea Delights Fans & Herself," *Washington Daily News*, June 15, 1959.
Althea as sports correspondent: clippings from *London Evening Standard*, AGC.
"Her finesse on the tennis courts . . .": Izzy Rowe, "Izzy Rowe's Notebook," *Pittsburgh Courier*, May 9, 1959.
"Yawn" and "ho-hum": Gene Roswell, "Working Press," *New York Post*, September 11, 1959.
Ralph Bunche: "Negro Defends Tennis Site," *Sunday Star*, July 12, 1959; Hicks, "Another Angle: Althea Gibson," *New York Amsterdam News*, July 18, 1959; "USLTA to Discuss Club's Bias," *New York Post*, July 12, 1959; Al Laney, "The West Side Story," *Herald Tribune*, undated, AGC.

131 Contract with Abe Saperstein: Wendell Smith, "Tennis Queens Bring Beauty to QB Meeting," *Chicago's American*, November 17, 1959, AGC.
Karol Fageros: Ibid.; Eleanor Peeler, "Have Tennis Racket, Will Travel," *San Jose News*, January 27, 1960; "Globetrotters Net Althea and Karol," *United Press International*, undated, AGC; Harold Weissman, "Althea Planning Pro Femme Tour," undated, AGC; Gibson, *So Much to Live For*, pp. 56–57.
New Year's Eve: Howard M. Tuckner, "Garden Offering a Sportspourri," *New York Times*, December 31, 1959.

132 "If you lobbed a ball high enough . . .": Gibson, *So Much to Live For*, p. 53.
"Traveling is more tiring . . .": K. O'Connor and R. Reusch, "Tennis Champ Prefers Singing," *Peace Points*, March 15, 1960.
"I found them wonderful gentlemen . . .": Gibson, *So Much to Live For*, p. 62.

133 "We played as if our lives and honor depended on winning": Ibid., p. 63.
"I'm getting a real kick out of it": Smith, "Tennis Queens Bring Beauty to QB Meeting," *Chicago's American*.
"That sort of thing rubbed against the grain . . .": Gibson, *So Much to Live For*, p. 60.

133 Interview with Gordon Parks.
 Interview with Robert Ryland, former ATA champion and first black male professional.
 "I got myself a beautiful apartment . . .": George Barner, "Althea Finally Gets Apartment," undated, AGC.

134 Furnishings: AGC.
 "Giddy with greed": Gibson, *So Much to Live For*, p. 71.
 "Most-publicized tennis players . . .": Bob Addie's Column, *The Washington Post*, June 9, 1959.
 Ranking on newsworthiness: Eleanor Pollock, "Newsworthy Women of the '50s." *The Sunday Bulletin*, December 27, 1959.
 "I was, in effect, ruined": Gibson, *So Much to Live For*, p. 79.

135 "The most significant black athlete in America . . .": Bill Rhoden, "A Fruitful Past, but a Shaky Future," *Ebony*, August 1977, pp. 60–64.
 "The fact that I did have a run of bad luck . . .": Gibson, *So Much to Live For*, p. 115.

136 "I wanted to stay in sports a little longer": John Brockmann, "Althea Gibson, at 50, Seeks First LPGA Victory," *Sarasota Herald-Tribune*, February 26, 1978.

Chapter 7. Swing Time

137 Opening quotation "Anything I do, I want to be the best at it": Gene Roswell, "Althea: Next Golf Champ," *New York Post*, September 14, 1958.
 "That girl hits just like a man": Roswell, "Working Press," *New York Post*, October 30, 1959.
 "My style of play . . .": Ibid.

138 Interview with William Hayling, friend and doctor.
 "No sport seems to be beyond her capability": Roswell, "Working Press," *New York Post*, October 30, 1959.
 Visit to Spaulding's: Roswell, "Althea: Next Golf Champ," *New York Post*.
 Interview with Hansel Tookes, former golf coach at FAMU.

140 Sealy Posturepedic and Eve Cigarettes: "Lady Pros Seek Golf Glory," *Ebony*, July 1971, pp. 106–109.
 Comparison to Didrikson: Roswell, "Althea: Next Golf Champ," *New York Post*, LPGA.
 "It's no secret . . .": Carolyn White, "LPGA Pioneer Now Pursuing Age Standard," *USA Today*, August 24, 1990; Karin Miller, "Sports News," *Associated Press*, January 9, 1991.

141 "I want to be the only woman . . .": Dick Young, "Young Ideas," *New York Daily News*, April 2, 1967.
 "Maybe because I'm a champion . . .": "Pride, Desire Keep Althea Going," *New York Daily News*, June 18, 1967.
 "That ball just sits up there . . .": Roswell, "Althea: Next Golf Champ," *New York Post*.
 "You're never too old . . .": Gene Roswell, "Golf Is Driving Althea Off the Tennis Court," *New York Post*, May 3, 1961.

141 Golf equipment: Roswell, "Althea: Next Golf Champ," *New York Post*.

142 "Just walking after that ball . . .": Ibid.

"And she can practice endlessly . . .": "Althea Gibson Making Fine Golfing Progress," *The Record*, August 2, 1962.

Ward Baking Company: AGC.

"Once I had my game together, I entered local amateur contests": Barbara Kukla, "Tennis Great Loves to Teach," *The Star-Ledger*, May 7, 1972.

Black tournaments: Roswell, "Golf Is Driving Althea Off the Tennis Court," *New York Post*; "Althea Gibson 20 Strokes Ahead," *New York Times*, February 23, 1962; "Althea Gibson Leads Golfers," *Associated Press*, February 23, 1962; Lincoln A. Werden, "Althea Gibson Draws Plaudits in Debut on Metropolitan Links," *New York Times*, June 21, 1962.

143 "Althea has great potential": "Althea Gibson Making Fine Golfing Progress," *The Record*.

"As far as my progress is concerned . . .": Werden, "Althea Gibson Draws Plaudits in Debut on Metropolitan Links," *The New York Times*.

Qualifying for the LPGA: LPGA, AGC.

LPGA debut: AGC.

144 "You have to be a trouper . . .": Kukla, "Tennis Great Loves to Teach," *The Star-Ledger*.

145 Will Darben: Gibson, *So Much to Live For*, pp. 113–114, 153–155.

146 Lake Venice: Young, "Young Ideas," *New York Daily News*.

"A rare type of female . . .": Jim Obert, "She Made the Switch," *Peoria Journal Star*, August 19, 1967.

147 Interview with David N. Dinkins, friend, tennis partner, and former New York mayor.

148 Father's death: Gibson, *So Much to Live For*, pp. 143–144.

Interview with Renee Powell, friend and fellow LPGA member.

Interview with Marlene Hagge-Vossler, friend and fellow LPGA member, 2003.

149 Interview with Kathy Whitworth, friend and fellow LPGA member, 2004.

Sealy Posturepedic Pro-Amateur Classic: "Lady Pros Seek Golf Glory," *Ebony*, July 1971.

150 "Althea was a good player": Pete McDaniel, *Uneven Lies: The Heroic Story of African-Americans in Golf* (Greenwich, CT: The American Golfer, 2000), p. 77.

Golf history: Ibid., pp. 69, 76, 77; Calvin H. Sinnette, *Forbidden Fairways* (Chelsea, MI: Sleeping Bear Press, 1998), pp. 89, 117, 166, 204; John H. Kennedy, *A Course of Their Own: A History of African American Golfers* (Kansas City, Mo.: McMeel, 2000).

152 Judy Rankin: LPGA.

153 "If my being out here . . .": "Pride, Desire Keep Althea Going," *New York Daily News*.

St. Petersburg Women's Open: Bob LeNoir, "Welcome Back, Althea Gibson," undated newspaper article, AGC.

154 Charlie Sifford: Sinnette, *Forbidden Fairways*, p. 131.

154   Interview with Lenny Wirtz, friend and former LPGA commissioner, 2004.

        "There were a lot of tournaments that wouldn't accept me": Bruce Phillips, "For Althea Gibson, Two Barriers Broken," undated newspaper article, AGC.

        "I don't know if they thought I was going to eat the grass": "Lady Pros Seek Golf Glory," *Ebony*.

158   Dewey Brown: Sinnette, *Forbidden Fairways*.

        PGA's "Caucasian clause": Ibid.

        LPGA vote against clause: Ibid.

        Sifford: Ibid.

159   Shoal Creek: Ibid.

        Tiger Woods: Todd Gutner with Mark Hyman, "More Heat on the Masters," *Business Week*, August 12, 2002.

        "I knew what it would be like . . .": Phillips, "For Althea Gibson, Two Barriers Broken," AGC.

160   Interview with Marilynn Smith, friend and fellow LPGA member, 2004.

161   "I haven't been giving my all to golf . . .": Ibid.

        "I was born too soon": Beth Hightower, "Althea Gibson Wanted to Be Somebody," *The Sacramento Union*, April 8, 1976.

        "It's pretty phenomenal . . .": Dave Anderson, "Sports of The Times: A New Hall Opens for Althea Gibson," *New York Times*, September 7, 1980.

Chapter 8. The Comeback Kid

162   Opening quotation "As long as God has given me the strength . . .": Murray Janoff, "Tennis' Greatest Trailblazer," *The Sporting News*, June 24, 1972.

        Debut of open tennis: Ashe, *A Hard Road to Glory*, 3:172.

        "I want at least one more crack at Wimbledon as a professional": "Althea Working Hard on Tennis Comeback," *The Evening Star*, December 24, 1968.

        "I feel great . . .": Janoff, "Tennis' Greatest Trailblazer," *The Sporting News*.

163   Interview with Billie Jean King.

        "My hands aren't as strong . . .": "Althea Working Hard on Tennis Comeback," *The Evening Star*, December 24, 1968.

        "It seems a little strange . . .": "Althea Trying Court Comeback," *New York Daily News*, December 24, 1968.

164   Interview with Art Carrington, Sydney Llewellyn's protégé.

        "There are a lot of black women . . .": "Althea Gibson's New Ambition: To Get Back Into Competition," *New York Daily News*, May 14, 1972.

        "Why should a former world champion have to do that?": Mike Lackey, "Althea Gibson: 'I Still Have Desire to Play,'" undated newspaper article, AGC.

        Mixed doubles with Arthur Ashe: AGC.

        Chris Evert: Al Picker, "Match Point: Connors Climbing," *The Star-Ledger*, February 24, 1974.

165 ABC "Superstars": AGC.
Interview with Rosemary Darben.
Interview with Daniel "Bubba" Gibson Jr.
Divorce decree: AGC.

166 "The fact that it didn't work out . . .": Kay Gilman, "Althea Gibson . . . Still Every Inch a Queen," *New York Daily News*, June 30, 1974.
Interview with Evelyn Cunningham.

167 "I can't cry over spilt milk": Craig Stolze, "Not Cashing . . . Not Crying," *The Times-Union*, July 19, 1973.
"When I came out of tennis . . .": Gene Roswell, "Working Press: The Pro Gets a Lesson," *New York Post*, July 23, 1969.
Bent Tree Classic: Brockmann, "Althea Gibson, at 50, Seeks First LPGA Victory," *Sarasota Herald-Tribune*, February 26, 1978.
American Defender Golf Classic: Phillips, "For Althea Gibson, Two Barriers Broken," AGC.
Physical shape; Brockmann, "Althea Gibson, at 50, Seeks First LPGA Victory," *Sarasota Herald-Tribune*.

168 LPGA letter: AGC.
Comeback attempts: AGC.
"I don't want to talk about it": C. Neff, "Teeing It Up," *Sports Illustrated*, September 10, 1990.
"I want to get back my LPGA tour card . . .": White, "LPGA Pioneer Now Pursuing Age Standard," *USA Today*.
Doral-Ryder Open: Tenley Jackson-Hawkins, "Althea Gibson: Portrait of a Competitor," *Black Elegance*, undated magazine article, AGC.

169 Interview with Gordon Parks.

171 Interview with Sandra Givens.
Interview with Mary Ann Drayton.

Chapter 9. Ambassador for Excellence

172 Opening quotation "I had help . . .": Kukla, "Tennis Great Loves to Teach," *The Star-Ledger*.
"I love to get high . . .": Anne Lee, " 'Ace' Writers: Pupils 'Persuade' Althea Gibson to Visit," *The Star-Ledger*, May 2, 1991.
Letter from Christina Martin: AGC.

173 "If you have a little bit of talent . . .": Lee, " 'Ace' Writers," *The Star-Ledger*.

174 "I just let all of that roll off my back . . .": Kukla, "Tennis Great Loves to Teach," *The Star-Ledger*.

175 "I'm motivated . . .": Ibid.
"I learned how to play tennis with a paddle . . .": Barbara Kukla, "Althea Gibson Brings Tennis to Newark Kids," *The Star-Ledger*, July 6, 1973.

176 "The loser is always a part of the problem": *Magic Year in Sports*.
Interview with Art Carrington.
"I've been playing tennis for twenty-some years . . .": Richard Zitrin, "Althea Gibson Has Conquered Modesty, Too," *Akron Beacon Journal*, March 3, 1973.

177   Support of various causes: AGC.

ATA reunion: "Playground in Harlem Renamed for Tennis Player and Coach," *New York Times*, October 24, 1971; "11-Year-Old Boy Faces Former Tennis Star at Playground Ceremony," *New York Times*, October 24, 1971.

Akron Open Tennis Tournament: Zitrin, "Althea Gibson Has Conquered Modesty, Too," *Akron Beacon Journal*.

Celebrity benefits: "The Pros Take to the Pavements," *New York Daily News*, August 12, 1975, AGC.

Vanguard Sports: George Kanzler Jr., "Starcity Looks to Bridge Jersey's Communications Gap," *The Star-Ledger*, May 16, 1977, AGC.

178   "Our aim is to discover and develop potential talent": Joan Babbage, "Althea Gibson Keeps Determined Drive," *The Star-Ledger*, January 20, 1974.

Interview with Rosemary Darben.

Nomination as State Athletic Commissioner: Linda Lamendola, "Byrne Nominates Althea as Athletic Commissioner," *The Star-Ledger*, September 19, 1975.

179   "I will do everything in my power . . .": Swearing-in ceremony speech, November 17, 1975, AGC.

"Why should people have to travel into New York . . .": Mary Amoroso, "Althea Gibson, Champion for N.J.," *The Record*, December 11, 1975.

"What can I do for you, babe?": Ibid.

Memo to Governor Byrne: Althea Gibson, "Expanding the Functions and Scope of the State Athletic Commission and Commissioner," December 23, 1975, AGC.

180   State senator Frank J. Dodd: Frank J. Dodd, "Round 2: Senator Dodd vs. Althea Gibson," *New York Times*, May 23, 1976.

Resignation: "Althea Gibson Quits as N.J. Sports Chief," *New York Post*, January 19, 1977.

Interview with Hamilton Richardson.

Campaign for State Senate: "Into a New Court?" *Staten Island Advance*, April 28, 1977; "Althea Set for New Game," *New York Post*, April 28, 1977; Jacqueline Trescott, "Update," *Washington Post*, June 5, 1977.

182   "Battle of the Senior Sexes": AGC.

Awards and honorary degrees: Cindy Schmerler, "A Salute to Women in Sports WSF Dinner," *Women's Sportscape*, New York Women's Sports Association newsletter, Winter 1980–1981, Volume 2, p. 1, AGC.

185   Return to Florida A&M: "Your University Invites Althea Back," *The FAMU Alumni News*, May-June 1976, p. 5.

Chapter 10. Revolutionizing the Sports World

186   Opening quotation "Preparation implies hard work . . .": AG.

"All the girls thought I was the worst tomboy . . .": Gibson, *I Always Wanted to Be Somebody*, p. 48.

187   Title IX and girls in sports: Women's Sports Foundation.

Interview with Billie Jean King.

189 Cheryl Miller: Cheryl Miller, "50 Years of Black Women in Sports," *Ebony*, November 1995, p. 163.
Cynthia Cooper: "Stage: One-Act Plays About Heroines," Mel Gussow, *New York Times*, April 6, 1986.

190 Interview with Mocha Lee, 2003.
Zina Garrison: Zina Garrison, *Zina: My Life in Women's Tennis* (Berkeley, CA: Frog Ltd., 2001), pp. 1, 2, 50, 79, 150; 2004 interview.

191 Black winners of Grand Slams: USTA.
"She was a born coach . . .": Bob Duffy, "Hidden Treasure: Althea Gibson Made History But Not Money in Tennis and Has Become a Virtual Recluse," *Boston Globe*, June 24, 2001.

193 "monstrous breakthrough . . .": "Althea Gibson Echoes Ashe's Prediction: Stardom Influx Premature; Few 'tigers' on Tennis Circuit Today," *Indianapolis Recorder*, August 16, 1980, pp. 16–17.
Interview with Leslie Allen, protégé.

194 Sylvia Hooks: Zitrin, "Althea Gibson Has Conquered Modesty, Too," *Akron Beacon Journal*; Grace Lichtenstein, "Where Is the Next Althea Gibson?" *Ms. Magazine*, December 1973.
"What I've accomplished . . .": Zitrin, "Althea Gibson Has Conquered Modesty, Too," *Akron Beacon Journal*.
Comparison to Wilma Rudolph: Rhoden, "A Fruitful Past, but a Shaky Future," *Ebony*, pp. 60–64.

195 Interview with William Hayling.

196 Interview with Bill Davis.
Interview with Gordon Parks.

197 Charlie Sifford: Sinnette, *Forbiden Fairways*.
Interview with Renee Powell.
"Someone once wrote that the difference between me and Jackie Robinson . . .": AGC.
Segregated seating in Norfolk, Virginia: "Althea Gibson 'Didn't Know This Sort of Thing Existed,'" *New York Post*, December 21, 1959.

198 "I wasn't fighting any cause": AGC.
Interview with Marlene Hagge-Vossler.

199 African Americans in LPGA: LPGA.
LaRee Sugg: Niki Herbert, "Women's Golf Seeks Diversity," *The News and Observer*, August 10, 2001.

Chapter 11. A Private Life, A Public Legacy

201 Opening quotation "I'm not complaining; I'm just explaining": AG.

203 Awards and honors: AGC.
Prize money: Joel Stein, "The Power Game," *Time*, September 3, 2001, pp. 57, 58, 61, 63, USTA.
Interview with David Dinkins.

204 Giving voice to her disappointments: Gibson, *So Much to Live For*, p. 76.

205 Fundraising efforts: Ron Thomas, "Championing the Cause for Althea Gibson," *Emerge*, April 1997, p. 64; "FAMU Raising Funds for Ailing Tennis Great Althea Gibson," *Washington Afro-American*, July 26, 1997; AGC.

205 Interview with William Hayling.
Interview with Bill Davis.
206 "emotional toll . . .": Arthur Ashe with Neil Amdur, *Off the Court* (New York: The New American Library, 1981), p. 42.
Interview with Billie Jean King.
Interview with Leslie Allen.
207 Interview with Arvelia Myers.
Muhammad Ali: Cal Fussman, "Ali Now," *Esquire*, October 2003, pp. 132–139, 201–202.
209 Interview with Mattie Bryant.
Interview with Mary Ann Drayton.
Interview with Sandra Givens.
Interview with Daniel "Bubba" Gibson Jr.
Interview with Gordon Parks.
212 Interview with Zina Garrison, 2004.
213 Lucky one: Howie Evans, "Althea Gibson Was a Role Model for the Ages," *The New York Amsterdam News*, October 9, 2003.
214 Interview with Robert Ryland.
Interview with Hamilton Richardson.

Index